COMPLETE

ENTERTAINING

COOKBOOK

WILLIAMS-SONOMA

COMPLETE

ENTERTAINING

COOKBOOK

GENERAL EDITOR

Chuck Williams

RECIPES

Joyce Goldstein

PHOTOGRAPHY

Allan Rosenberg
and Allen V. Lott

WELDON OWEN
PUBLISHING

First published in the USA, 1998, by Weldon Owen Inc.

Originally published as *Festive Occasions* (© 1993 Weldon Owen Inc.) and *Casual Occasions* (© 1995 Weldon Owen Inc.).

In collaboration with Williams-Sonoma Inc.
3250 Van Ness Avenue, San Francisco, CA 94109

WILLIAMS-SONOMA
Founder & Vice-Chairman: Chuck Williams
Book Buyer: Cecilia Michaelis

PRODUCED BY WELDON OWEN INC.
Chief Executive Officer: John Owen
President: Terry Newell
Chief Operating Officer: Larry Partington
Creative Director: Gaye Allen
Vice President International Sales: Stuart Laurence
Sales Manager: Emily Jahn
Associate Publisher: Val Cipollone
Managing Editors: Sally W. Smith, Tori Ritchie, Genevieve Morgan
Copy Editors: Sharon Silva, Carolyn Miller
Consulting Editor: Norman Kolpas
Original Design: John Bull, The Book Design Company
Additional Design: Patty Hill; Nancy Campana;
    Kari Ontko, India Ink
Production: Chris Hemesath, Stephanie Sherman, Jen Dalton,
    Linda Bouchard
Proofreader: Desne Border
Indexer: Ken DellaPenta
Food Photographers: Peter Johnson, Allan Rosenberg, Allan V. Lott
Locations and Prop Styling: Sandra Griswold, Elizabeth Davis,
    Karen Nicks
Food Stylists: Heidi Gintner, Susan Massey
Wine Consultant: Evan Goldstein
Menu Illustrations: Diane Reiss-Koncar, Gretchen Shields
Appendix Illustrations: Alice Harth
Front Cover Photographer: Peter Johnson
Back Cover Photographers: Allan Rosenberg, Allan V. Lott

The Williams-Sonoma Complete Cookbook series
conceived and produced by Weldon Owen Inc.
814 Montgomery Street, San Francisco, CA 94133

First printed in 1998
20 19 18 17 16 15 14 13 12

Library of Congress Cataloging-in-Publication Data is available.
ISBN 978-1-887451-15-4

Separations by Colourscan Overseas Co. Pte. Ltd.
Printed in China by SNP Leefung Printers Ltd.

A Note on Weights and Measures
All recipes include customary U.S., U.K. and metric measurements.
Conversions are based on a standard developed for these books
and have been rounded off. Actual weights may vary.

Contents

Introduction

Casual Gatherings

Holidays & Occasions

Elements of Entertaining

$\mathcal{I}$NTRODUCTION

SO MANY OF LIFE'S MOMENTS, big and small, are worthy of special celebration: a traditional holiday, a birthday or engagement, a reunion with old friends. Any such occasion becomes even more memorable when recognized with good food, lovingly prepared and served.

Think back to the gatherings you've ever given or attended that stand out in your memory and you'll probably discover that one word applies to them all: *effortless*. A truly special occasion flows with a life and style all its own. Of course, magical though they seem, such events—grand or intimate—don't happen by magic. From the first inspiration to the final cleanup, great entertaining results from organization and creativity, in equal parts. This book aims to provide you with both. Whether you use it for a grand holiday feast or a casual dinner party, its goal is to make the event as easy and enjoyable for you as it is for your guests.

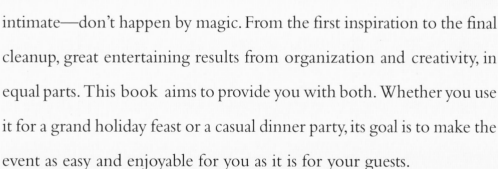

ENTERTAINING WITH EASE AND STYLE

This book is designed to guide you through effortless entertaining while also inspiring you. Like a personal party consultant, it takes care of the particulars of planning, leaving you free not only to add your own inimitable style, but also to enjoy the occasion as it happens.

෫ The twenty-six menus are divided into two sections, one for casual get-togethers, the other for more elaborate parties celebrating special occasions and holidays. Created and planned by master chef and cookbook author Joyce Goldstein, the menus are geared both to particular events and to the seasons and are organized in each section in a yearly pattern. What all of these occasions have in common is easy hospitality and the underlying principle that pleasure comes whenever good food is generously shared.

෫ Each menu begins with all the practical information you will need to organize the meal, from preparation tips and decorating ideas to beverage recommendations and strategies for cooking in advance. In most cases, the recipes can easily be multiplied for larger parties.

෫ Cooking methods are straightforward, and much of the work can be done ahead. While all the dishes in each menu work together, the menus are designed to be flexible. You can prepare as many or as few dishes as suit your needs, or you can mix recipes from more than one menu. Most also work for everyday meals, in all sorts of combinations. Note, too, that variations on recipes are frequently offered. As you cook from this book, you'll probably find that many of the recipes will become new favorites, permanent parts of your culinary repertoire.

෫ All entertaining, whether casual or formal, calls for some thought and planning. When you're getting ready to entertain, let this introduction serve to remind you of useful strategies.

෫ To find the dishes that suit your specific occasion, or for fresh ideas, browse through the menus. For step-by-step instructions on how to set a table, fold a napkin, arrange flowers and more, consult Elements of Entertaining at the back of the book (pages 292–314), which also includes a glossary (pages 304–7) that explains cooking terms, special ingredients and useful techniques.

STRATEGIES FOR FESTIVE PARTIES

The success of a party depends on the guest list. It is essential that your guests enjoy one another. To that end, try to select a dynamic blend of invitees.

෫ Think, too, about mixing guests in a way likely to encourage conversation. For cocktail parties, pay attention to the positioning of the food tables and bar area so that people can gather in comfortable spaces.

෫ To assist you in such deliberations, keep a party logbook, entering details of each occasion's guest list, seating, menu and other pertinent details. Refer back to it when planning future events, and you'll soon gain a reputation as someone who entertains wisely and well.

EXTENDING AN INVITATION

In these busy times, it is important to invite guests well in advance. For an informal gathering, invitations should be extended at least a week ahead. More formal occasions, or parties to which you're inviting people you don't know particularly well, require the courtesy of at least two weeks' notice. Traditional holidays or gala events like a wedding, engagement or anniversary call for invitations to be sent at least one month ahead.

෫ The more formal the occasion, the more appropriate are printed or written invitations. Formal rules of etiquette call for them to include your name(s) and the words "request(s) the pleasure of your company," followed by the occasion, date and time, suggested attire and the letters RSVP—an abbreviation of the French request for a response, *répondez s'il vous plaît*. Position your phone number beside or beneath the RSVP if a telephone response is acceptable.

෫ For a casual occasion, an invitation can be extended orally, but a handwritten note, including date, time and an RSVP request, is a courtesy—it will provide your invitee with a more tangible, accurate reminder.

KEEPING IT RUNNING SMOOTHLY

Observe good hosts or hostesses in action and you'll see that no detail of their guests' comfort goes unnoticed. Excelling in the role is a matter of making a personal commitment to your guests.

❧ Make a mental checklist and refer to it as the party progresses. Keep a constant eye out for guests' needs. If you see someone monopolizing a conversation, or another person standing alone, diplomatically encourage mingling. Informal introductions performed by you, rather than by your guests, help break the ice, too.

❧ You may want to consider bringing in help, particularly for large or very formal gatherings. Word of mouth can lead you to reliable firms that supply caterers, wait staff, bartenders and others to share the work or do it all. You'll also find listings in the telephone directory, but be sure to ask for and check references. Consider recruiting friends, or your teenage children or their friends, to help out.

❧ If anything does go wrong, don't call attention to it and don't panic. More likely than not, a recipe you accidentally overcooked will not be noticed by your guests as long as you don't announce the mistake. Remember that a great party, one that you've carefully planned, usually develops a life of its own, independent of your design. Relax and enjoy it yourself and your guests will too.

DECIDING ON THE MENU & WINES

The occasion itself is your first guide to the foods you might serve. Holidays seem to demand traditional dishes. Celebrations call for more elaborate presentations. Casual gatherings, usually not bound by custom, naturally lend themselves to informal foods. Remember, though, that a few dishes well prepared and served are better than too many that are not done well.

❧ Whatever the occasion, try to include seasonal ingredients at their best. Review your guest list and records of past parties to make sure you'll cater to special tastes or dietary needs. And don't serve too much food; guests leave a table happier when they're satisfied rather than overfed.

❧ Once you've selected the menu, the next step is to choose the accompanying wines. For every menu in this book, master sommelier Evan Goldstein has provided general wine guidelines and specific varietal suggestions. But some basic rules also bear repeating.

❧ "Red with meat, white with fish" is the oldest maxim in the canon of wine wisdom. But today the rule is flexible. Poultry, lighter meats like veal or pork, and richer seafood like salmon or lobster go well with either light red wines or robust whites. Sauces and garnishes also influence your choice, as does the number of courses.

❧ Despite these considerations, the decision need not be complicated. Start with the suggestions found with each menu. Then, seek out a knowledgeable local wine merchant to help you in your deliberations, and pay strong attention to your personal preferences. Furthermore, don't feel that you have to pay a lot to ensure quality; good wine doesn't have to be expensive nowadays.

SHOPPING & COOKING AHEAD

The more cooking you can do beforehand, the lighter your workload and anxiety on the day of the party. Several days before, double-check your selected recipes, as well as the preparation list that appears with each menu. This way, you will have ingredients needing advance preparation (meat requiring marination, for example) on hand at the right moment.

❧ No matter how few people are invited, the importance of making a list cannot be overemphasized. First, read carefully through each recipe and prepare a master shopping list. Divide it into those items you can purchase at the supermarket and those that come from specialty food or wine shops. (You'll find that most of the ingredients in this book can be purchased from a good-quality food shop. It is helpful, too, to have access to a reliable butcher and fishmonger.) Check the list against your supplies, marking off the things that you already have. Also check that you have all the necessary cooking utensils, pots, pans, baking dishes and so on. Make another list of flowers, candles, linens and any decorations you might need. Purchase, borrow or rent whatever is necessary to fill in the gaps.

❧ For a big event, if time allows, do a trial run: prepare and serve at least part of the menu for your family a week or so before the party.

SETTING THE SCENE

The dining room is the most obvious place to set a meal. But try thinking beyond those four walls. A casual party could be held happily in a spacious kitchen, family room or den. For a large, formal dinner, consider clearing an area in the living room for the table. An intimate dinner may call for a small table by the fireside or near a

window. When the weather allows, move the feast outdoors.

ɕ Don't forget to clean the house well in advance. Check the guest bathroom for sufficient hand towels, soap and other supplies. Designate an area for hanging coats, too; if the weather is inclement, you don't want wet garments thrown on your bed.

TABLES & CHAIRS

For a small gathering, your dining table and chairs will no doubt meet your needs. As the guest list increases, feel free to press into service tables and chairs from other rooms and to use additional surfaces as buffet counters. Consider rentals if you don't have enough furniture to meet your needs.

ɕ Above all, anticipate your guests' comfort. Try sitting in every seat to make sure there is enough leg room and that the height is correct, then move chairs around and provide cushions as necessary.

CHOOSING TABLEWARE

Throughout this book, a variety of dishware, glassware and cutlery is used, each chosen to match the occasion and the food or drink being served. Let these selections inspire your own choices. Ideally, dishware should flatter the food you are serving and play to any theme (such as Italian ceramics for a Mediterranean menu). On a more practical level, however, count to be sure you have enough pieces for the menu and for the number of guests. Don't hesitate to mix patterns. Borrow, buy or rent additional pieces if needed, calling at least a week ahead for rentals.

FLOWERS & OTHER CENTERPIECES

Well-planned centerpieces enhance a party's festive air. Flowers are the most obvious choice, but all kinds of items can be incorporated, such as shells, ribbons, twigs and leaves. Beautifully arranged seasonal vegetables, fruits or herbs also make stunning nonfloral decorations. Always bear in mind that the best centerpieces are low and spread out, allowing guests to see each other across the table.

LIGHTING & MUSIC

For an evening party, a night or two before, turn on all the lights and look over the setting. If you can, reposition lamps to help define conversation areas.

ɕ Candlelight always adds to the ambience and flatters anyone seen in its glow. But be sure to use supplementary electric lights, or the room may be too dark. It's best to use good-quality drip-free candles such as beeswax. Avoid scented candles, which can detract from your guests' appreciation of the food and wine.

ɕ Any music you select should serve to enhance the mood subtly. Your personal tastes will certainly play a part in the music you choose, but bear in mind guests' inclinations as well. For a very special occasion, you might want to employ musicians. Always keep music low enough that it doesn't compete with normal conversational levels.

GIFTS & FAVORS

Special events become all the more lasting when guests are offered mementos to take home. Whether it is a jar of homemade preserves, a bottle of wine with a personalized label, or even a small framed instant photograph used as a placecard, remember that a host gift should not be so grand that it causes embarrassment, requires a special acknowledgment or makes guests feel obliged to reciprocate. Throughout this book, you'll find suggestions for host gifts that you may find useful or inspiring.

PUTTING IT ALL TOGETHER

In the end, however, the success of any party depends less on how you set the scene, or even on the food or drink you serve, than on how welcome you make your guests feel. In the belief that a relaxed host or hostess is the best party giver, this book is de-signed to be an all-encompassing resource—a resource guaranteed to put you as much at ease as your guests are sure to be.

Casual Gatherings

૭৶

No matter what the time of day or the season of the year, a casual party
is always in order, from a dinner with co-workers or dear friends to an
engagement shower, from a cookout celebrating summer to a Sunday
morning brunch, from seafood chowder by the fireside to a beer-and-
pizza extravaganza where everyone lends the cook a hand.

Regardless of the size of the guest list, the menus that follow ensure
a relaxed experience. Created with an eye to busy schedules, the food
can either be gradually put together over the course of a week or
assembled in just an afternoon. The suggested decorations, too, are easily
achieved, providing maximum effect with minimal effort. With a little
planning and advance preparation, any of these casual get-togethers can
be as much fun for the host or hostess as it is for the guests.

Welcome Home Dinner

THE SIMPLE PHRASE "Welcome Home" may do more to warm the heart than any other words. Whether it marks the return of a family member or of a friend, and whether it falls on a special holiday, during a school break or after a long trip, a homecoming dinner delights guests and hosts alike with its informal, generous hospitality.

The style of the party setting matters far less than the spirit with which you stage the event. Whether you invite close friends of the guest of honor or celebrate with just family, bring out your long-cherished dishes and other memorabilia to help rekindle fond memories. This menu, in all its charm and simplicity, would suit almost any close-knit gathering. For our party, we kept the decorations comfortingly casual: flowers grouped in antique containers and baskets and favorite collectibles scattered here and there.

Left uncovered to show off its lovingly worn finish, an old pine table is set with new and old Majolica dishware. Separate plates are set atop the dinner plates for the first-course crab cakes.

OUR WELCOME HOME menu features recipes that are time-honored favorites: a crab cake appetizer, roast leg of lamb and a rich chocolate dessert.

While carving and serving the lamb with its accompaniments at table may best suit this close-knit occasion, the crab cakes look most attractive presented on individual plates. We suggest serving them from the kitchen. The chocolate mousse torte also looks best brought to the table in individual slices.

Menu

BEVERAGE IDEAS

This traditional meal demands classic companions. A smoky single-malt scotch before dinner will begin things on the right note. Later, move to an aromatic Sauvignon Blanc, Vernaccia or Semillon to accompany the crab cakes. The lamb calls for a Bordeaux or a California Cabernet Sauvignon. Pour a late-harvest Zinfandel or ruby port with dessert.

Deviled Crab Cakes on Mixed Greens
with Ginger-Citrus Vinaigrette

❧

Roast Leg of Lamb
with Braised Garlic, Sherry & Thyme

Herbed Mashed Potatoes

Glazed Carrots with Grapes & Walnuts

❧

Chocolate Mousse Torte
with Cold Zabaglione Sauce

A bottle of wine brought by a guest is displayed with glasses in
an antique wine holder decorated with grapes and a bow.

PREPARATION LIST

◆ One day before, assemble the crab cake mixture, form into cakes and coat with bread crumbs; prepare the leg of lamb for roasting and refrigerate.

◆ Up to eight hours before, make the torte and the zabaglione sauce. At the same time, make the vinaigrette and wash and crisp the greens; ready the carrots and grapes for cooking and poach the garlic cloves.

◆ One and one-half hours before, begin to bake the potatoes and roast the lamb.

EACH RECIPE YIELDS 6–8 SERVINGS.

An old ceramic mixing bowl from the kitchen becomes an impromptu vase
for snapdragons, ranunculi, freesias and assorted wildflowers.

DEVILED CRAB CAKES ON MIXED GREENS WITH GINGER-CITRUS VINAIGRETTE

SERVES 6–8

Seek out fresh crab meat for these special cakes. They are moist and flavorful but not too spicy. The crab cake mixture can be made the night before and the cakes formed and breaded and then covered and refrigerated. The vinaigrette can be made and the greens washed and crisped 8 hours in advance. Cook the crab cakes just before serving or keep warm in a 300°F (150°C) oven for up to 15 minutes. If you like, use watercress for part of the lettuce and/or garnish the greens with diced avocado or mango and then drizzle with the vinaigrette.

FOR THE CRAB CAKES:

3 tablespoons unsalted butter
1 cup (5 oz/155 g) finely chopped
 yellow onion
⅓ cup (1½ oz/45 g) finely chopped
 celery
¼ cup (1½ oz/45 g) finely chopped
 red or green bell pepper (capsicum)
1 tablespoon dry mustard
½ teaspoon cayenne pepper
1 lb (500 g) fresh crab meat, picked
 over for shell fragments and cartilage
⅓ cup (3 fl oz/80 ml) mayonnaise
1 egg, lightly beaten
½ cup (1 oz/30 g) fresh bread crumbs
1 tablespoon finely grated lemon zest
 (see glossary)
4 tablespoons chopped fresh flat-leaf
 (Italian) parsley
salt and freshly ground pepper
1 cup (4 oz/125 g) fine dried bread
 crumbs

FOR THE GINGER-CITRUS VINAIGRETTE:

¾ cup (6 fl oz/180 ml) peanut oil
finely grated zest of 1 lemon or lime
 (see glossary)
¼ cup (2 fl oz/60 ml) lemon or lime
 juice
2 tablespoons grated, peeled fresh
 ginger
1 fresh jalapeño (hot green) chili
 pepper, seeded, if desired, and minced
sugar
salt

8 cups mixed torn lettuces
peanut oil for frying

To make the crab cakes, in a sauté pan over medium heat, melt the butter. Add the onion and sauté until translucent, about 8 minutes. Add the celery and bell pepper and sauté until tender, about 5 minutes longer. Stir in the mustard and cayenne pepper and cook for 1–2 minutes, stirring constantly to prevent scorching. Transfer to a bowl and let cool completely. Add the crab meat, mayonnaise, egg, fresh bread crumbs, lemon zest and parsley. Fold together gently until all the ingredients are thoroughly incorporated; do not overmix. Season to taste with salt and pepper. Form into 8 cakes each about ½ inch (12 mm) thick.

❧ Place the dried bread crumbs on a plate or in a shallow bowl and, working with 1 cake at a time, coat the cakes evenly with the crumbs. Cover and refrigerate for at least 1 hour or as long as overnight; the cakes will hold together better if they have been chilled.

❧ To make the vinaigrette, in a bowl, whisk together the peanut oil, lemon or lime zest and juice, ginger and jalapeño. Season to taste with sugar and salt.

❧ Toss the lettuces with half of the vinaigrette and divide among the 6–8 individual plates.

❧ To cook the crab cakes, in a large frying pan over medium-high heat, pour in oil to a depth of 1 inch (2.5 cm). When the oil is shimmery, slip the cakes into the pan, working in batches if the pan is too crowded. Fry, turning once, until golden, 2–3 minutes on each side.

❧ To serve, place the warm crab cakes atop the greens and drizzle with the remaining vinaigrette. Serve at once.

The occasion's happy informality inspires a whimsical display of family collectibles playing on the theme of coming home to roost.

Deviled Crab Cakes on Mixed Greens with Ginger-Citrus Vinaigrette

Roast Leg of Lamb with Braised Garlic, Sherry & Thyme; Herbed Mashed Potatoes

ROAST LEG OF LAMB WITH BRAISED GARLIC, SHERRY & THYME

SERVES 6–8

The lamb can be roasted with the bone in, or you can ask the butcher to bone the leg and tie it for easier carving and more uniform slices. It is best to insert the garlic and thyme sprigs into the leg the day before roasting to flavor the meat more intensely, but this step can also be done just before the leg goes into the oven. Be sure to remove the lamb from the refrigerator about an hour before putting it in the oven.

1 leg of lamb, about 6 lb (3 kg)
3 or 4 cloves garlic, cut into slivers
12–14 small fresh thyme sprigs, each
    ½ inch (12 mm) long
salt and freshly ground pepper

FOR THE BRAISED GARLIC:

3 heads garlic, cloves separated and
    peeled
beef stock, to cover (see page 294)
3 fresh thyme sprigs
1 bay leaf

FOR THE SAUCE:

beef stock as needed
1 cup (8 fl oz/250 ml) dry sherry
4 teaspoons chopped fresh thyme
salt and freshly ground pepper

Cut 12–14 small, shallow slits into the surface of the lamb. Insert a sliver of garlic and a thyme sprig into each slit. Cover and refrigerate for up to 1 day.
❧ Preheat an oven to 400°F (200°C). Sprinkle the lamb with salt and pepper and place in a roasting pan.
❧ Roast for about 1¼ hours for rare with the bone in, or until a meat thermometer registers 130°F (54°C). A boneless leg will take about 1 hour.

❧ While the lamb is roasting, prepare the braised garlic. In a saucepan over medium heat, combine the garlic cloves, stock to cover barely, thyme sprigs and bay leaf. Cover, bring to a simmer and continue to simmer over medium heat until the garlic is tender when pierced with a fork, about 25 minutes. Remove from the heat and, using a slotted spoon, transfer the garlic to a small bowl. Strain the cooking liquid into a 2-cup (16-fl oz/500-ml) measuring cup.
❧ To make the sauce, add stock to the strained liquid to measure 2 cups (16 fl oz/500 ml) and transfer to a saucepan. Add the sherry and bring to a boil. Boil, uncovered, over high heat until reduced by one-third. Add the chopped thyme and reserved braised garlic cloves. Adjust the seasoning with salt and pepper and keep warm.
❧ When the lamb is done, remove from the oven and cover loosely with aluminum foil. Let rest for 10 minutes. Carve the lamb and divide evenly among individual plates. Spoon some of the sauce, including the garlic cloves, over each serving of the lamb. Serve immediately.

HERBED MASHED POTATOES

SERVES 6-8

Who doesn't love mashed potatoes? They are in the true spirit of a casual meal. You can use light cream, heavy cream or milk. And if you like the sharp flavor, buttermilk is lower in fat and will work well, too. The potatoes should be baked on a separate baking sheet. They can be mashed ahead of time and held over warm water until ready to serve.

6 large baking potatoes, about
    3 lbs (1.5 kg)
1 cup (8 fl oz/250 ml) light (single)
    cream, heavy (double) cream or milk
6 tablespoons (3 oz/90 g) unsalted butter
2 teaspoons chopped fresh parsley
2 teaspoons chopped fresh thyme
2 teaspoons chopped fresh marjoram
salt and freshly ground pepper

Preheat an oven to 400°F (200°C).
❧ Pierce the potatoes several times with a fork and place them directly on the oven rack or on a baking sheet and bake until very tender, about 1 hour. Remove from the oven and let cool just until they can be handled.
❧ While the potatoes are cooling, heat the cream in a small saucepan over medium-low heat until small bubbles form at the edge of the pan. Cut the potatoes in half and scoop out the pulp into a bowl. Then pass the pulp through a potato ricer or a food mill placed over a large saucepan. Alternatively, scoop out the pulp into a bowl and mash with a potato masher, then transfer to a large saucepan.
❧ Add the butter to the potatoes and mash it into them with a spoon or fork. Then, with the saucepan over low heat, gradually add the hot cream to the potatoes, stirring constantly. Continue to stir well until the desired consistency is achieved.
❧ Mix in the herbs and season to taste with salt and pepper. If you're not ready to serve, transfer potatoes to the top pan of a double boiler or to a heatproof bowl and place over (but not touching) hot water. When ready, transfer to a serving dish and serve immediately.

Glazed Carrots with Grapes & Walnuts

GLAZED CARROTS WITH GRAPES & WALNUTS

SERVES 6–8

The carrots and grapes can be prepared for cooking up to 8 hours in advance. For a citrusy accent, add 2 teaspoons grated lemon or orange zest (see glossary) with the stock. This dish is also good prepared with currants instead of grapes (see below). A sprinkling of chopped fresh mint makes a good garnish.

1 large bunch carrots, peeled and sliced about ¼ inch (6 mm) thick (about 6 cups/1½ lb/750 g)

¼ cup (2 oz/60 g) unsalted butter

1 cup (8 fl oz/250 ml) chicken stock (see page 295) or water

3 tablespoons sugar

1 cup (6 oz/185 g) seedless red grapes, cut in half

½ cup (2 oz/60 g) chopped walnuts

salt and freshly ground pepper

In a wide sauté pan over high heat, combine the carrots, butter, stock or water and sugar. Bring to a boil, then reduce the heat to medium-low. Simmer, uncovered, until the carrots are tender and the pan juices are reduced to a syrupy glaze, 8–10 minutes.

❧ Stir in the grapes and walnuts and season to taste with salt and pepper. Serve immediately.

GLAZED CARROTS WITH CURRANTS AND WALNUTS

Omit the grapes. In a small bowl, combine 1 cup (6 oz/185 g) dried currants and hot water to cover. Let stand for 20 minutes until plumped, then drain, reserving the soaking liquid. Measure the soaking liquid and use in place of part or all of the stock or water. Add the currants with the walnuts.

To decorate everyday candlesticks, attach grapes, flowers or ivy to your candleholders with florist's tape, then conceal the tape with ribbon.

CHOCOLATE MOUSSE TORTE WITH COLD ZABAGLIONE SAUCE

SERVES 6–8

Utterly rich, this would make a special birthday cake for a chocoholic. The cold zabaglione is a dramatic addition. The torte can be made the day before, but it will taste best if made no more than 8 hours ahead. Serve at room temperature. The sauce can also be spooned over fresh berries or simple pound cake. Served right off the heat, this rich wine custard is called zabaglione *in Italy and* sabayon *in France. It can be chilled for up to 8 hours.*

8 oz (250 g) bittersweet chocolate
1 cup (8 oz/250 g) unsalted butter
1 cup (8 oz/250 g) sugar
¼ cup (2 fl oz/60 ml) brewed coffee
10 eggs, separated
1 teaspoon vanilla extract (essence)
½ cup (2½ oz/75 g) all-purpose
   (plain) flour
½ teaspoon salt

FOR THE ZABAGLIONE:

1 cup (8 fl oz/250 ml) dry Marsala (see
   glossary)
7 egg yolks
7 tablespoons (3½ oz/105 g) sugar
1 cup (8 fl oz/250 ml) heavy (double)
   cream

2 cups (8 oz/250 g) raspberries or
   strawberries

Preheat an oven to 350°F (180°C). Butter the bottom and sides of a 9-inch (23-cm) springform pan, then line the bottom of the pan with parchment paper.

*Chocolate Mousse Torte with
Cold Zabaglione Sauce*

❧ In the top pan of a double boiler or in a heatproof bowl placed over (but not touching) hot water, combine the chocolate, butter, sugar and coffee. Heat until the chocolate and butter are melted, then stir until smooth. Remove from the heat and whisk in the egg yolks and vanilla. Then fold in the flour and salt.

❧ In a bowl, using an electric mixer set on medium speed, beat the egg whites until frothy. Increase the speed to high and beat until medium-firm peaks form. Gently fold the egg whites into the batter just until they fully disappear. Do not overmix. Transfer the batter to the prepared pan.

❧ Bake the torte until it springs back when touched lightly in the center, 45–60 minutes.

❧ While the torte is baking, make the zabaglione. In a bowl, whisk together the Marsala, egg yolks and sugar until well blended. Pour through a fine-mesh sieve into the top pan of a large double boiler or into a large heatproof bowl. Place the pan or bowl over (but not touching) simmering water. Using a whisk or an electric mixer set on medium speed, beat until thickened, pale and fluffy, 10–15 minutes. The mixture should double in volume.

❧ Remove the pan or bowl from the heat and immediately nest in a bowl of ice to cool it down completely. In a chilled bowl with chilled beaters, whip the cream until stiff peaks form. Fold the cold custard into the whipped cream. Cover and refrigerate.

❧ Remove the torte from the oven when done and let cool completely in the pan on a wire rack. Remove the pan sides and transfer the torte to a serving plate. Cut into wedges and serve with the zabaglione sauce and the berries.

DATE DINNER FOR TWO

A FIRST-EVER INVITATION to dinner presents a delicate balancing act. It aims, as it should, both to make a good impression on your guest and to express your interest without fanning the flames of romance too vigorously.

Gracious informality, we believe, is the key, and to that end we decided to place a small table in the living room, setting it with a subtly checked cloth, woven place mats, simple pottery plates and nice tumblers to replace the usual stemmed wineglasses. In the same casual spirit, we chose to arrange pretty but understated bouquets in a simple glass vase and in a tin florist's bucket, and we lit the table with votive candles rather than more formal tapers. A bowl of seasonal fruit and, perhaps, one or two favorite objects make the table for two appear pleasingly personal but not overdone.

If you like, precede the meal with a glass of Champagne or, as shown here, sparkling wine. Two delicate tumblers strike a more casual tone than tall Champagne flutes would.

Menu

OUR MENU FOR two impresses subtly by offering courses based on popular but light ingredients: shrimp, chicken breast, white rice and seasonal green beans or asparagus. More important still, it encourages animated conversation with exotic but unintimidating dishes inspired by the cuisines of Asia. A rich chocolate mousse, enlivened with a hint of orange, provides an appropriately sweet finale.

All of the recipes are easy to prepare and some of the work can even be done up to two days in advance; only brief cooking is required before serving—leaving you free to devote your full attention to your guest.

BEVERAGE IDEAS

Start with a half bottle or split of brut Champagne or sparkling wine. Continue with a zesty white with just a snap of sweetness, such as a German or American Riesling. If you prefer a red, try a Beaujolais or an Italian Dolcetto or Barbera. End the meal with an orange Muscat wine or chilled Cointreau.

Asian-Inspired Shrimp Salad
with Tropical Fruit

❧

Satay with Peanut Dipping Sauce

Rice Pilaf

Asparagus or
Green Beans with Ginger

❧

Chocolate-Orange Mousse

At each place setting, a shallow glass bowl atop a simple pottery dinner plate awaits the first-course salad.

PREPARATION LIST

◆ You can make the peanut dipping sauce for the satay a day or two before.

◆ One day before, cube the meat for the satay; peel and cook the shrimp and make the chocolate mousse.

◆ In the morning or during the day, make the vinaigrette and cut up the papaya, mango or cucumber. Wash, dry and crisp the lettuces for the salad.

◆ Three to five hours before, marinate the meat for the satay and trim the asparagus or green beans.

EACH RECIPE YIELDS 2 SERVINGS.

With little fuss, small seasonal bouquets may be arranged with other attractive mementos to form a decorative display on a mantel or sideboard.

ASIAN-INSPIRED SHRIMP SALAD WITH TROPICAL FRUIT

SERVES 2

Tangy fruit and opalescent pink shrimp dressed with a spicy sweet-and-tart vinaigrette make a nice light beginning for a special meal. If you cannot find a mango or papaya in the market, 2 oranges, peeled and sectioned, or ½ cantaloupe, peeled, seeded and diced, can be substituted. Or the salad can be made without fruit and with the addition of cucumber (see below). The shrimp can be poached the night before or earlier in the day when you prepare the vinaigrette. Dice or slice the fruit as you like. Assemble at the last minute.

2 cups (16 fl oz/500 ml) water or dry
   white wine
½ lb (250 g) medium-sized shrimp
   (prawns), peeled and deveined
   (about 10) (see glossary)
1 ripe papaya or mango
3 cups (6 oz/185 g) torn mixed lettuces
3 tablespoons torn fresh mint leaves
3 tablespoons torn fresh basil leaves

FOR THE VINAIGRETTE:

⅓ cup (3 fl oz/80 ml) peanut oil or
   olive oil
finely grated zest of 1 lime (see glossary)
3 tablespoons fresh lime juice
1 tablespoon brown sugar
½ teaspoon red pepper flakes or
   ½ teaspoon diced fresh jalapeño (hot
   green) chili pepper, or to taste
salt

In a saucepan over high heat, bring the water or wine to a boil. Add the shrimp and cook until they turn pink and curl, 3–5 minutes. Using a slotted spoon, transfer to a bowl. Cover and refrigerate until needed.

❧ If using a papaya, peel, then cut in half lengthwise and scoop out and discard the seeds. Dice or slice the flesh. If using a mango, cut off the flesh from either side of the large central pit, then dice or slice the flesh. (There will be some tasty flesh still clinging to the pit; eat it off while standing over the sink for a true chef's treat.)

❧ In a bowl combine the lettuces, mint and basil and toss to mix.

❧ To make the vinaigrette, in a small bowl, thoroughly whisk together the peanut or olive oil, lime zest and juice, brown sugar, pepper flakes or jalapeño pepper and the salt to taste.

❧ Add a few tablespoons of the vinaigrette to the shrimp, toss well and let stand for a few minutes. Drizzle half of the remaining vinaigrette over the lettuces and herbs and toss thoroughly. Divide the lettuce mixture between 2 individual plates. Top with the shrimp and papaya or mango. Drizzle the remaining vinaigrette over the top.

SHRIMP SALAD WITH CUCUMBER

Omit the fruit. Peel 1 small cucumber, cut in half lengthwise and scoop out and discard the seeds. Slice the cucumber thinly and place in a bowl. Add 2 tablespoons of the vinaigrette to the cucumber, toss well and let stand for 10 minutes. Proceed as directed for the shrimp and lettuce mixture, then assemble the salad, substituting the cucumber for the fruit.

The key to stress-free cooking is to have all the ingredients assembled beforehand. Here, the components of the dish are readily accessible on a countertop; only the fruit needs last-minute attention.

*Asian-Inspired Shrimp
Salad with Tropical Fruit*

SATAY WITH PEANUT DIPPING SAUCE

SERVES 2

The meat can be cubed the day before and then marinated in the refrigerator 3 to 5 hours in advance or at room temperature for 30 minutes while you assemble the rest of the meal. Lemongrass can be found in Southeast Asian stores and well-stocked food stores. For the coconut cream, purchase a can of coconut milk and, without shaking the can, open it and skim off the thick layer of cream that has settled on the top. The peanut sauce can be made 2 days in advance and reheated. Fruit salsa (recipe on page 295) may be substituted for the peanut sauce if you have prepared the shrimp salad with cucumber rather than fruit.

FOR THE MARINADE:

2 cloves garlic

1 piece fresh ginger, about 1 inch (2.5 cm) long, peeled and sliced

2 tablespoons minced green (spring) onions

2 tablespoons minced lemongrass or 2 teaspoons finely grated lemon zest (see glossary)

2 tablespoons soy sauce

2 tablespoons bourbon, rice wine or dry sherry

1 tablespoon Asian sesame oil

½ teaspoon freshly ground white pepper

CHOICE OF ONE:

4 half chicken breasts, boned and skinned, 4–6 oz (125–185 g) each

2 beef fillet steaks, 6–8 oz (185–250 g) each

2 small pork tenderloins, about 6 oz (185 g) each

FOR THE PEANUT DIPPING SAUCE:

½ cup (5 oz/155 g) unsalted peanut butter

2 tablespoons fresh lemon or lime juice

2 tablespoons coconut cream

¼ cup (2 fl oz/60 ml) water

2 tablespoons soy sauce

¼ teaspoon cayenne pepper, or to taste

½ teaspoon curry powder

sugar

olive oil or peanut oil

salt and freshly ground pepper

To make the marinade, in a food processor fitted with the metal blade or blender, combine the garlic, ginger, green onions and lemongrass or lemon zest. Using on-off pulses, process to form a purée. Add the soy sauce, bourbon or wine, sesame oil and white pepper and process just until blended.

❧ To make the satay, select one of the meats and cut into 1-inch (2.5-cm) cubes. Place in a glass or plastic container, add the marinade and toss to distribute evenly. Cover and refrigerate for 3–5 hours, turning occasionally, or marinate at room temperature for 30 minutes.

❧ To make the dipping sauce, in a heavy saucepan over medium heat, combine the peanut butter, lemon or lime juice, coconut cream, water, soy sauce, cayenne pepper, curry powder and sugar to taste. Bring to a simmer, stirring constantly. Transfer to the top pan of a double boiler or to a heatproof bowl and place over (but not touching) hot water until serving.

❧ Preheat a broiler (griller), or make a fire in a charcoal grill. Soak 6 bamboo skewers in water to cover for about 15–30 minutes.

❧ Drain and thread the meat cubes onto the soaked skewers. Brush the meat with olive or peanut oil and sprinkle with salt and pepper to taste.

❧ Place the skewers on an oiled grill and grill, turning once, until cooked, 2–3 minutes on each side for chicken or beef and 4–5 minutes on each side for the pork. Serve with the warm dipping sauce.

Peanut butter, coconut cream, citrus juice, soy sauce, spices and sugar meld their flavors to make a Southeast Asian–style peanut sauce.

Satay with Peanut Dipping Sauce

RICE PILAF

SERVES 2

Here is a classic rice pilaf that may be embellished with any number of additions. If you are serving the peanut sauce with the satay, do not top the pilaf with toasted nuts. Do not use the currants if you are serving the fruit salsa with the satay.

2 tablespoons peanut oil or olive oil
1 small yellow onion, diced (4–5 tablespoons/1½ oz/45 g)
1 cup (7 oz/220 g) basmati or jasmine rice, rinsed and drained
2 cups (16 fl oz/500 ml) water or chicken stock (see page 295)
1 piece fresh ginger, about 1 inch (2.5 cm) long, peeled and smashed
salt

SUGGESTED ADDITIONS:

2 tablespoons toasted pine nuts or almonds (see glossary)
2 tablespoons dried currants, plumped in hot water to cover for 20 minutes and drained
3 tablespoons minced green (spring) onions, green tops only
1 small ripe tomato, peeled, seeded and diced
2 tablespoons flaked coconut, lightly toasted in a dry frying pan

In a saucepan over medium heat, warm the peanut or olive oil. Add the onion and sauté until translucent, about 8 minutes. Add the rice and sauté for a few minutes until the kernels are thoroughly coated with the oil.

❧ Add the water or stock, ginger and salt to taste and bring to a boil. Cook for 2 minutes, reduce the heat to low, cover and simmer until the water is absorbed, 15–20 minutes.

❧ Stir in the additions of choice and remove from the heat. Let rest for 10 minutes, then fluff with a fork, remove ginger and serve at once.

ASPARAGUS OR GREEN BEANS WITH GINGER

SERVES 2

A green vegetable is the perfect accompaniment to the satay and rice. The asparagus or green beans can be readied 3–5 hours in advance. Asparagus are most flavorful when still crisp, while green beans taste best when they are cooked until somewhat tender. You can also use spinach (see variation at right) in place of the asparagus or green beans.

10 oz (315 g) asparagus or green beans
2 tablespoons peanut or vegetable oil or unsalted butter
¼ cup (1½ oz/45 g) minced yellow onion
1 tablespoon grated, peeled fresh ginger or ½ teaspoon red pepper flakes
1 teaspoon minced garlic
⅔ cup (5 fl oz/160 ml) water or chicken (see page 295) or vegetable stock
finely grated zest of 1 lemon (see glossary) or fresh lemon juice, optional
salt and freshly ground pepper

If using the asparagus, break off the ends, where they snap easily. Peel the stalks with a paring knife or vegetable peeler if they are thick. Cut on the diagonal into 2-inch (5-cm) lengths. If using the green beans, trim off their tops and tails and cut in half crosswise if they are longer than 2 inches (5 cm).

❧ In a sauté pan over medium heat, warm the peanut or vegetable oil or melt the butter. Add the onion and sauté until tender, about 5 minutes. Add the ginger or pepper flakes and garlic and sauté, stirring often, for 2 minutes longer. Add the water or stock and the beans or asparagus and cook, uncovered, over medium heat until the vegetables are tender and have absorbed most of the water or stock, 5–6 minutes for the beans and about 4 minutes for the asparagus.

❧ Stir in the lemon zest or juice to taste, if using, and then season to taste with salt and pepper. Serve immediately.

SPINACH WITH GINGER
Carefully wash 1 lb (500 g) spinach and trim off the stems. Sauté the onion, ginger and garlic as directed, then add the spinach with its washing water still clinging to its leaves. Omit the ⅔ cup (5 fl oz/160 ml) water or stock. Cook uncovered as directed, turning the spinach occasionally with a fork, just until wilted and tender, 3–5 minutes. Season as directed.

Rice Pilaf; Asparagus with Ginger

CHOCOLATE-ORANGE MOUSSE

SERVES 2, WITH LEFTOVERS

This is an ideal dessert for two, as it can be prepared fully the night before and poured into individual ramekins ready for serving. The recipe makes about two or three 1-cup (8 fl oz/250 ml) portions, depending upon how much air you whip into the egg whites and cream. But it is so good you may not mind having an extra serving on hand. Look for high-quality candied orange peel in specialty-food stores.

2 oz (60 g) semisweet chocolate

2 tablespoons fresh orange juice or
　orange-flavored liqueur

2 eggs, separated

pinch of salt

¼ cup (2 oz/60 g) sugar

½ cup (4 fl oz/125 ml) heavy (double)
　cream

2 teaspoons minced candied orange
　peel, optional

Combine the chocolate and orange juice or liqueur in the top pan of a double boiler or in a heatproof bowl. Place over (but not touching) simmering water and stir until melted and smooth. Remove the pan or bowl from over the water and let cool a bit, then whisk in the egg yolks until well blended.

❧ In a bowl combine the egg whites and salt. Using an electric mixer, beat until soft peaks form. Gradually add the sugar, continuing to beat until stiff, but not dry, peaks form. Stir one-third of the beaten whites into the melted chocolate to lighten it, and then gently fold in the remaining whites into the mixture.

❧ In a chilled bowl with chilled beaters, beat the cream until stiff peaks form. Gently fold the cream into the chocolate mixture.

❧ Divide the mixture evenly among 2 or 3 attractive ramekins. Cover and refrigerate until set, at least 2 hours or for up to 1 day.

❧ To serve, garnish with the candied orange peel, if desired.

Gourmet coffee shops now sell a variety of sweeter roasts that go especially well with dessert. Serve freshly brewed regular or decaffeinated coffee and offer Muscat wine or an orange-flavored liqueur, such as Cointreau.

Chocolate-Orange Mousse

FAMILY BIRTHDAY PARTY

A BIRTHDAY DINNER SHARED with family and close friends calls for a particularly light and cheerful mood. There's no need to dress up, to spend hours in the kitchen or to set an elaborate table. The party should instead focus on honoring the birthday celebrant.

We decided to hold our party late in the afternoon on a spring day, letting the bright sunshine add to the occasion's glow. But even if your guest of honor's day falls during the winter, an array of brightly colored tableware and linens, as well as centerpieces of complementary-colored flowers, peppers and lemons, can give the room a festive air just as surely as the more traditional balloons and streamers would. To set the table, we used more napkins as place mats, letting them hang slightly over the edge, instead of a tablecloth.

If you have a garden of blooming flowers, pick some to decorate the birthday table. Here, Icelandic poppies and anemones (both seasonally available from florists) form a colorful bouquet in a watering can before they are arranged.

Menu

INDIAN SPICES ENLIVEN the main course and side dishes in our birthday dinner menu. To leave you free to enjoy the celebration, most of the dishes are prepared ahead of the party day.

For such a close-knit gathering, we recommend serving most of the meal family style. The first-course soup might be ladled into bowls in the kitchen and carried out on a tray. The chicken, rice and vegetables follow on serving platters or in bowls, to be passed around the table. Dessert, however, calls for a special presentation: decorate a serving of profiteroles with a few brightly burning tapers for the celebrant to blow out.

Just inside the front door, an oversized basket with a handle holds birthday gifts that can be carried with ease to the honoree for opening.

Cold Cucumber Soup

❧

Ginger & Orange Curried Fried Chicken

Mango Chutney

Saffron Rice

Corn with Chilies & Coconut Milk

Spinach with Peas & Mint

❧

Almond Profiteroles with
Banana Ice Cream & Hot Fudge Sauce

A glazed earthenware plate reflects the bright, primary colors of the table linens and centerpieces. Napkins are informally rolled and secured with woven napkin rings.

PREPARATION LIST

◆ A few weeks before, make the chutney and store in the refrigerator.

◆ Two weeks before, make the fudge sauce.

◆ Two days before, mix the ice cream base.

◆ A day before, make the soup and the profiteroles; roast the chilies and wash the spinach. Freeze the ice cream.

◆ About two hours before, marinate the chicken and make the flour coating; prepare the corn base and soak the saffron rice. Shell and cook the peas.

EACH RECIPE YIELDS 6 SERVINGS.

BEVERAGE IDEAS

Champagne or sparkling wine is a must to celebrate the occasion. A light, red wine (Beaujolais, American Pinot Noir or Gamay) or a medium-bodied white (California Chardonnay, off-dry Riesling or Alsatian Gewürztraminer), or both, may accompany the food. For dessert, offer amaretto coffee or a Godiva chocolate liqueur.

COLD CUCUMBER SOUP

SERVES 6

An ideal soup for a hot summer day. It can also be served hot instead of cold (see below). Mint, dill or basil is a refreshing and appropriate garnish to sprinkle on top. If you would like some added crunch, garnish each serving with chopped toasted walnuts, pine nuts or almonds. Prepare the soup the day before serving and chill well. Adjust seasoning at serving time.

2 tablespoons unsalted butter

1 yellow onion, diced

3–4 cups (24–32 fl oz/750 ml–1 l) chicken stock (see page 295)

1 small potato, about 4 oz (125 g), peeled and diced

3 cucumbers, peeled, seeded and diced

1 cup (8 oz/250 g) plain yogurt or ½ cup (4 fl oz/125 ml) heavy (double) cream

salt and freshly ground pepper

3 tablespoons chopped fresh dill, mint or basil

In a medium saucepan over medium heat, melt the butter. Add the onion and sauté until tender and translucent, about 10 minutes. Add 3 cups (24 fl oz/ 750 ml) of the chicken stock and the potato, raise the heat to high and bring to a boil. Reduce the heat to medium and simmer, uncovered, for 10 minutes. Add the cucumbers and continue to simmer until the cucumbers are soft, about 10 minutes longer.

&❧ Working in batches, transfer to a food processor fitted with the metal blade or to a blender and purée until smooth. If the purée is too thick, add as much of the remaining 1 cup (8 fl oz/ 250 ml) stock as needed to thin to a soup consistency. Transfer to a bowl, let cool slightly and then whisk in the yogurt or cream. Cover and refrigerate the soup until well chilled.

&❧ Add salt and pepper to taste and ladle into chilled bowls. Garnish with herb of choice and serve.

HOT CUCUMBER SOUP

To serve the soup hot, omit the yogurt. Add ½ cup (4 fl oz/125 ml) sour cream or heavy (double) cream to the processor or blender and then purée the soup. Add the stock as needed to thin the purée and reheat gently. Season to taste with salt and pepper. Alternatively, omit the sour cream or heavy cream, reheat the purée and serve garnished with a dollop of plain yogurt.

These bright blue and green oversized bottles make creative decanters for wine.

Cold Cucumber Soup

GINGER & ORANGE CURRIED FRIED CHICKEN

SERVES 6

Although frying the chicken must be done at the last minute, it marinates in the refrigerator for about 2 hours. Buttermilk and ginger tenderize the meat, so do not allow the chicken to stand in the marinade longer than the specified time. The curry-flavored flour can be mixed in a large paper bag or on a deep plate. You can also use bone-in chicken parts, but marinate them 3 hours and then fry, turning often, for 20–25 minutes. Offer 1 or 2 chicken breast halves per person.

2 cups (16 fl oz/500 ml) buttermilk
2 tablespoons grated, peeled fresh
 ginger
3 tablespoons grated orange zest (see
 glossary)
salt and freshly ground black pepper
12 half chicken breasts, boned,
 (5–6 oz/155–185 g each)
1½ cups (7½ oz/235 g) all-purpose
 (plain) flour
4–5 teaspoons curry powder
¾ teaspoon ground ginger
pinch cayenne pepper, optional
peanut oil for deep-frying
mango chutney (recipe on page 297) or
 high-quality bottled chutney

In a shallow glass or plastic dish, combine the buttermilk, grated ginger, orange zest and salt and pepper to taste and mix well. Add the chicken, turning to coat well. Cover and marinate for 1–2 hours in the refrigerator.

*Ginger & Orange Curried
Fried Chicken; Saffron Rice*

❧ In a large paper bag or on a deep plate, combine the flour, curry powder, ground ginger, salt and black pepper to taste and the cayenne pepper, if using.
❧ Remove the chicken from the marinade and, a few pieces at a time, shake them in the bag of seasoned flour or coat them evenly in the seasoned flour on the plate.
❧ In a large frying pan (or in 2 pans) over medium heat, pour in oil to a depth of 3 inches (7.5 cm) and heat to 375°F (190°C), or until a small cube of bread turns golden within moments of being dropped into it. When the oil is ready, add the chicken pieces and fry, turning once, until golden brown, 3–4 minutes on each side.
❧ Using a slotted spatula, transfer to paper towels to drain briefly. Arrange on a warmed platter or individual plates and serve immediately with the chutney.

SAFFRON RICE

SERVES 6

Fragrant with whole spices, this golden yellow rice can be soaked about 2 hours before serving and then baked while you are frying the chicken, or it can also be baked in advance and then kept warm in the top pan of a double boiler or in a heatproof bowl placed over (but not touching) hot water. If you are not including fruits or nuts in other dishes in the meal, raisins or almonds are a good addition to the rice (see below).

2 cups (14 oz/440 g) basmati rice
6 qt (6 l) water
salt
¼ cup (2 fl oz/60 ml) dry white wine
 or water
1 teaspoon saffron threads
4–6 tablespoons (2–3 oz/60–90 g)
 unsalted butter

1 cinnamon stick, about
 3 inches (5 cm) long
8 whole cloves
seeds from 8 cardamom pods
freshly ground pepper

In a bowl combine the rice and water to cover by 1 inch (2.5 cm). Let stand for 2 hours; drain.
❧ Preheat an oven to 350°F (180°C).
❧ In a saucepan, bring the 6 qt (6 l) water to a boil and add salt to taste. Add the drained rice and boil for 10 minutes.
❧ Drain the rice and rinse with warm water. Drain again and place in a shallow 1½-qt (1.5-l) baking dish measuring about 9 inches (23 cm) by 11 inches (28 cm) by 2 inches (5 cm).
❧ Meanwhile, in a small pan over low heat, warm the wine or water; remove from the heat. Crush the saffron threads gently and add to the warm liquid. Let stand for 10 minutes.
❧ In a small frying pan or saucepan over medium heat, melt the butter. Add the saffron and its soaking liquid, cinnamon, cloves, cardamom and pepper to taste and toss with the butter. Add the butter mixture to the rice, toss well and then cover the baking dish with aluminum foil.
❧ Bake until the butter has been absorbed and the rice is tender but still firm, about 25 minutes. Remove the cinnamon stick and cloves and discard. Serve the rice hot.

SAFFRON RICE WITH RAISINS OR ALMONDS

Soak ½ cup (3 oz/90 g) raisins in hot water to cover until soft and plump, about 20 minutes. Drain and add to the butter with the spices. Or add ½ cup (3 oz/90 g) toasted almonds (see glossary) to the butter with the spices.

CORN WITH CHILIES & COCONUT MILK

SERVES 6

Curried corn is incredibly sweet and aromatic. Summer white corn is best, but during the winter you may use frozen corn as well. You can also use corn stock in place of the chicken stock: combine the corn cobs with water to cover and boil for 30 minutes, then discard the cobs. The dish can be prepared up to the point where the coconut milk, stock and lemon zest are added 2 hours in advance and then finished just before serving.

1 teaspoon cumin seeds
2 tablespoons unsalted butter
¼ cup (¾ oz/20 g) minced green
   (spring) onions, including tender
   green tops
1 tablespoon ground coriander
⅛ teaspoon cayenne pepper
1 teaspoon curry powder
1 cup (8 fl oz/250 ml) coconut milk
½ cup (4 fl oz/125 ml) chicken stock
   (see page 295)
1 teaspoon finely grated lemon zest
   (see glossary)
4 cups (1½ lb/750 g) corn kernels
   (6–8 ears)
2 fresh pasilla chili peppers, roasted,
   peeled, deribbed and diced (see
   glossary)
4 tablespoons chopped fresh cilantro
   (fresh coriander)
salt and freshly ground black pepper

In a small, dry frying pan over medium heat, toast the cumin seeds, stirring or shaking the pan, until fragrant, about 3 minutes. Transfer to a spice grinder or a mortar and finely grind; set aside.

❧ In a large saucepan over medium heat, melt the butter. Add the green onions and sauté, stirring, until tender, about 5 minutes. Stir in the coriander, cumin, cayenne and curry powder and sauté for 3 minutes longer.

❧ Add the coconut milk, stock and lemon zest and bring to a simmer, stirring to mix well. Add the corn and continue to simmer until the corn is almost tender, about 3 minutes.

❧ Fold in the chilies and the cilantro and cook for 1 minute longer. Season to taste with salt and pepper.

❧ Transfer to a serving dish and serve at once.

SPINACH WITH PEAS & MINT

SERVES 6

This leafy curry is a fine foil for the richness of the chicken and the sweetness of the corn. Swiss chard (silverbeet) can be used in place of the spinach. The greens can be washed and dried up to a day ahead and stored in the crisper section of the refrigerator; shell and cook the peas up to 2 hours in advance. Thawed frozen peas can be substituted for the cooked fresh peas.

1 teaspoon fennel seeds
1 teaspoon cumin seeds
¼ cup (2 oz/60 g) unsalted butter or
   (2 fl oz/60 ml) olive oil
1 tablespoon grated, peeled fresh ginger
¼ teaspoon ground cloves
3 lb (1.5 kg) spinach, carefully washed,
   stems removed and cut into strips
   ½ inch (12 mm) wide
2 teaspoons finely grated lemon zest
   (see glossary)
1 cup (5 oz/155 g) shelled green peas
   (about 1 lb/500 g unshelled), cooked
   in boiling water until tender-crisp,
   2–5 minutes, and drained
salt and freshly ground pepper
½ cup (¾ oz/20 g) chopped fresh mint

In a small, dry frying pan over medium heat, toast the fennel and cumin seeds, stirring or shaking the pan, until fragrant, about 3 minutes. Transfer to a spice grinder or a mortar and finely grind; set aside.

❧ In a large, wide sauté pan over medium heat, melt the butter or warm the olive oil. Add the ground fennel and cumin, ginger and cloves and stir until heated through. Add the spinach and stir and toss until wilted, 3–5 minutes, adding a bit of water if the spinach begins to scorch.

❧ Stir in the lemon zest and peas and heat through. Season to taste with salt and pepper.

❧ Add the mint, toss well and transfer to a serving dish. Serve immediately.

Corn with Chilies & Coconut Milk;
Spinach with Peas & Mint

ALMOND PROFITEROLES WITH BANANA ICE CREAM & HOT FUDGE SAUCE

SERVES 6

Instead of a birthday cake, why not surprise everyone with these mini–cream puffs filled with banana ice cream and topped with a thick, rich hot fudge sauce. Put a candle on the birthday celebrant's portion and enjoy the party. The profiteroles can be prepared the day before, stored in a covered metal container and then warmed in a 350°F (180°C) oven for 5 minutes to recrisp them. The fudge sauce can be made up to 2 weeks in advance, refrigerated and then gently reheated. The ice cream base can be made 2 days in advance and then frozen the day before serving. Since bananas quickly darken after peeling, don't purée them until the moment you are ready to mix the bananas into the ice cream base.

FOR THE ICE CREAM:

6 egg yolks

2 cups (16 fl oz/500 ml) milk

2 cups (16 fl oz/500 ml) heavy (double) cream

¾ cup (6 oz/185 g) sugar

½ teaspoon freshly grated nutmeg

1 cup (8 oz/250 g) puréed ripe bananas (about 2 bananas)

1 teaspoon vanilla extract (essence)

¼ teaspoon salt

FOR THE PROFITEROLES:

1 cup (8 fl oz/250 ml) water

¼ teaspoon salt

½ cup (4 oz/125 g) unsalted butter, cut into pieces

1 cup (5 oz/155 g) all-purpose (plain) flour

1 tablespoon sugar

5 eggs

½ cup (2½ oz/75 g) chopped toasted almonds (see glossary)

hot fudge sauce (recipe on page 297)

To make the ice cream, place the egg yolks in a bowl and beat lightly with a fork until blended.

❧ In a saucepan over medium heat, combine the milk, cream, sugar and nutmeg. Heat, stirring to dissolve the sugar, until small bubbles form along the edge of the pan. Stir in the bananas. Gradually add a little of the hot cream mixture to the yolks, whisking constantly. Whisk in a bit more of the cream mixture, then whisk the yolk mixture into the hot cream mixture. Cook over medium heat, stirring constantly, until the custard coats the back of a spoon, 3–5 minutes.

❧ Strain the custard through a fine-mesh sieve into a bowl and then nest in an ice bath. Stir in the vanilla and salt. When cool, remove from the ice bath, cover and refrigerate overnight to develop the flavors.

❧ The next day, taste and adjust the sweetness and amount of vanilla or nutmeg, as necessary. Pour into an ice cream maker and freeze according to the manufacturer's instructions.

❧ To make the profiteroles, preheat an oven to 375°F (190°C). In a saucepan, combine the water, salt and butter and bring slowly to a boil. Remove from the heat and add the flour and sugar all at once. Return the pan to medium heat and cook, stirring vigorously, until the mixture forms a dry ball and pulls away from the sides of the pan, about 4 minutes.

❧ Remove from the heat and transfer the dough to a bowl. Then, using an electric mixer set on medium speed, beat in the eggs, one at a time, beating well after each addition. When all the eggs have been added, the mixture should be smooth and glossy and stiff enough to hold its shape. Spoon the profiterole pastry onto ungreased baking sheets, forming mounds about 1 inch (2.5 cm) in diameter for small profiteroles or 1½–2 inches (4–5 cm) in diameter for medium-sized profiteroles. You should have 18 small or 12 medium pastries in all. Sprinkle with the almonds.

❧ Bake until golden brown, about 20 minutes. Turn off the oven. Make 1 or 2 tiny slits in the side of each profiterole to let the steam escape. Position the oven door slightly ajar and leave the puffs in the oven to cool and dry, about 20 minutes.

❧ To serve, split the pastries in half and arrange on individual plates. Fill the bottom halves with the banana ice cream and replace the tops. Spoon the hot fudge sauce over the tops and serve immediately.

Almond Profiteroles with Banana Ice Cream & Hot Fudge Sauce

BACKYARD BARBECUE

THE WARMEST, MOST leisurely time of the year lures us outdoors to entertain, whether we are celebrating a public holiday, a family anniversary or nothing at all. The meal itself, cooked in the open air, becomes the occasion.

We set our early evening party in a large garden with a built-in stone barbecue. But, you could hold it on any patio large enough for an outdoor grill or even in an apartment, with the food cooked on a small barbecue on the balcony or in the kitchen broiler (griller). Oversized, brightly colored dishware, in this case Provençal pottery, holds generous servings and emphasizes the sunny spirit of the season, as do blossoms gathered from the garden or bought from the florist and, if space allows, pots and urns of live seasonal flowers.

SEVERAL SUN-DRENCHED cuisines contribute to our backyard barbecue menu. India, where foods are often cooked in a tandoor oven, inspired the appetizer. A Middle Eastern marinade flavors the pork loin, and South-western corn and Mediterranean tomato salads round out the offerings. The only cooking to do during the party itself is grilling the shrimp and pork, both quick, simple tasks. All recipes double or triple easily if the guest list grows.

The menu is meant to be served buffet style, so have dishes and platters on hand, with plates, napkins and cutlery stacked nearby. If you have picnic baskets or hampers, you might use them to carry all the serving pieces outside, and then leave them in view to underscore the ambience of an at-home picnic. Provide guests with seating at tables, on benches, or, should they succumb fully to summer's allure, on blankets or cushions on the grassy lawn.

Menu

BEVERAGE IDEAS

Wine spritzers or a zesty summer punch make a good start. Follow with an assortment of medium-bodied beers, red wines such as Zinfandel, Beaujolais or Italian Dolcetto and fragrant whites: Chardonnay, Chenin Blanc or a white Rhône.

Tandoori Shrimp

*Pork Loin with
Pomegranate & Orange Glaze*

Apricot Mustard

Cheddar Chive Biscuits

*Tomato Salad with
Basil-Honey Vinaigrette*

Corn Salad

Peach Bread Pudding

*Summer flowers and foliage are gathered from the garden for
decorations. Proper gloves, clippers and a basket ease the work.*

PREPARATION LIST

◆ You can make the apricot mustard two to three weeks (or up to several months) before.

◆ If serving the raspberry-lime purée with the bread pudding, make it the day before.

◆ The night before, marinate the pork and prepare the tandoori marinade.

◆ Make the corn salad, the bread pudding and the vinaigrette six hours before.

◆ Two hours before, slice the tomatoes.

◆ An hour before, marinate the shrimp, make the fire and form the biscuits.

EACH RECIPE YIELDS 6 SERVINGS.

*Guests can help
themselves to chilled
white wine in wicker-
insulated carafes or a
selection of beers on ice
in any lined container.
Arrange good-sized
glasses nearby and don't
forget the bottle opener.*

TANDOORI SHRIMP

SERVES 6

Shrimp is always popular, but if your budget is tight, cubes of fish or boneless chicken breast meat can be substituted (see below). The marinade can be made the night before, but be sure to marinate the shrimp only 1–2 hours. The shrimp can also be skewered and cooked in a preheated broiler (griller), or they can be sautéed in unsalted butter or peanut or olive oil. Soak the skewers while the charcoal heats in the grill.

2 cloves garlic, minced

1 piece fresh ginger, about 2 inches (5 cm) long, peeled and cut up

3 tablespoons fresh lemon or lime juice

¼ teaspoon ground turmeric

1 tablespoon ground cumin

½ teaspoon salt

2 fresh jalapeño (hot green) chili peppers, seeded, if desired, and minced (see glossary)

1 cup (8 oz/250 g) nonfat plain yogurt

1 tablespoon paprika, plus paprika for garnish

1½ lb (750 g) large shrimp (prawns), peeled and deveined (see glossary)

lemon or lime wedges

In a food processor fitted with the metal blade or in a blender, combine the garlic, ginger, lemon or lime juice, turmeric, cumin, salt, jalapeños, yogurt and the 1 tablespoon paprika. Process until well blended. Transfer to a glass or plastic bowl, add the shrimp and toss to coat evenly. Cover and marinate in the refrigerator for about 1 hour.

❧ Place 12 bamboo skewers in water to cover to soak for 15–30 minutes. Prepare a fire in a charcoal grill.

❧ Drain the skewers, then remove the shrimp from the marinade. Holding 2 skewers parallel, thread 4 or 5 of the shrimp onto the pair of skewers, holding the shrimp flat. (Parallel skewers make turning the shrimp on the grill easier.) Repeat with the remaining shrimp and skewers. Place on an oiled grill rack and grill for 2 minutes. Turn the shrimp and grill until the shrimp turn pink, about 2 minutes longer.

❧ Sprinkle with paprika and serve immediately with lemon or lime wedges.

FISH OR CHICKEN TANDOORI

If using fish, substitute any firm white fish fillets, such as bass, swordfish or flounder, for the shrimp. Cut into 1½-inch (4-cm) cubes, marinate for no longer than 1–2 hours and thread onto single rather than parallel skewers. Grill as directed for the shrimp, cooking until opaque at the center. If using chicken, cut chicken breast meat into 1½-inch (4-cm) cubes for skewering. Marinate for as long as 4–5 hours and then thread onto single skewers. Grill as directed for shrimp, cooking until opaque at the center.

Tandoori Shrimp

PORK LOIN WITH POMEGRANATE & ORANGE GLAZE

SERVES 6

Pomegranate syrup is available in specialty markets. Fresh or bottled pomegranate juice can be reduced over high heat to a syrupy consistency. Marinate the pork in the spice paste overnight for fullest flavor. The tenderloins can also be cooked in a broiler (griller) or the loin can be roasted in the oven (see right).

1 boneless pork loin, about 3 lb (1.5 kg), tied for roasting, or 3 pork tender-loins, about 1 lb (500 g) each

FOR THE SPICE PASTE:

2 teaspoons minced garlic

2 tablespoons apricot mustard (opposite) or hot Dijon mustard

finely grated zest of 1 orange (see glossary)

⅓ cup (3 fl oz/80 ml) fresh orange juice

2 tablespoons grated, peeled fresh ginger

2 tablespoons pomegranate syrup

2 tablespoons soy sauce

FOR THE BASTING SAUCE:

⅓ cup (3 fl oz/80 ml) fresh orange juice

3 tablespoons honey

3 tablespoons pomegranate syrup

2 tablespoons soy sauce

Place the pork in a glass or plastic dish. To make the spice paste, in a bowl, combine the garlic, mustard, orange zest and juice, ginger, pomegranate syrup and soy sauce. Rub onto the meat, cover and marinate for at least 6 hours or overnight in the refrigerator. Bring to room temperature before grilling.

❧ Prepare a fire in a charcoal grill.

❧ To make the basting sauce, in a small bowl, mix the orange juice, honey, pomegranate syrup and soy sauce.

❧ Place the pork loin or tenderloins on an oiled grill rack not too close to the heat source. Grill, brushing with the basting sauce and turning often until nicely glazed, 15–20 minutes on each

Pork Loin with Pomegranate & Orange Glaze; Apricot Mustard; Cheddar Chive Biscuits

side for the large loin and 5 minutes per side for the smaller tenderloins, or until an instant-read meat thermometer registers 140°F (60°C) for medium.

❧ Transfer the pork to a work surface, cover with an aluminum foil tent and let rest for 8–10 minutes. Snip the strings if tied and thinly slice across the grain. Serve at once.

ROAST PORK LOIN

To roast the pork loin in the oven, preheat the oven to 400°F (200°C). You will need to make only half a recipe of the basting sauce. Place the marinated pork loin in a roasting pan and roast, brushing often with the basting sauce, until nicely glazed, about 1 hour and 10 minutes or until an instant-read meat thermometer registers 140°F (60°C) for medium.

APRICOT MUSTARD

MAKES ABOUT 3 CUPS (1½ LB/750 G)

This mustard must be made 2–3 weeks in advance of serving to allow the flavors to mellow. It can be stored in the refrigerator for up to several months. Or, ladle it into hot, sterilized jars and process for 10 minutes (see Canning Preserves, glossary), in which case it can be stored for 6 months.

1 cup (3 oz/90 g) dry mustard
½ cup (4 fl oz/125 ml) cider vinegar
6 oz (185 g) dried apricots
1 cup (8 fl oz/250 ml) hot water, or to cover
½ cup (4 fl oz/125 ml) orange juice, or as needed
1 cup (7 oz/220 g) firmly packed dark brown sugar
½ teaspoon salt
½ teaspoon ground cinnamon
¼ teaspoon ground ginger

In a bowl, whisk together the dry mustard and vinegar. Let stand for 1 hour. Meanwhile, in a small saucepan, combine the apricots and the water. Let stand for 30 minutes.

❧ Place the pan with the apricots over medium heat, bring to a simmer and simmer, uncovered, for 5 minutes to soften. Remove from the heat.

❧ In a food processor fitted with the metal blade, combine the apricots and any liquid remaining in the pan and the orange juice and purée until smooth. Add the mustard-vinegar mixture, brown sugar, salt, cinnamon and ginger and process to mix well.

❧ Transfer to a container, cover tightly and refrigerate.

An assortment of colorful cotton throws, pillows and straw hats invites guests to relax. Keep a good supply of sunscreen on hand, too.

CHEDDAR CHIVE BISCUITS

MAKES 1 DOZEN

A nice variation on the basic biscuit, these are a fine foil for the richness of the pork. The biscuits can be cut out and arranged on a baking sheet 1 hour before baking.

2 cups (10 oz/315 g) all-purpose (plain) flour
1 tablespoon baking powder
1 teaspoon baking soda (sodium bicarbonate)
1 teaspoon salt
1 teaspoon sugar
½ cup (4 oz/125 g) unsalted butter, chilled
4 tablespoons minced fresh chives
1 cup (8 fl oz/250 ml) buttermilk
½ cup (2 oz/60 g) coarsely shredded Cheddar cheese

Preheat an oven to 400°F (200°C).

❧ In a bowl, stir together the flour, baking powder, baking soda, salt and sugar. Using a pastry blender or 2 table knives, cut in the butter until the mixture resembles cornmeal. Make a well in the center of the mixture.

❧ In a small bowl, stir the chives into the buttermilk. Pour the buttermilk into the well and add the cheese. Stir quickly to combine, just until the dough pulls away from the sides of the bowl, 1–2 minutes. Turn out onto a floured work surface and knead gently and quickly until the dough is no longer sticky, 3 or 4 turns. Pat into a square ½ inch (12 mm) thick. Dip a 2½ inches (6 cm) in diameter or square biscuit cutter or glass in flour, then cut out 12 round or square biscuits.

❧ Place biscuits on an ungreased baking sheet and bake until pale gold, 12–15 minutes. Serve hot.

TOMATO SALAD WITH BASIL-HONEY VINAIGRETTE

SERVES 6

This aromatic dressing also complements avocados and pears or melon. Some balsamic vinegars are sharper than others, so start with 3 tablespoons and add more as needed to taste. Do not use strong olive oil for this recipe or the balance of sweet and sour will be overwhelmed. If you cannot find beefsteak tomatoes, any ripe, fresh variety will do. The vinaigrette can be made 6 hours in advance and the tomatoes can be sliced 2 hours in advance, but do not drizzle the vinaigrette over the tomatoes until just before serving.

FOR THE VINAIGRETTE:

3–4 tablespoons balsamic vinegar

3 tablespoons full-flavored honey

1 teaspoon salt

¾ cup (6 fl oz/180 ml) mild olive oil

½ cup (¾ oz/20 g) tightly packed
  chopped fresh basil

2–2½ lb (1–1.25 kg) ripe beefsteak or
  other flavorful tomatoes

To make the vinaigrette, in a small bowl, whisk together the vinegar, honey and salt. Add the olive oil and basil and whisk to blend well. Taste and adjust the seasonings.

❧ Slice the tomatoes and arrange on a platter. Drizzle the vinaigrette over the tomatoes and serve.

*Tomato Salad with
Basil-Honey Vinaigrette*

CORN SALAD

SERVES 6

This salad says summer. Of course, just-picked sweet corn can make a difference. The tomatoes can be peeled, if you like. The salad will hold for up to 6 hours and is best served at room temperature.

6 ears corn
½ cup (4 fl oz/125 ml) olive oil
1 cup (5 oz/155 g) minced red
  (Spanish) onion
2 teaspoons chili powder
1 teaspoon ground cumin
1 red bell pepper (capsicum), seeded,
  deribbed and cut into ¼-inch
  (6-mm) dice (see glossary)

1 green bell pepper (capsicum), seeded,
  deribbed and cut into ¼-inch
  (6-mm) dice (see glossary)
1–1½ cups (6–9 oz/185–280 g) seeded
  and diced tomatoes
4 tablespoons chopped fresh cilantro
  (fresh coriander)
3 tablespoons sherry vinegar, or to taste
salt and freshly ground pepper

Shuck corn and rub off the silk. Using a sharp knife, hold each ear of corn firmly and cut off the kernels. You should have approximately 3 cups (18 oz/560 g) of kernels.

❧ Bring a saucepan three-fourths full of salted water to a boil. Add the corn kernels and boil for 1–2 minutes. Drain and immerse in cold water to stop the cooking. Drain again and pat dry with paper towels.

❧ In a small sauté pan over medium heat, warm ¼ cup (2 fl oz/60 ml) of the olive oil. Add the onion and sauté for a few minutes, just to take the sharp bite out. Add the chili powder and cumin and sauté for 1 minute longer.

❧ In a serving bowl, combine the corn, red and green bell peppers, tomatoes and cooled onions. Toss to mix. Add the cilantro, the remaining ¼ cup (2 fl oz/60 ml) olive oil and the vinegar. Toss well to combine. Season to taste with salt and pepper, toss again and serve.

Corn Salad

PEACH BREAD PUDDING

SERVES 6

The lime-scented raspberry purée is a particularly nice touch but not absolutely necessary for this old-fashioned dessert. All you truly need for this delicate summer pudding are flavorful ripe peaches. The almond-scented amaretto liqueur gives the peaches a pleasing fragrance and flavor. The pudding can be baked up to 6 hours before serving. If you are serving the raspberry purée as well, it can be made 1 day ahead. Be sure to have a kettle or saucepan full of hot water on hand while assembling.

6 tablespoons (3 oz/90 g) unsalted butter, melted and clarified (see glossary)

12 slices fine-textured white bread or brioche, cut into 1-inch (2.5-cm) cubes

4 cups (32 fl oz/1 l) heavy (double) cream

6 large ripe peaches, peeled, pitted and cut into ¾-inch (2-cm) cubes

¼ cup (2 fl oz/60 ml) amaretto liqueur

4 whole eggs, plus 4 egg yolks

¾ cup (6 oz/185 g) sugar

1 teaspoon vanilla extract (essence)

½ teaspoon almond extract (essence)

raspberry-lime purée (recipe on page 90), optional

Preheat an oven to 300°F (150°C).

❧ In a large frying pan over medium-high heat, warm 3 tablespoons of the butter. Add half of the bread cubes and fry, stirring, until golden on all sides, 3–4 minutes. Using a slotted spoon, transfer to paper towels to drain. Repeat with 3 more tablespoons butter and the remaining bread cubes.

❧ In a saucepan over medium heat, warm the cream until small bubbles appear at the edge of the pan. Meanwhile, in a bowl, combine the peaches and amaretto and toss to mix.

❧ In another bowl, combine the whole eggs, egg yolks and sugar and, using a whisk, beat until frothy.

❧ Whisk about ½ cup (4 fl oz/125 ml) of the hot cream into the egg mixture, then gradually whisk in the remaining cream. Stir in the vanilla and almond extracts. To remove any lumps, pour the mixture through a fine-mesh sieve into a clean pitcher or bowl.

❧ Combine the peaches and bread cubes in a 3-qt (3-l) shallow rectangular or oval baking dish. Mix to distribute evenly. Slowly pour in the custard, being careful not to disturb the peach mixture. Place the baking dish in a large roasting pan and pour hot water into the pan to reach halfway up the sides of the dish. Bake until the custard is just set, about 1½ hours; it should still be slightly wobbly in the center.

❧ Let cool on a wire rack. Serve with the raspberry-lime purée, if desired.

Peach Bread Pudding

ENGAGEMENT PARTY

LIFE SENDS OUR way many happy moments. Today we can observe these milestones without the fuss of a more traditional, formal party. Here we celebrate a young couple's engagement by throwing open the doors and serving a filling but easy meal suitable for a small gathering or a large crowd.

We felt buffet-style service starting in mid to late afternoon would suit the leisurely tone of the party and would encourage guests to mingle on into the evening. You could arrange the food on a sideboard in the dining room, or on any table that is large enough to hold oversized platters and serving dishes. Small containers of flowers and clusters of cathedral candles lend a relaxed air. The open-hearted, Spanish feel of this menu makes it adaptable for other occasions, too, such as a house-warming or *bon voyage* party.

WHEN GUESTS ARRIVE for the celebration, they are welcomed with pitchers of ice-cold sangría. Although you can serve it in any glasses that hold a generous amount, we used oversized glass goblets to show off the Spanish wine punch to its most striking effect.

Most of the preparation for the meal is easily done in advance. The recipes can be doubled or tripled for a larger group, but plan on the additional time and expense a bigger affair will demand. We chose to present the paella in a wide rustic earthenware dish, but you can use any serving dish large enough to show off the assortment of seafood and chicken or serve already-plated portions.

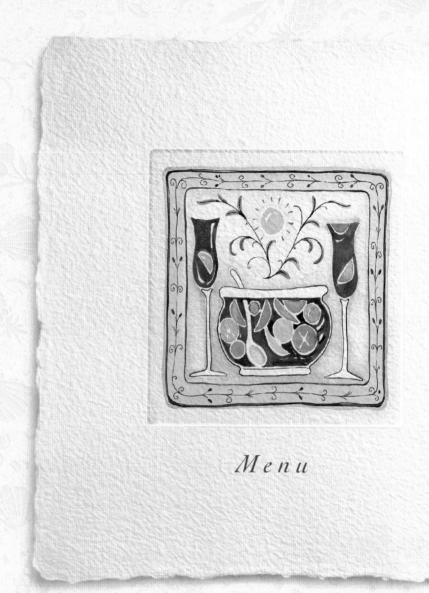

Menu

Simple gifts for the engaged couple could range from a set of thick kitchen towels for their new home, or fabric-wrapped bottles of wine to help start their bar or wine cellar, to fireplace tools and wood.

BEVERAGE IDEAS

Although sangría (recipe on page 69) can be sipped throughout the meal with satisfaction, a selection of red and white wines is welcome. For the whites, choose more rustic types such as Pouilly Fumé, Sancerre or a simple French Chablis, Italian Vernaccia or American Sauvignon Blanc or Chardonnay. For the reds, select from Spanish Riojas, American Pinot Noirs, Merlots or Syrahs from the Rhône or elsewhere. Chilled kirschwasser would make a fine climax to the meal.

Roasted Eggplant & Peppers

*Asparagus & Beets with
Romesco Mayonnaise*

❧

Simple Country Paella

Sangría

❧

Bing Cherry Cheese Tart

*Mussels, clams, shrimp, chicken and saffron-tinted rice
transform the surface of a paella into an edible landscape.*

PREPARATION LIST

◆ The day before, make and freeze the tart shell, cook the beets and make the mayonnaise; roast the eggplants, peppers and the onion(s), if using, and assemble. Marinate the chicken, pit the cherries and prepare the sangría base.

◆ That morning, brown the chicken, assemble the paella base and cook the asparagus. Combine the cherries and the liqueur, make the cheese filling for the tart and prebake the tart shell.

◆ An hour before, assemble and bake the tart and debeard the mussels.

EACH RECIPE YIELDS 6 SERVINGS.

Citrus fruits form a backdrop for goblets of thirst-quenching sangría.

ROASTED EGGPLANT & PEPPERS

SERVES 6

On another occasion, offer this versatile dish as part of an antipasto spread or an assortment of tapas. It also doubles as a robust topping for bread, in which case you should coarsely chop the eggplants, peppers and onions for easier spreading. Put all of the vegetables into the oven at the same time and then remove them as they are ready. This dish can be assembled the day before, but the salt and vinegar will need to be adjusted to taste just before serving.

2 small eggplants (aubergines)
1 large or 2 small red (Spanish) onions, unpeeled (optional)
3 red bell peppers (capsicums)
olive oil for rubbing on onion(s), plus ½ cup (4 fl oz/125 ml) olive oil
2 teaspoons ground cumin
2 tablespoons sherry vinegar
salt and freshly ground pepper
4 tablespoons chopped fresh flat-leaf (Italian) parsley
handful of sharply flavored black or green olives

Preheat an oven to 400°F (200°C).
❧ Prick the eggplant in a few places with a fork and place in a baking pan. If using the onion(s), rub them with olive oil and add them to the pan. Roast the eggplants, turning occasionally to ensure even cooking, until tender, 35–45 minutes. Set aside until cool enough to handle. Continue to roast the onion(s), until tender when pierced with a knife, about 50 minutes, then set aside to cool.
❧ To roast the peppers, preheat a broiler (griller). Place the peppers on a baking sheet and slip under the broiler.

Broil (grill), turning occasionally, until the skins are evenly blackened and blistered. Transfer to a closed paper bag or plastic container and let stand until cool enough to handle, about 10 minutes.
❧ Using your fingers, peel off the charred skin from the peppers. Cut the peppers in half and pull out and discard the stems, seeds and ribs. Cut the peppers into long, thin strips. Peel the eggplants and cut the flesh into 1½–2-inch (4–5-cm) cubes. Place in a colander to drain. Then peel the onion(s) and cut into long, thin strips. Set aside.
❧ Combine the drained eggplant, the bell peppers and onion(s) in a large bowl. In a small bowl, whisk together the ½ cup (4 fl oz/125 ml) olive oil, cumin and sherry vinegar and toss the vegetables with the mixture. Season to taste with salt and pepper.
❧ At serving time, garnish with the parsley and olives.

Marketed in a range of shapes and in hues from white to purple-black, an assortment of eggplants is available in today's produce markets.

ASPARAGUS & BEETS WITH ROMESCO MAYONNAISE

SERVES 6

Beets and asparagus with a spicy tomato-almond mayonnaise are a wonderful beginning to a meal. If asparagus are out of season, use green beans in their place. To transform this dish into a main course, add cooked potatoes to the assortment. The beets can be either baked or boiled. They can be cooked and the Romesco mayonnaise made 1 day in advance. The asparagus can be cooked 4 hours ahead of serving.

FOR THE ROMESCO MAYONNAISE:

1 tablespoon minced garlic
coarse salt
1½ cups (12 fl oz/375 ml) mayonnaise
1 cup (4 oz/125 g) sliced almonds, toasted and chopped (see glossary)
½ cup (3 oz/90 g) seeded and finely chopped, drained canned plum (Roma) tomatoes
½ teaspoon cayenne pepper
¼ cup (2 fl oz/60 ml) tomato purée
¼ cup (2 fl oz/60 ml) red wine vinegar
salt and freshly ground pepper to taste

1½ lb (750 g) asparagus
12 small beets (beetroots)

To make the Romesco mayonnaise, in a mortar, combine the garlic with a little coarse salt and, using a pestle, grind them together to form a paste. Alternatively, in a bowl and using a fork or the back of a spoon, mash together the garlic and salt to form a paste. Place the mayonnaise in a bowl and stir in the garlic paste. Fold in the almonds, tomatoes, cayenne pepper, tomato purée, vinegar and salt and pepper to taste until well mixed. Cover and refrigerate.

Roasted Eggplant & Peppers; Asparagus & Beets with Romesco Mayonnaise

❧ Break off the tough ends of the asparagus where they snap easily and trim the spears to a uniform length. If the stalks are thick, peel them with a paring knife or vegetable peeler.

❧ Half fill a large, wide frying pan with salted water and bring to a boil. Add the asparagus and boil until tender-crisp, 4–6 minutes; the timing will depend upon the thickness of the stalks. Drain well and immerse immediately in ice water to stop the cooking and set the color. Drain well again and pat dry.

❧ To bake the beets, preheat an oven to 375°F (190°C). Trim the greens off the beets but leave about ½ inch (12 mm) of the stems intact. Scrub the beets and wrap them together in aluminum foil, sealing tightly. Place in a baking dish and add water to a depth of 1–2 inches (2.5–5 cm). Bake until tender when pierced with a knife, about 1 hour, adding additional water to the pan as needed to make steam. Remove from the oven, let cool and then remove and discard the foil. Peel the beets and cut into wedges.

❧ Alternatively, to boil the beets, trim as directed. Bring a saucepan three-fourths full of water to a boil. Add the beets and boil until tender, 30–40 minutes. Drain well and immerse in warm water. When cool enough to handle, peel the beets and cut into wedges.

❧ To serve, place the beets and asparagus on a platter. Pass the mayonnaise in a bowl. Or arrange the vegetables on individual plates and garnish each plate with a dollop of the mayonnaise.

Simple Country Paella; Sangría

SIMPLE COUNTRY PAELLA

SERVES 6

Paella need not be an elaborate and expensive dish. Some of the very best versions are the simplest. Of course you can add chunks of diced ham or chorizo, or shrimp, but the dish will be satisfying even without these embellishments. Begin marinating the chicken the day before. Four hours before, brown the chicken and cook the onion, garlic and tomato base in the same pan. The rest of the dish must be done at the last minute, but why not sip sangría and talk with your guests while you cook and stir?

FOR THE MARINADE:

2 tablespoons minced garlic

2 tablespoons dried oregano, crumbled

2 teaspoons salt

1 tablespoon coarsely ground pepper

3–4 tablespoons red wine vinegar

5–6 tablespoons (2½–3 fl oz/75–90 ml) olive oil

12 small half chicken breasts, or 6 small chicken thighs and 6 small half chicken breasts

¼ cup (2 fl oz/60 ml) dry white wine or water, plus dry white wine or water for cooking clams or mussels

½ teaspoon saffron threads

6 tablespoons (3 fl oz/90 ml) olive oil

2 large yellow onions, chopped

1 tablespoon minced garlic

3–4 cups (18–24 oz/560–750 g) seeded and diced canned plum (Roma) tomatoes

2 cups (14 oz/440 g) short-grain white rice

4–5 cups (32–40 fl oz/1–1.25 l) chicken stock (see page 295)

24 shrimp (prawns), peeled and deveined, optional (see glossary)

1 cup (5 oz/155 g) shelled peas or tender, young lima beans

36 clams and/or mussels in the shell, scrubbed and debearded if using mussels (see glossary)

To make the marinade, in a small bowl, combine the garlic, oregano, salt and pepper. Add the vinegar and stir to form a paste. Stir in the olive oil.

❧ Place the chicken pieces in a glass or plastic container. Rub the marinade on the chicken pieces, coating evenly. Cover and refrigerate overnight.

❧ In a small saucepan over low heat, warm the ¼ cup (2 fl oz/60 ml) wine or water; remove from the heat. Crush the saffron threads gently and add to the warm liquid. Let stand for 10 minutes.

❧ In a large, deep frying pan over medium-high heat, warm the olive oil. Add the chicken in batches and brown quickly on all sides. Remove from the pan and set aside. To the oil remaining in the pan, add the onions and sauté over medium heat, stirring often, until tender and translucent, about 10 minutes. Add the garlic and tomatoes and sauté, stirring, for 5 minutes.

❧ Add the rice, reduce the heat to low and stir for 3 minutes. Add the chicken stock (the amount you add will depend on the absorbency of the rice) and the saffron and its soaking liquid and bring to a boil. Reduce the heat and simmer, uncovered and without stirring, for 10 minutes. Add the browned chicken and continue to cook, uncovered, until the liquids are absorbed and the rice is tender, about 10 minutes longer, adding the shrimp, if using, and the peas or lima beans during the last 5 minutes. Alternatively, once the chicken is added, place the pan in an oven preheated to 325°F (165°C) and bake until the liquids are absorbed and the rice is tender, about 15 minutes, adding the

shrimp and peas or lima beans during the last 5 minutes.

❧ Meanwhile, in a saucepan, place the clams and/or mussels, discarding any that do not close to the touch. Add wine or water to a depth of 1 inch (2.5 cm). Cover, place over medium-high heat and cook until the shellfish open, about 5 minutes. Add them to the paella 1–2 minutes before it is ready, discarding any that did not open.

❧ Remove the paella from the stove top or oven and let rest for 10 minutes before serving.

SANGRÍA

SERVES 6

A wine punch popular in Spain as well as Portugal, especially during the hot summer months. Combining the wine, sugar, lemons and oranges the night before serving intensifies the flavors.

1 bottle (3 cups/24 fl oz/750 ml) dry red wine such as Rioja

3 tablespoons sugar

2–3 tablespoons fresh lemon juice

½ cup (4 fl oz/125 ml) fresh orange juice

2 lemons, thinly sliced

2 oranges, thinly sliced

3–4 cups (24–32 fl oz/750 ml–1 l) club soda

ice cubes

In a glass bowl or other nonreactive container, stir together the wine, sugar, and lemon and orange juices and slices. Cover and refrigerate overnight to blend the flavors.

❧ At serving time, transfer the wine mixture to 1 or 2 pitchers. Add the club soda and plenty of ice cubes.

BING CHERRY CHEESE TART

SERVES 6, WITH LEFTOVERS

The tart shell can be made 1 or 2 days ahead and frozen. The cherries can be pitted the night before and refrigerated; combine them with the liqueur 4 hours before assembling the tart. The cheese mixture can be assembled at the same time. Serve the tart slightly warm or at room temperature.

2 cups (8 oz/250 g) stemmed Bing cherries, pitted, or raspberries or blueberries
2 tablespoons Tuaca, amaretto or Frangelico

FOR THE TART SHELL:
1¼ cups (6½ oz/200 g) all-purpose (plain) flour
¼ cup (2 oz/60 g) sugar
½ cup (4 oz/125 g) unsalted butter, chilled, cut into slivers
1 egg yolk
2 tablespoons heavy (double) cream
1 tablespoon Tuaca, amaretto or Frangelico
1 teaspoon finely grated lemon zest (see glossary)

FOR THE CHEESE TOPPING:
1 cup (8 oz/250 g) cream cheese at room temperature
⅓ cup (3 oz/90 g) sugar
2 whole eggs or 1 whole egg and 2 egg yolks
2 tablespoons Tuaca, amaretto or Frangelico
½ teaspoon almond extract (essence)

In a bowl, toss together the cherries and liqueur. Cover and let stand for 4 hours to blend the flavors.

❧ To make the tart shell pastry by hand, in a bowl, stir together the flour and sugar. Drop the butter into the bowl and, using two knives or a pastry blender, cut in the butter until the mixture resembles cornmeal. In a small bowl, whisk together the egg yolk, cream, liqueur and lemon zest. Add to the flour mixture and, using a fork, stir together until the dough forms a rough mass. Gather the dough into a ball, flatten it, and wrap in plastic wrap. Chill for 1 hour or for up to 1 day. (If the dough has been chilling for a day, allow it to soften a bit before rolling it out.)

❧ To make the tart shell pastry in a food processor, place the flour and sugar in a processor fitted with the metal blade. Add the butter pieces and, using rapid on-off pulses, process until the mixture resembles cornmeal. In a small bowl, whisk together the egg yolk, cream, liqueur and lemon zest. Add to the flour and process briefly just until the dough forms a rough mass, then gather, shape, wrap and chill as for hand method.

❧ Preheat an oven to 400°F (200°C). On a well-floured surface, roll out the dough into a round about 11 inches (28 cm) in diameter. Carefully transfer the round to a 9-inch (23-cm) tart pan with a removable bottom. Alternatively, if the dough is difficult to roll out, press by hand into the tart tin. In either case, do not fit the dough too snugly to the pan, as the crust will shrink as it bakes. Make the sides slightly higher than the tart rim, so that there will be enough of an edge to hold the filling. Trim off any excess overhang.

❧ Using a fork, prick a few holes in the bottom of the crust. Line the tart shell with aluminum foil and fill with pie weights or beans. Bake for 15 minutes, then remove the foil and weights. Lower the oven temperature to 350°F (180°C) and bake for about 15 minutes longer. Transfer to a wire rack to cool for about 15 minutes. Leave the oven set at 350°F (180°C).

❧ Meanwhile, to make the cheese filling, in a bowl combine the cream cheese, sugar, whole eggs or whole egg and egg yolks, liqueur and almond extract. Using an electric mixer set on medium, beat until well combined. Alternatively, place the ingredients in a food processor fitted with the metal blade and process until well combined.

❧ Distribute the cherries evenly on the bottom of the tart shell. Pour the cheese mixture over the cherries. Bake until the custard is set, about 25 minutes. Cool on a wire rack.

To pit summertime's fresh cherries easily, use a cherry pitter, which holds the fruit and pushes out the pit when pressure is applied.

Bing Cherry Cheese Tart

CASUAL PIZZA PARTY

WHAT COULD BE more casual than letting your guests assemble and cook their own food? Many people love to participate in making a pizza, and the method we chose for this menu is well within anyone's culinary abilities.

Such an occasion is best suited to a weekend afternoon or early evening, when guests have more time to join in. With so many people preparing their pizzas, it makes good sense to set the event in the kitchen or as close to the kitchen as possible. If you have a large enough kitchen, make the pizzas in there and then serve them with the rest of the meal in an informal dining room; but, if the kitchen has a dining area, you could have seating there. After preparing the pizzas everyone could gather in the family room to watch a movie or sporting event on television, in which case, you might arrange chairs, tables and trays around the set.

ALTHOUGH YOUR GUESTS will do much of the final food compilation, you still have to make the pizza dough, sauces and toppings. The work is time-consuming, but it can be spread out over a couple of weeks. If you're pressed for time, you can prepare only as many of the toppings suggested on page 76 as seems manageable. A whimsical salad accompanies the pizzas, and biscotti and fruit end the meal in similarly relaxed style.

Provide a wide variety of beers and soft drinks on ice for guests to choose from. Use your imagination to create an ice chest from whatever container you have on hand; just be sure to line it with plastic first. We placed some large goblets nearby, but any tall glass will do.

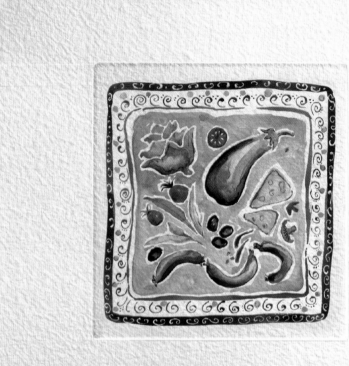

Menu

Cluster extra aprons and cooking utensils within easy reach for guests who wish to participate in the cooking.

BEVERAGE IDEAS

Offer a wide array of beers, assembling an assortment of styles (pilsners, lagers, ales and stouts) and countries. Pour medium-bodied Italian reds, such as Chianti, Rosso di Montalcino and Nebbiolo, for the wine drinkers and nonalcoholic beers and a selection of soft drinks and mineral waters for the nondrinkers.

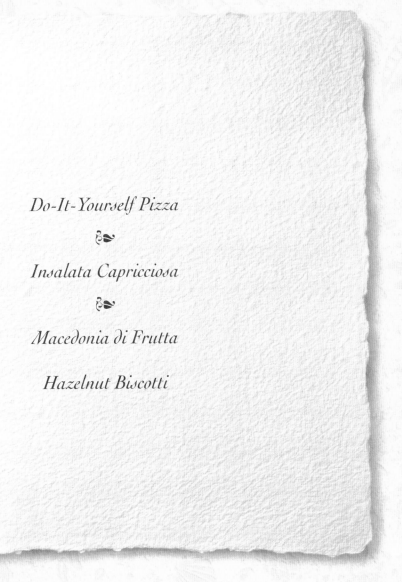

Do-It-Yourself Pizza

❧

Insalata Capricciosa

❧

Macedonia di Frutta

Hazelnut Biscotti

Terra-cotta plates, sturdy tumblers and colorful table linens complement the bright palette of pizza ingredients.

PREPARATION LIST

◆ Make the tapenade up to two weeks before and the pesto and the sun-dried tomato spread up to one week before.

◆ During the week, make the biscotti.

◆ The day before, make the tomato purée and the cooked pizza toppings.

◆ In the morning, make the pizza dough and vinaigrette. Wash and crisp the lettuce and ready the vegetables for the salad.

◆ Prepare the uncooked pizza toppings and make the *macedonia* a few hours before.

◆ One and one-half hours before, marinate the chick-peas for the salad.

EACH RECIPE YIELDS 6 SERVINGS.

Instead of a standard cooler, we used a large terra-cotta pot for icing beers and soft drinks, but any large container lined with plastic and filled with ice may be substituted.

DO-IT-YOURSELF PIZZA

SERVES 6

This is a versatile recipe. Prepare as many of the suggested spreads and toppings as you like. The topping amounts given are conservative suggestions and should be enough to top 12 small pizzas with an assortment of ingredients. If your guests favor certain ingredients, have plenty of those on hand. Judge and adjust according to your own personal tastes and those of the party goers—if you know them.

The tapenade can be made up to 2 weeks in advance. The pesto and sun-dried tomato spread can be made up to 1 week in advance and the tomato purée can be made up to 2 days in advance. Prepare the cooked toppings 1 day in advance and cut the uncooked ones 4 hours before the party.

A sponge is a type of starter that gives a particularly resilient texture to the crust. The addition of rye or buckwheat flour to the dough deepens the flavor of the crust. The dough can be made 8 hours before the party, left to rise at room temperature, and then divided into 12 equal portions, covered with plastic wrap and refrigerated. Remove the dough balls from the refrigerator about 30 minutes before forming them into crusts.

If you have one or two baking stones, place them in the oven when you turn it on; the stones will ensure a crisp crust. You will need a baker's peel or a rimless baking sheet to slide the pizzas onto the stone.

When it is time for the guests to top their pizzas, set out all the spreads and toppings in bowls or on platters and let the guests choose from among them.

This recipe yields 12 small pizzas; bake 6 pizzas at a time so everyone eats together.

SUGGESTED SPREADS FOR THE CRUST:

tapenade (recipe on page 296)

pesto (recipe on page 297)

sun-dried tomato spread (recipe on page 296)

tomato purée (recipe on page 296)

SUGGESTED TOPPINGS:

4 medium-sized red (Spanish) onions, sliced and lightly sautéed

4 large red or green bell peppers (capsicums), seeded, deribbed, sliced and lightly sautéed (see glossary)

1 lb (500 g) fresh mushrooms, sliced and lightly sautéed

1 lb (500 g) small new potatoes, roasted and sliced ¼ inch (6 mm) thick

2 eggplants (aubergines), sliced ¼ inch (6 mm) thick and baked or grilled

2 lb (1 kg) escarole or Swiss chard, chopped, lightly sautéed and well drained

1 lb (500 g) Italian sausages, cooked and then sliced

½ lb (250 g) sliced pancetta, cut into strips and sautéed (see glossary)

1½ lbs (750 g) tomatoes, diced and drained

2 cups (8 oz/250 g) freshly grated Parmesan cheese

1 lb (500 g) fresh mozzarella cheese, sliced

¾ lb (375 g) Fontina cheese, shredded or sliced

FOR THE SPONGE:

3 tablespoons active dry yeast

1½ cups (12 fl oz/375 ml) warm (110°F/43°C) water

1½ cups (7½ oz/235 g) unbleached all-purpose (plain) flour

FOR THE DOUGH:

2¼ cups (18 fl oz/560 ml) warm (110°F/43°C) water

½ cup (4 fl oz/125 ml) plus 1 tablespoon olive oil

1 tablespoon salt

9 cups (2¾ lb/1.4 kg) unbleached all-purpose (plain) flour, plus additional flour as needed

1 cup (3 oz/90 g) rye or buckwheat flour or 1 additional cup (5 oz/155 g) all-purpose (plain) flour

½ cup (¾ oz/20 g) finely chopped rosemary or sage

cornmeal for baking sheets

olive oil for brushing on crust, optional

Select and prepare the spreads and the toppings for the pizzas.

☙ To make the sponge, in a heavy-duty electric mixer fitted with a paddle attachment, dissolve the yeast in the warm water. Add the flour and beat at medium speed until all the ingredients are fully combined. (Or combine the ingredients in a large bowl and mix with a wooden spoon.) Cover the bowl with a dampened kitchen towel or plastic wrap and let rest in a warm, draft-free place for 30 minutes.

☙ To make the dough, add the warm water, olive oil, salt, flour(s) and rosemary or sage to the sponge. Beat with the paddle attachment until all the ingredients come together and are well mixed. Then attach the dough hook and beat until the dough pulls away from the sides of the bowl and is smooth and elastic, 5–10 minutes, adding more flour as necessary to reduce stickiness.

☙ Turn out the dough onto a lightly floured work surface and knead for 1–2 minutes to be sure it has achieved the proper consistency. (Or add the ingredients to the sponge and beat with a wooden spoon until well mixed, then turn out onto a floured surface and knead until smooth and elastic, 15–20 minutes, adding more flour as needed to reduce stickiness.)

❧ Shape the dough into a ball, place in a lightly oiled bowl, and turn the dough to coat all surfaces with the oil. Cover with a dampened kitchen towel or plastic wrap and let rise in a warm, draft-free place until doubled in size, about 1 hour.

❧ Turn out the dough onto a lightly floured work surface. Punch it down and divide it into 12 equal portions; shape each portion into a ball. Place

the balls on a baking sheet, cover with plastic wrap and refrigerate for 30 minutes or for up to 8 hours (see note above).

❧ Preheat an oven to 475°F (245°C).

❧ To form the crusts, punch down one dough portion at a time on a lightly floured work surface. Flatten it into a disk about 3 inches (7.5 cm) in diameter. Then, using your fingers and the heels of your hands, gently press and stretch the dough into a 4–5-inch (10–13-cm) round about ¼ inch (6 mm) thick. The edges of the dough round

should be a little thicker than the center. Lift the dough round occasionally as you work, to prevent sticking.

❧ Dust 2 large baking sheets with cornmeal and transfer 6 of the pizza crusts to them. Have the bowls of spreads and toppings ready. Encourage each guest to top his or her own pizza according to their own individual taste.

❧ Bake the pizzas until the crusts are golden brown, 12–15 minutes. Remove from the oven, brush the edges of the crusts with olive oil, if using, and serve immediately.

Do-It-Yourself Pizza

Insalata Capricciosa

INSALATA CAPRICCIOSA

SERVES 6

The perfect salad for a do-it-yourself pizza party. Capricciosa more or less means "with whimsy," so use your imagination when putting this salad together. Start with romaine and then add whatever you like, such as diced cucumbers, sliced carrots, cooked chick-peas, a few olives. If you like, cut the carrots into narrow, thin strips rather than slices. If only thick-skinned cucumbers are available, peel them. You can also use canned chick-peas in place of home-cooked ones; rinse and drain them well before adding to the salad. Mix the chick-peas well with a garlicky vinaigrette and add a few croutons (see Green Salad with Gruyère & Croutons, page 134), if desired. You can make the vinaigrette, wash and crisp the lettuce and cut the vegetables 8 hours before serving. Combine the chick-peas and the vinaigrette 1½ hours before serving.

FOR THE GARLIC VINAIGRETTE:

⅔ cup (5 fl oz/160 ml) mild olive oil
⅓ cup (3 fl oz/80 ml) extra-virgin olive oil
¼ cup (2 fl oz/60 ml) red wine vinegar
1 tablespoon balsamic vinegar, optional
2 teaspoons minced garlic
salt and freshly ground pepper

1½–2 cups (9–12 oz/280–375 g) drained, cooked chick-peas (garbanzo beans)
1 small head cauliflower, cut into florets, optional
12 cups (1½ lb/750 g) torn romaine (cos) lettuce
2 cups (10 oz/315 g) seeded, diced English (hothouse) cucumber
1 cup (4 oz/125 g) thinly sliced carrot

To make the vinaigrette, in a small bowl, whisk together the mild and extra-virgin olive oils, wine vinegar, balsamic vinegar (if using), garlic and salt and pepper to taste. Set aside.

❧ Place the chick-peas in a bowl and add ½ cup (4 fl oz/125 ml) of the vinaigrette. Stir to coat the chick-peas well and let marinate for 1½ hours. Set the remaining vinaigrette aside.

❧ If using the cauliflower florets, bring a saucepan three-fourths full of water to a boil. Add the florets and boil until tender-crisp, 3–5 minutes. Drain well and immerse in ice water to cool completely. Drain well again and pat dry with paper towels.

❧ In a large salad bowl, combine the lettuce, cucumber, carrot, chick-peas and the cauliflower, if using. Drizzle the remaining vinaigrette over the top, toss well and serve.

Flowerpots in various shapes and sizes, glued or arranged together on a board (see page 313), form an innovative container for a mostly edible centerpiece of fresh herbs, mushrooms, cherry tomatoes and baby carrots.

MACEDONIA DI FRUTTA

SERVES 6, WITH LEFTOVERS

After a filling meal of pizza and a hearty salad, a light fruit dessert such as this Italian macedonia is all that is needed. The Italians love to flood this favorite dolce with injudicious amounts of maraschino liqueur, but you may enhance it with the liqueur of your choice; Grand Marnier or kirsch is nice. Or you can omit the alcohol altogether. The macedonia must be prepared 4 hours before serving to allow the flavors to blend. Do not, however, prepare it further than 8 hours ahead, as the fruits will lose their crispness. Any leftovers are great for breakfast.

3 apples, peeled, cored and diced
3 pears, peeled, cored and diced
3 bananas, sliced
2 cups (8 oz/250 g) strawberries, stems removed and sliced
2 or 3 oranges, peeled and sectioned
2 cups (16 fl oz/500 ml) fresh orange juice
1 cup (8 fl oz/250 ml) fresh lemon juice
¼ cup (2 fl oz/60 ml) orange-flavored liqueur, optional
sugar

In a large attractive bowl, combine the fruits, orange and lemon juices, orange liqueur (if using) and sugar to taste. Toss gently to mix well.

❧ Cover bowl and refrigerate for at least 4 hours or for up to 8 hours, but not longer. Serve chilled.

HAZELNUT BISCOTTI

MAKES 18–20

These cookies can be made 3–5 days before the party and stored in an airtight container. If they soften before serving, recrisp them in a 250°F (120°C) oven. Savor them with espresso, tea or dessert wine.

2½ cups (12½ oz/390 g) all-purpose (plain) flour
1½ teaspoons baking powder
½ teaspoon salt
1 teaspoon ground cinnamon
½ cup (4 oz/125 g) unsalted butter at room temperature
1 cup (8 oz/250 g) sugar
3 eggs
juice and finely grated zest of 1 lemon (see glossary)
1 tablespoon vanilla extract (essence)
½ teaspoon almond extract (essence)
2 cups (10 oz/315 g) toasted hazelnuts (filberts), coarsely chopped (see glossary)

Preheat an oven to 325°F (165°C).

❧ In a bowl, stir together the flour, baking powder, salt and cinnamon. Set aside. In another bowl, combine the butter and sugar. Using an electric mixer set on medium speed, beat the mixture until light and fluffy. Add the eggs, one at a time, beating well after each addition. Beat in the lemon juice and zest and vanilla and almond extracts. Reduce the speed to low and beat in the flour mixture, one third at a time. Fold in the nuts. The dough will be slightly granular.

❧ Turn the dough out onto a floured work surface and divide it in half. Using the palms of your hands, roll each half into an oval log about 1½ inches (4 cm) in diameter. Place well spaced on an ungreased baking sheet.

❧ Bake until golden brown, about 30 minutes. Remove from the oven and let rest until cool to the touch. Reduce the oven temperature to 250°F (120°C).

❧ Cut each log on the diagonal into slices ⅓ inch (1 cm) thick. The slices will flatten slightly when you cut them. Arrange the slices, cut side down, on the ungreased baking sheet and return to the oven. Bake until biscotti are lightly toasted and the edges are golden brown, about 10 minutes. Let cool either on the pan or on a wire rack.

Biscotti are twice-baked cookies: the dough is shaped into a log, baked, and then sliced and baked again to produce a delightfully crunchy texture.

*Macedonia di Frutta;
Hazelnut Biscotti*

KITCHEN BREAKFAST

AS CHILDREN, WE are all taught that a good breakfast is the best way to launch the day. That homespun truth has been adopted by hosts and hostesses who know that a generous morning meal served to weekend houseguests, friends assembling for a daytime outing or family members celebrating a special event gets everyone off to a great start.

We created a relaxed mood by serving breakfast at an island that doubles as the kitchen table. If your kitchen is small, you can have the meal in the dining room, family room or other comfortable space. Any breakfast calls for minimal fuss. After all, who wants to get up early to set a fancy table? We settled on simple potted flowers for decoration, complementing everyday dishware in a colorful floral pattern.

SINCE WEEKEND breakfasts tend to be more hearty, we chose to feature contemporary variations on rustic Italian favorites: polenta and sausage patties. Both dishes are also good served later in the day, should you change the occasion to a brunch. A classic sour cream coffee cake and papaya with raspberry-lime purée round out the menu.

Offer one or more fresh-squeezed juices to guests as well. We used the juice of blood oranges, available in well-stocked markets and good produce stores, as the basis for mimosas—a popular morning drink made of equal parts orange juice and Champagne or sparkling wine.

Menu

The bright floral pattern of everyday family china, including generously sized coffee mugs, establishes a festive tone. Vibrant red placemats boldly define each setting.

BEVERAGE IDEAS

Offer a choice of mimosas, juices and spiced coffees to your guests. Then, if you like, switch to a brut-style Champagne or sparkling wine. In addition, serve an off-dry white wine such as American Chenin Blanc, German Riesling or French Vouvray or a white Zinfandel or similar-styled blush wine with the meal.

*Butternut Squash Polenta
with Greens & Fontina*

Turkey Sausage Patties

❧

Sour Cream Coffee Cake

Papaya with Raspberry-Lime Purée

Small pots holding geraniums or primroses become cheerful centerpieces when wrapped or swagged with squares of colorful fabric (see page 312).

To coat glass rims with sugar for mimosas or juice, spread the sugar on a plate. Moisten the rims with a cut lemon and then dip in the sugar. Garnish each glass with organically grown edible flowers.

PREPARATION LIST

◆ The day before, bake the squash, make the polenta, shred the cheese and wash and sauté the greens. Assemble the sausage mixture and form into patties; make the raspberry-lime purée.

◆ The night before, bake the coffee cake.

◆ An hour before breakfast, peel and slice the papayas; assemble the ramekins or gratin dish for the polenta.

EACH RECIPE YIELDS 6 SERVINGS.

BUTTERNUT SQUASH POLENTA WITH GREENS & FONTINA

SERVES 6

This blends a classic northern Italian ravioli filling and baked polenta. The greens provide a nice contrast between the sweetness of the squash and the richness of the cornmeal. The squash and polenta can be cooked 1 day in advance; the greens can be washed and cooked at the same time. An hour before, assemble the ramekins or gratin dish. For a simpler preparation to include with this menu, omit the greens and serve fried polenta with maple syrup (see below).

1 butternut squash, about 2½ lb (1.25 kg)

¼ cup (2 fl oz/60 ml) milk

¼ cup (2 oz/60 g) unsalted butter at room temperature

1 teaspoon freshly grated nutmeg, plus grated nutmeg to taste

pinch of ground cinnamon, optional

salt and freshly ground pepper

1½ cups (9 oz/235 g) medium-grind polenta or yellow cornmeal

5 cups (40 fl oz/1.25 l) water

⅔ cup (3 oz/90 g) freshly grated Parmesan cheese

2 tablespoons chopped fresh sage

2 tablespoons olive oil

1 yellow onion, diced

2 lb (1 kg) Swiss chard, kale or dandelion greens, or a mixture, carefully washed and cut into strips

a few drops of balsamic vinegar or water

1 cup (4 oz/125 g) finely shredded Fontina cheese

Preheat an oven to 400°F (200°C). Place the squash in a baking pan and puncture with a knife in a few places. Bake until soft to the touch, about 1 hour. Remove from the oven and, when cool enough to handle, cut in half and scoop out the seeds and discard. Peel the squash and then mash the pulp in a bowl with a potato masher or fork, or pass it through a ricer into a bowl. Beat in the milk and butter until smooth. Season with the 1 teaspoon nutmeg, the cinnamon, if using, and salt and pepper to taste. Set aside.

❧ Butter or line with parchment paper a 16-by-12-by-1-inch (40-by-30-by-2.5-cm) baking pan or a large, sided baking sheet.

❧ In a large saucepan, combine the polenta and water. Bring to a boil over medium heat, stirring constantly. Reduce the heat to low and simmer uncovered, stirring often, until thickened and the polenta no longer tastes grainy. If the polenta is not yet cooked but is quite dry, add a little water.

❧ When the polenta is ready, whisk in the squash mixture, Parmesan and sage until well mixed. Season to taste with salt, pepper and nutmeg. Pour into the prepared baking pan and refrigerate. When it has firmed up, cover well with plastic wrap and return to the refrigerator until very firm and well chilled.

❧ In a large sauté pan or frying pan over medium heat, warm the olive oil. Add the onion and sauté until golden, about 15 minutes. Add the greens and sprinkle with the balsamic vinegar or water. Cook, stirring occasionally, until wilted and tender, about 8 minutes. Drain well and chop coarsely. Season to taste with salt and pepper.

❧ Preheat an oven to 400°F (200°C). Butter six 4–6-inch (10–15-cm) individual ramekins or one 11-by-18-inch (28-by-46-cm) oval gratin dish.

❧ Using a knife or biscuit cutter (for rounds), cut the polenta into desired shapes such as triangles, rectangles, rounds, squares or strips. Using a spatula, remove from the baking pan.

❧ Layer half of the greens in the ramekins or gratin dish. Top with the polenta cutouts. (Reserve any leftover cutouts for another use.) Layer with the remaining greens; top with the Fontina.

❧ Bake until heated through and the cheese is melted, about 20 minutes. Serve immediately.

FRIED POLENTA WITH MAPLE SYRUP

Increase the ground cinnamon to 1 teaspoon and add the finely grated zest of 1 orange to the squash purée; omit the sage and the Parmesan. When the polenta is cold and firm, cut it into strips or triangles.

❧ In a frying pan over medium-high heat, fry the polenta pieces in a few tablespoons of unsalted butter or olive oil until golden on both sides. Serve with maple syrup and with sautéed apple slices, if you like.

Butternut Squash Polenta with Greens & Fontina

For guests who prefer tea with breakfast, offer full-flavored yet mild morning varieties such as Darjeeling, orange pekoe and English or Irish breakfast blends, along with herbal teas. If you use loose leaves instead of bags, tea infusers such as the one shown here—available in well-stocked kitchen stores and tea shops—brew individual cups in charming style.

TURKEY SAUSAGE PATTIES

SERVES 6

Here is a very lean sausage. You can increase the amount of nutmeg, allspice or mace for a more fragrant and sweeter taste. Adding the Calvados (an apple brandy), an orange-flavored liqueur and/or the orange zest deepens the flavor. You can make the sausage and form the patties 1 day ahead of serving.

2 lb (1 kg) ground (minced) turkey
2 teaspoons salt
2 teaspoons freshly ground pepper
2 teaspoons chopped fresh sage or
  ½ teaspoon dried sage
2 teaspoons chopped fresh thyme or
  ½ teaspoon dried thyme
½ teaspoon ground ginger
½ teaspoon ground nutmeg, allspice
  or mace
¼ cup (2 fl oz/60 ml) Calvados or
  orange-flavored liqueur, optional
2 teaspoons finely grated orange zest,
  optional (see glossary)
olive oil for frying

In a large bowl, combine the turkey, salt, pepper, sage, thyme, ginger and the nutmeg, allspice or mace, the Calvados or orange-flavored liqueur, if using, and the orange zest, if using. Mix together well. Scoop out a small nugget of the mixture, fry in a little olive oil, taste and adjust the seasonings.

• Form the turkey mixture into 6–8 patties each about ½ inch (12 mm) thick.

• In a large frying pan over high heat, warm a thin film of olive oil. Fry the patties, turning once, until golden and cooked through, about 4 minutes on each side. Serve immediately.

Butternut Squash Polenta with Greens & Fontina (page 87); Turkey Sausage Patties; Sour Cream Coffee Cake (page 90)

SOUR CREAM COFFEE CAKE

SERVES 6, WITH LEFTOVERS

Although this is not an unusual recipe for coffee cake, it is one of the very best you will find. The sour cream in the dough gives the cake a moist, rich texture. The traditional filling is made with pecans, but almonds or walnuts are equally suitable. If you like, add the raisins, dried currants, dates or apricots along with the nuts. A bundt pan or a tube pan works beautifully. The cake can be baked the night before, wrapped well and stored at room temperature.

Though coffee should be offered throughout the meal, it goes especially well with the cake. Be sure to brew only from freshly ground beans.

1 cup (4 oz/125 g) chopped pecans (see glossary)

1 tablespoon plus 2 cups (1 lb/500 g) sugar

1 teaspoon ground cinnamon

½ cup (3 oz/90 g) coarsely chopped raisins, apricots, pitted dates or whole dried currants, optional

2 cups (10 oz/315 g) all-purpose (plain) flour

1 teaspoon baking powder

¼ teaspoon salt

1 cup (8 oz/250 g) unsalted butter at room temperature

2 eggs

1 cup (8 fl oz/250 ml) sour cream

½ teaspoon vanilla extract (essence)

Preheat an oven to 350°F (180°C). Butter and flour a 9-inch (23-cm) tube or bundt pan. In a small bowl, stir together the pecans, the 1 tablespoon sugar, the cinnamon and the dried fruits, if using. Set aside.

❧ In a bowl, sift together the flour, baking powder and salt. Set aside. In another bowl and using an electric mixer set on medium speed, beat together the butter and the remaining 2 cups (1 lb/500 g) sugar until light and fluffy. Beat in the eggs, one at a time, beating well after each addition. Reduce the speed to low and mix in the sour cream and vanilla. Then beat in the flour at low speed, one third at a time, just until incorporated. Spoon one third of the batter into the prepared pan. Sprinkle with the nut mixture. Spoon the remaining batter over the nut mixture, smoothing the top.

❧ Bake until golden, about 1 hour. Let cool completely in the pan on a wire rack, then invert onto a serving plate.

PAPAYA WITH RASPBERRY-LIME PURÉE

SERVES 6

Easy and delicious, this is the ideal fruit accompaniment for this menu. The berry purée looks brilliant over the orange of the papaya. A few whole berries or thin strips of lime zest may be added as a garnish. The papaya can be peeled 2 hours before serving.

3 ripe papayas

3 cups (12 oz/375 g) raspberries

finely grated zest of 1 lime (see glossary)

2 tablespoons fresh lime juice

2 tablespoons sugar, or to taste

Peel the papayas, then cut in half lengthwise. Scoop out the seeds and discard. Cut lengthwise into slices ½ inch (12 mm) thick and arrange on individual plates.

❧ In a food processor fitted with the metal blade or in a blender, purée the raspberries until smooth. Strain the purée through a fine-mesh sieve to remove any seeds and stir in the lime zest and juice and the sugar. Pour the raspberry purée over the papaya and serve at once.

Sour Cream Coffee Cake; Papaya with Raspberry-Lime Purée

AUTUMN SUNDAY SUPPER

IN THE AUTUMN, as the days grow shorter and the nights turn cooler, people enjoy coming together to share the season's harvest. A casual Sunday supper for family and friends offers the opportunity to enjoy the first glimpses of winter in a warm atmosphere built upon wholesome food and close companionship.

Autumn's early twilight can often carry with it a hint of darkness, so we decided to brighten our table with lively Asian touches, including Japanese stoneware dishes, bamboo-handled cutlery and orchid plants displayed in red lacquerware baskets. It also makes a pleasing contrast to this classically Western menu. Of course, any assortment of accessories in burnished autumn colors will suit the occasion equally well, and such graceful touches as tangerines and fallen leaves only enhance the ambience.

FOR THIS MENU suited to a cozy gathering of six, we felt a roast chicken would be the ideal centerpiece. Autumnal side dishes include baked yams, a stuffing with seasonal mushrooms and a spiced cranberry sauce flavored with tangerine juice and zest. The chicken could be served on an oversized platter and carved at the table.

For the soup that starts the meal, we used an heirloom tureen. The table was set with soup bowls already in place, each one nestled in a napkin that we folded into a nest. Once the guests have finished the soup, the bowls and napkins are cleared away.

Menu

To chase autumn's chill, offer cups or mugs of hot tea soon after guests arrive or at the end of the meal. Green, jasmine or herbal teas, which require no milk, go especially well with the dessert.

BEVERAGE IDEAS

Begin with an aperitif of dry sherry or Madeira and follow it with a medium- to full-bodied white (Chardonnay, a Bordeaux Graves or an Australian Semillon). A fragrant medium-bodied red, such as Beaujolais Nouveau, a young Pinot Noir or a Merlot, will marry well with the chicken. End with a pear eau-de-vie chilled or in coffee.

Spinach Soup with
Madeira Cream

Roast Chicken with
Mushroom-Pancetta Stuffing

Cranberry-Tangerine Conserve

Gratin of Yams

Green Beans & Celery

Pear Clafouti

Bamboo, available in art or garden supply shops, can be cut into varying lengths, attached to the sides of votive candles with hot glue and then tied with cord.

PREPARATION LIST

◆ Make the conserve well in advance, up to four days ahead of the dinner.

◆ The night before, make the stuffing.

◆ Early in the morning, make the soup up to the point where it is puréed. Prepare the pears for the *clafouti* and place in the baking dish.

◆ Up to four hours before, assemble the gratin and stuff the chicken.

◆ Two hours before, boil the beans, roast the chicken and ready the ingredients for the *clafouti* batter.

◆ Just before sitting down to dinner, assemble and bake the *clafouti*.

EACH RECIPE YIELDS 6 SERVINGS.

An attractive table runner was put together by sewing a band of fabric similar to the napkins around an inexpensive woven beach mat. It can be used again and again.

SPINACH SOUP WITH MADEIRA CREAM

SERVES 6

To ensure this soup keeps its bright green color, add the spinach at the last minute and barely wilt it in the stock. Then purée the soup and reheat gently with the cream and wine. The soup can be made up to 8 hours in advance to the point where it is puréed. Finish it just before serving. As an alternative to stirring the cream directly into the soup, whip the cream until soft peaks form, beat the Madeira into it and top each serving with a dollop of the cream.

¼ cup (2 oz/60 g) unsalted butter
2 cups (8 oz/250 g) diced yellow onion
1 baking potato, about 8 oz (250 g),
　peeled and thinly sliced
2 cups (16 fl oz/500 ml) chicken stock,
　plus chicken stock as needed for
　thinning soup (see page 295)
1½–2 lb (10–12 oz) spinach, stems
　removed, carefully washed and
　drained (10–12 firmly packed cups)
1 cup (8 fl oz/250 ml) heavy (double)
　cream
¼ cup (2 fl oz/60 ml) Madeira or dry
　sherry
¼ teaspoon freshly grated nutmeg
salt and freshly ground pepper

In a large, wide saucepan over medium heat, melt the butter. Add the onion and sauté, stirring, until tender and translucent, 8–10 minutes. Add the potato and the 2 cups (16 fl oz/500 ml) chicken stock and bring to a boil. Cover, reduce the heat to low and simmer until the potato is soft, 8–10 minutes.

❧ Raise the heat to high and start adding the spinach leaves by the handful, pushing them down into the hot stock with a spoon. When all of the spinach has been immersed in the stock, cook until it is barely wilted, 1–2 minutes.

❧ Working in batches and using a slotted spoon, transfer the soup solids to a blender or food processor fitted with the metal blade and blend or process until smooth; it will be very thick. Pour the purée into a clean saucepan and add the liquid from the original pan.

❧ Stir in the cream and Madeira or sherry and reheat gently, thinning with additional stock if necessary; do not allow to boil. Season with the nutmeg and salt and pepper to taste. Serve in warmed bowls.

For centerpieces with an Asian simplicity, set orchid plants in decorative containers and surround them with moss.

Spinach Soup with Madeira Cream

ROAST CHICKEN WITH MUSHROOM-PANCETTA STUFFING

SERVES 6

The stuffing can be made up to 24 hours ahead, or use packaged cubed bread for the stuffing. Stuff the bird and put it in the oven about 2 hours before mealtime.

FOR THE STUFFING:

4 cups (8 oz/250 g) cubed day-old
   bread (about ½ loaf)
½ cup (4 oz/125 g) unsalted butter
½ lb (250 g) pancetta, cut into slices ¼
   inch (6 mm) thick and then cut into
   strips ¼ inch (6 mm) wide
1 cup (4 oz/125 g) diced yellow onion
2 cups (6 oz/185 g) sliced fresh flavorful
   mushrooms, wild or cultivated, such
   as chanterelle or portobello
2 teaspoons chopped fresh thyme
2 teaspoons chopped fresh sage
½–¾ cup (4–6 fl oz/125–180 ml)
   chicken stock (see page 295)
salt and freshly ground pepper

FOR THE CHICKEN:

1 large roasting chicken, about
   6 lb (3 kg)
1 lemon, cut in half
salt and freshly ground pepper
paprika, optional

FOR THE BASTE:

½ cup (4 fl oz/125 ml) olive oil
¼ cup (2 fl oz/60 ml) fresh lemon juice
3 cloves garlic, smashed with the side
   of a knife
1 tablespoon chopped fresh sage
1 teaspoon chopped fresh thyme
1 teaspoon freshly ground pepper

Roast Chicken with Mushroom-Pancetta Stuffing;
Cranberry-Tangerine Conserve

To make the stuffing, preheat an oven to 300°F (150°C). Spread the cubed bread in a large rimmed baking sheet and toast in the oven, stirring from time to time, until dried out, about 1 hour.

❧ Meanwhile, in a large sauté pan over medium heat, melt ¼ cup (2 oz/60 g) of the butter. Add the pancetta and sauté until it is nearly crisp, 5–8 minutes. Using a slotted spoon, transfer the pancetta to a large bowl and set aside. To the fat remaining in the pan, add the onion and sauté over medium heat until tender and translucent, 8–10 minutes. Transfer the onion to the bowl holding the pancetta.

❧ In the same pan over medium heat, melt the remaining ¼ cup (2 oz/60 g) butter. Add the mushrooms and sauté until they give off some liquid, about 5 minutes. Stir in the thyme and sage. Transfer the mushrooms and liquid to the bowl holding the pancetta and onion.

❧ Add the bread cubes to the bowl and pour ½ cup (4 fl oz/125 ml) of the stock evenly over the top. Toss until all the bread cubes are evenly moistened, adding more stock as needed if the stuffing seems too dry. Season with salt and a generous amount of pepper. Cover and refrigerate for as long as overnight before stuffing the chicken.

❧ Preheat an oven to 375°F (190°C). Wipe the bird inside and out with a damp cloth and then with a cut lemon. Rub the cavity lightly with a little salt and pepper. Spoon the stuffing loosely into the body and sew or truss closed. (Place any extra stuffing in a buttered baking dish, cover tightly and slip it into the oven with the chicken about 45 minutes before the chicken is done.)

❧ Place the chicken, breast side down, on a rack in a roasting pan. Sprinkle the flesh with salt, pepper and with a little paprika, if desired.

❧ To make the baste, in a small bowl, stir together the olive oil, lemon juice, garlic, sage, thyme and pepper.

❧ Place the chicken in the oven and roast for 45 minutes, brushing or spooning the basting juice over the bird every 15 minutes.

❧ Turn the chicken, breast side up, and continue to roast, basting every 15 minutes, until tender and juices run clear when a thigh is pierced with a skewer or long fork, 30–45 minutes longer. To test with a roasting thermometer, insert it into the thickest part of the thigh away from the bone; it should register 180°F (82°C).

❧ Remove from the oven, cover loosely with aluminum foil and let rest for about 15 minutes. Using a spoon, remove the stuffing from the cavity and place in a serving bowl. Carve the chicken and serve immediately.

To better highlight the bright red color of the cranberry conserve, present it in a clear glass bowl or pottery in a bright, contrasting color.

CRANBERRY-TANGERINE CONSERVE

MAKES ABOUT 6 CUPS (3 LB/1.5 KG)

It doesn't have to be a holiday to serve a tangy cranberry conserve to accompany roast chicken or turkey. Frozen cranberries can be found throughout the year. The conserve can be made up to 4 days in advance, covered and stored in the refrigerator.

finely grated zest of 3–4 tangerines (see glossary)
2 cups (16 fl oz/500 ml) fresh tangerine juice
1½ cups (12 oz/375 g) sugar
½ teaspoon ground ginger
½ teaspoon ground cinnamon
4 cups (1 lb/500 g) cranberries

In a saucepan over high heat, combine the tangerine zest, 1½ cups (12 fl oz/375 ml) of the tangerine juice, sugar, ginger and cinnamon. Bring to a boil, stirring to dissolve the sugar. Reduce the heat to medium and simmer, uncovered, for 10 minutes. Add the cranberries and cook until the berries pop and the mixture starts to bubble, 5–7 minutes longer.

❧ Stir in the remaining ½ cup (4 fl oz/125 ml) tangerine juice and continue to simmer, stirring occasionally, until the cranberries are tender and the juices are syrupy but not too thick, 10–15 minutes. The syrup will continue to thicken as the conserve cools.

❧ Remove from the heat, transfer to a bowl and let cool. Serve at room temperature.

GRATIN OF YAMS
SERVES 6

This delicious cream-free gratin is made with what Americans call yams, although these dark-skinned tubers with deep orange flesh are actually a variety of sweet potato and unrelated to the true yam. Assemble the gratin about 4 hours before serving. Toasted hazelnuts make a nice topping if you are not using almonds on the Green Beans & Celery (see following recipe).

6–9 yams (3 lb/1.5 kg)

½ cup (4 fl oz/125 ml) apple cider

¼ cup (2 fl oz/60 ml) maple syrup

¼ cup (2 oz/60 g) firmly packed
   brown sugar

1 tablespoon fresh lemon juice

½ teaspoon ground ginger or freshly
   grated nutmeg

½ teaspoon ground cinnamon

6 tablespoons (3 oz/90 g) unsalted
   butter

salt

toasted hazelnuts (filberts), peeled and
   chopped, optional (see glossary)

Preheat an oven to 375°F (190°C). Butter a large rectangular baking dish or two 9-inch (23-cm) square baking dishes.

&❧ Bring a large saucepan three-fourths full of water to a boil. Add the yams and boil, uncovered, until they can be pierced but are still quite firm, about 30 minutes. Drain, immerse in cool water to stop the cooking and drain again.

&❧ Peel the yams and then slice crosswise ½ inch (12 mm) thick. Arrange the slices in a single layer, overlapping them (or in 2 layers), in the prepared baking dish(es).

&❧ Meanwhile, in a small saucepan over medium heat, combine the apple cider, maple syrup, brown sugar, lemon juice, ginger or nutmeg and cinnamon. Bring to a boil, stirring to dissolve the sugar, and boil for 10 minutes. Swirl in the butter, then pour the mixture evenly over the yams. Sprinkle lightly with salt and strew toasted hazelnuts (if using) over the top.

&❧ Bake uncovered, basting occasionally with the pan juices, until the yams are tender, 20–25 minutes. Serve immediately from the dish.

GREEN BEANS & CELERY
SERVES 6

If you are not topping the yam gratin with hazelnuts, sprinkle almonds over this dish. You can boil the green beans 2–4 hours in advance.

1½–2 lb (750 g–1 kg) green beans,
   trimmed

¼ cup (2 oz/60 g) unsalted butter or
   ¼ cup (2 fl oz/60 ml) olive oil

1 cup (3½ oz/105 g) sliced yellow
   onion

Gratin of Yams; Green Beans & Celery

4 large celery stalks, cut on the diagonal
   into strips ¼ inch (6 mm) wide
1 cup (4 oz/125 g) sliced toasted
   almonds, optional (see glossary)
salt and freshly ground pepper

Bring a large saucepan three-fourths full of salted water to a boil. Add the green beans and boil until tender-crisp, 3–5 minutes. Drain, immerse in ice water to stop the cooking and drain again. Pat dry with paper towels and cut into 2-inch (5-cm) lengths. Set aside.

❧ In a large sauté pan over medium heat, melt the butter or warm the oil. Add the onion and sauté, stirring, until tender and translucent, 8–10 minutes. Add the celery, raise the heat slightly and stir and toss for 3–4 minutes. Add the green beans and almonds (if using) and heat to serving temperature. Season to taste with salt and pepper. Transfer to a warmed dish and serve immediately.

PEAR CLAFOUTI

SERVES 6

A clafouti (also commonly spelled clafoutis for both the singular and the plural forms) is a rustic fruit "pancake" from France's Limousin region. It is traditionally prepared with cherries, but pears are a delicious alternative. The fruit can be arranged in the baking dish 8 hours before and the batter ingredients measured out up to 2 hours before. Before sitting down to dinner, blend the batter ingredients, pour the batter over the fruit and bake.

1½–2 lb (750 g–1 kg) ripe but firm
   Bosc or Anjou pears, peeled, halved,
   cored and cut into 1-inch (2.5-cm)
   pieces

Pear Clafouti

⅓ cup (3 fl oz/80 ml) pear brandy or
   ½ cup (4 fl oz/125 ml) sweet white
   wine
3 tablespoons minced candied
   ginger, optional
2 tablespoons unsalted butter
3 eggs
½ cup (2½ oz/75 g) all-purpose (plain)
   flour
½ cup (4 oz/125 g) granulated sugar
½ teaspoon ground cinnamon, optional
1 cup (8 fl oz/250 ml) milk
½ cup (4 fl oz/125 ml) heavy (double)
   cream
finely grated zest of 1 lemon or
   ½ orange (see glossary)
1 teaspoon vanilla extract (essence)
pinch of salt
confectioners' (icing) sugar

Preheat an oven to 375°F (190°C). In a small saucepan over medium heat, mix the pears, brandy or wine and candied ginger (if using). Cook gently, stirring occasionally, until the pears are tender but not mushy, about 10 minutes.

❧ Meanwhile, thoroughly grease a 10-inch (25-cm) pie plate or other shallow round baking dish with the butter. When the pears are ready, distribute them and their juices evenly on the bottom of the prepared pie plate.

❧ In a blender or in a bowl, blend or whisk together the eggs, flour, granulated sugar, cinnamon (if using), milk, cream, zest, vanilla and salt until well mixed. Scrape down the sides of the blender container and blend the batter again. Let the batter rest for about 5 minutes.

❧ Pour the batter evenly over the pears. Bake until puffed and set, 35–40 minutes. Remove from the oven and sift a light dusting of confectioners' sugar over the top. Serve warm.

AFTER-WORK SUPPER

SOONER OR LATER, an occasion arises when you want to invite colleagues home for a meal, whether to work on an ongoing project, to celebrate a job well done or to make a good impression. The challenge is to prepare and present a delicious meal with minimal effort in the midst of a busy workweek, while also striking the right casual tone.

Because guests may arrive with you from work, or show up soon after, it's a good idea to set the table the night before, using everyday flatware, dishes and napkins on simple place mats. Table decorations can be equally straightforward. We composed the centerpiece the night before by gathering a bunch of forced, flowering bulbs, although any cut flowers that are robust enough to last a few days, such as daisies, ranunculi, Queen Anne's lace or roses, can be purchased in advance and arranged in simple vases.

Previously forced to flower in glass vases, an assortment of white-blossomed bulbs—tulips, narcissi, hyacinths, and freesias—was grouped together on the dining table the night before to create an informal centerpiece.

Menu

OUR AFTER-WORK menu features Moroccan-style recipes that, while exotic enough to elicit comment, are nonetheless familiar and likely to appeal to everyone. Most of the dishes are prepared largely in advance. Quantities are easily doubled if you want to entertain a larger group of co-workers.

While you look after last-minute details, you might want to offer ice-cold cocktails. The classic martini of gin or vodka and a touch of dry vermouth has experienced a renaissance of late, and may be especially welcomed on a Friday evening as a way to launch the weekend. For nondrinkers, provide sparkling water.

Roasted almonds and marinated olives accompany freshly mixed martinis, prepared in a classic shaker.

Lentil Soup

White Fish with
Moroccan Spice Marinade

Couscous

Moroccan Vegetables

Dried Apricot or Melon Compote

PREPARATION LIST

◆ Up to three days before, make the dried apricot compote, if serving.

• The day before, make the lentil soup up to the point where the greens are added.

◆ The night before, make the fish marinade; prepare the onion base and cook the carrots and cauliflower for the Moroccan vegetables. Cook and chill the melon compote, if serving.

◆ An hour before dinner is served, marinate the fish, cook the couscous and wilt the greens for the soup.

EACH RECIPE YIELDS 4 SERVINGS.

BEVERAGE IDEAS

After cocktails (if serving), launch the meal with a glass of spicy and bright Pinot Noir from Oregon or a simple Burgundy or Côtes du Rhône. Stay with the same wine or switch to a crisp Vouvray or German or Pacific Northwest Riesling to accompany the fish. With dessert, serve an Asti Spumante or Muscat-based wine.

A sturdy, woven-raffia mat underscores a place setting with tasteful simplicity. Deep bowls await the lentil soup.

LENTIL SOUP

SERVES 4, WITH LEFTOVERS

Brown, red or green lentils can all be used in this soup. The green lentils are firmest, so they are best to use if you want to see whole lentils in the soup. The amount of water in which you cook the lentils will vary, depending upon how dry they are; older lentils will require the larger amount. The soup can be prepared the day before and reheated, but wilt and stir in the greens just before serving. A dollop of yogurt or crème fraîche adds a sharpness that cuts some of the richness of the lentils.

2 tablespoons olive oil
1 large yellow onion, diced
1 teaspoon ground cumin
1 large or 2 small carrots, peeled and
  diced
2 cups (14 oz/440 g) lentils
5–6 cups (40–48 fl oz/1.25–1.5 l)
  chicken stock (see page 295) or water
2 cups (4 oz/125 g) coarsely chopped
  spinach, Swiss chard or watercress,
  carefully washed
salt and freshly ground pepper
plain yogurt or crème fraîche for
  serving, optional

In a saucepan over medium heat, warm the olive oil. Add the onion and sauté until tender and translucent, about 8 minutes. Add the cumin, carrots, lentils and stock or water and bring to a boil. Reduce the heat to low, cover and simmer until the lentils are soft; begin testing for doneness after 20 minutes.

&❧ Meanwhile, in a large sauté pan over medium heat, place the spinach or other greens with just the washing water clinging to the leaves. Cook, turning occasionally, just until wilted. Remove from the heat and drain well.

&❧ Stir the greens into the soup. Season to taste with salt and pepper and serve at once, topped with the yogurt or crème fraîche, if desired.

Arrayed on the kitchen counter, choose from an appealing tableau of lentil varieties—(from left) red, green and brown—any of which can be used to make the first-course soup. Green lentils are often labeled "French Green" and may be smaller, denser beans. Regardless of color, the flavor of the lentils will be consistent.

Lentil Soup

WHITE FISH WITH MOROCCAN SPICE MARINADE

SERVES 4

An easy dish that goes together quickly to produce a wonderfully fragrant and exotic main course. The marinade can be prepared the night before or in the morning and takes just moments to combine. The fish should marinate for at least 40 minutes, but for no more than 1 hour before cooking. It can be baked or broiled, as you like.

FOR THE MARINADE:

2 tablespoons fresh lemon juice

¼ teaspoon saffron threads, steeped in 3
   tablespoons warm water for 30 minutes

3 tablespoons chopped fresh flat-leaf
   (Italian) parsley

3 tablespoons chopped fresh cilantro
   (fresh coriander)

1–2 cloves garlic, minced

1½ teaspoons paprika

2 teaspoons ground cumin

1 teaspoon freshly ground pepper

⅓ teaspoon ground cinnamon

½ teaspoon ground ginger

1 teaspoon salt

6 tablespoons (3 fl oz/90 ml) olive oil

4 firm white fish fillets such as cod,
   flounder, northern halibut or
   swordfish, about 6 oz (185 g) each

olive oil for brushing on fish, if broiling
   (grilling)

To make the marinade, in a bowl, mix spices with lemon juice and then add olive oil. Arrange the fish fillets in a glass or plastic container and spoon half of the marinade over them. Turn the fillets to coat evenly. Cover and marinate in the refrigerator for at least 40 minutes or for up to 1 hour.

❧ Preheat an oven to 450°F (230°C), or preheat a broiler (griller). If baking the fish, lightly oil a baking dish large enough to accommodate the fish in a single layer. Place the fillets in the dish and bake until opaque at the center when pierced, about 8 minutes.

❧ If broiling (grilling), lightly brush the fish fillets on both sides with olive oil and place on a broiler pan. Broil (grill), turning once, until opaque at the center, about 4 minutes on each side.

❧ Serve the baked or broiled fillets with the remaining marinade spooned over the top.

*A selection of pungent spices for the marinade
makes a fragrant display on a countertop.*

COUSCOUS

SERVES 4

A staple of North African cuisine, couscous is the name given to both the tiny pellets made from semolina and the dish made from them. With the advent of instant couscous, this dish takes but a few minutes to prepare. It can be made up to 1 hour in advance and transferred to the top pan of a double boiler over hot water to keep warm. Or place the baking pan in a warm place. It is important that the couscous puff up fully, so be sure to give it enough time to absorb all of the liquid. The grains will be light and fluffy.

1½ cups (7½ oz/235 g) instant
   couscous

2¼ cups (18 fl oz/560 ml) water or
   chicken stock (see page 295)

½ teaspoon salt

1–2 tablespoons unsalted butter or oil,
   optional

pinch of ground cinnamon, cumin or
   ginger, optional

Place the couscous in a 1½-qt (1.5-l) baking pan. In a saucepan, bring the water or stock to a boil. Add the salt and the butter or oil and one of the spices, if using. Pour the boiling liquid evenly over the couscous, stir well once and then cover the pan with aluminum foil. Set aside.

❧ After 10 minutes, remove the foil and fluff the couscous with a fork to separate the grains. Re-cover and keep warm until ready to serve (see note above). Fluff again just before serving.

*White Fish with Moroccan
Spice Marinade; Couscous*

MOROCCAN VEGETABLES

SERVES 4, WITH LEFTOVERS

Despite the numerous ingredients that go into this dish, it is actually quite easy to prepare and serve. Both the carrots and cauliflower can be parboiled and the seasoned onions prepared the night before. Then all you need to do before serving is reheat the onions and add the vegetables and seasonings. If fresh mint is unavailable, substitute 1 tablespoon dried mint, crumbled, adding it with the carrots and cauliflower to the onion mixture.

2 tablespoons olive oil
1 large yellow onion, diced
½ teaspoon salt
2 cloves garlic, minced
1 teaspoon paprika
½ teaspoon freshly ground black
    pepper
½ teaspoon cayenne pepper, or to taste
1 teaspoon ground ginger
½ teaspoon ground cinnamon
1 cup (8 fl oz/250 ml) chicken (see
    page 295) or vegetable stock or water
6 carrots, peeled and cut into 2-inch
    (5-cm) lengths
1 large cauliflower, cut into florets
2 tablespoons fresh lemon juice
4 tablespoons chopped fresh mint
Moroccan, Kalamata, Sicilian or other
    full-flavored black olives, optional
toasted almonds, optional (see glossary)

In a large sauté pan over medium heat, warm the olive oil. Add the onion and sauté until tender and translucent, about 8 minutes. Add the salt, garlic, paprika, black pepper, cayenne pepper, ginger and cinnamon and sauté, stirring from time to time, for 3 minutes longer. Add the stock or water and simmer for 1–2 minutes. Remove from the heat and set aside.

❧ Bring a saucepan three-fourths full of salted water to a boil. Add the carrots and boil until tender but still firm, 5–6 minutes. Using a slotted spoon, transfer the carrots to a bowl. Add the cauliflower florets to the same boiling water and boil until tender but still firm, about 5 minutes. Drain well.

❧ Reheat the onion mixture over medium heat. Add the carrots and cauliflower and toss well to coat with the onion mixture. When the mixture reaches a simmer, cover and heat until warmed to serving temperature. Stir in the lemon juice, then taste and adjust the seasonings.

❧ To serve, transfer to a serving dish and sprinkle with the mint and with the olives and almonds, if using.

Moroccan Vegetables

DRIED APRICOT OR MELON COMPOTE

SERVES 4

Dried fruits make a wonderful dessert compote in winter. However, in warmer months, you may want to choose a fresh fruit compote to serve with this menu. This recipe gives you a choice.

If you like, a mixture of dried fruits can be used in place of the apricots and raisins in the winter compote. Prepare it up to 3 days ahead of serving. The melon compote can be made up to 24 hours ahead.

FOR THE DRIED APRICOT COMPOTE:

1½ lb (750 g) dried apricots
⅓ cup (2 oz/60 g) golden raisins
5–6 cups (40–48 fl oz/1.25–1.5 l) water, Riesling, Moscato or other sweet wine, to cover
1 cup (8 oz/250 g) sugar, or to taste
2 orange zest strips (see glossary)
½ teaspoon ground cardamom
1–2 tablespoons orange flower water or rose water, or to taste (see glossary)
¾ cup (4 oz/125 g) toasted pine nuts or slivered almonds, optional (see glossary)

In a bowl, combine the apricots, raisins and enough of the water or wine to cover. Let stand overnight at room temperature. The next morning, transfer the fruits and their soaking liquid to a saucepan and add additional water or wine as needed to cover. Add the sugar, orange zest and cardamom and bring to a boil, stirring to dissolve the sugar. Reduce the heat to medium and simmer, uncovered, until the apricots are tender, about 30 minutes.

❧ Remove fruit from the heat and stir in orange flower water or rose water and nuts, if using. Transfer to a bowl; cool, cover and chill before serving.

FOR THE MELON COMPOTE:

1½ cups (12 fl oz/375 ml) water
¼ cup (2 fl oz/60 ml) fresh lemon juice
1 cup (8 oz/250 g) sugar
orange zest (see glossary)
2–3 lb (1–1.5 kg) cantaloupe or honeydew melon, peeled, seeded and scooped into balls or diced
½ teaspoon ground cardamom
1 tablespoon rose water
chopped pistachios or toasted slivered almonds (see glossary)

In a saucepan, combine water, lemon juice, sugar and orange zest to taste. Bring to a boil while stirring; cook 10 to 15 minutes, or until syrupy. Stir in the melon and the cardamom. Simmer 5 minutes. Remove from heat and stir in rose water. Transfer fruit to a bowl, cool, cover and chill before serving. Garnish with pistachios or almonds.

Dried Apricot Compote, left
Melon Compote, right

$\mathcal{S}$OUP SUPPER
BY THE FIRE

WINTER'S CHILLIEST DAYS bring out the natural desire to gather together beside the fire, seeking warmth in close companionship and good food. Any room that has a fireplace will do. If you don't have a fireplace, cozy seating and enough assorted votives and other candles to cast a warming glow will be just as inviting.

In this casual setting, a coffee table can become both the buffet and, for those seated close to it, the dining table. For other guests, an assortment of small end tables or folding trays within reach would do. A mantel is the perfect place to add seasonal decorations. Here, an arrangement of ivy, branches and moss is embellished with such serendipitous touches as early daffodils, urns of dried yarrow, a bird's nest and a wild porcini mushroom, freshly picked.

For a touch of springtime in midwinter, grow a variety of salad greens from seed indoors in individual glazed pots. Set on a sunny windowsill or in another bright location.

Menu

A HEARTY SOUP IS the ideal main course for a supper by the fire. Our zesty seafood chowder offers great leeway in the choice of ingredients— you can even turn it into a chicken chowder. Ladle it from a tureen, or serve it directly from the pot set on a trivet on the table, into deep bowls, mugs or—as we did—Italian *caffè latte* cups with saucers.

Accompanying the chowder is an array of other dishes, from which guests can choose: freshly baked breadsticks, a tossed salad and a selection of cheeses. Baked apples and ginger-snaps are a tasty, old-fashioned conclusion.

A choice of wines is set out with glasses on a sideboard or table. Through-out the meal guests can pour whichever vintage they prefer.

Seafood Chowder

*Green Salad with Cucumbers,
Walnuts & Mustard-Shallot Vinaigrette*

Sesame Breadsticks

Assorted Cheeses

Baked Apples

Gingersnaps

PREPARATION LIST

◆ A couple of days before, bake the ginger-snaps and store in an airtight container.

◆ In the morning, bake the breadsticks and the apples; prepare the base for the chowder through the point at which the potatoes are half-cooked. Make the vinaigrette.

◆ A few hours ahead, wash and crisp the salad greens; toast the walnuts for the salad.

EACH RECIPE YIELDS 6 SERVINGS.

BEVERAGE IDEAS

Despite the chill outside, white wines are best for this menu. Provide a medium-bodied, fragrant young Sauvignon Blanc or Chardonnay. A snifter of good brandy or Calvados will complement the flavors of the baked apples and gingersnaps.

Offset by a folded napkin, a plain glass bowl shows off a baked apple—garnished here with a mint leaf—in all its homey simplicity. An underplate allows gingersnaps to be served alongside.

SEAFOOD CHOWDER

SERVES 6

This Latin American–inspired chowder is versatile and easy to prepare. Use firm, white-fleshed fish, such as cod, snapper, halibut, angler, flounder or sea bass. A variety of shellfish can also be added, including shelled clams, shrimp (prawns) and scallops. If you cannot find fresh baby lima beans, more mature fresh limas can be used; they will need to be blanched for 2–3 minutes in boiling water and then drained before adding to the chowder. Prepare the soup base and half-cook the potatoes in it up to 8 hours in advance. At serving time, simply bring the soup base to a simmer and add the corn, limas and fish or fish and shellfish. Directions for transforming this soup into a chicken chowder follow.

3 tablespoons olive oil

2 yellow onions, chopped

3 cloves garlic, minced

1 tablespoon grated, peeled fresh
  ginger

finely grated zest of 1 lime or lemon
  (see glossary)

1 tablespoon paprika

3 celery stalks, chopped

4 tomatoes, peeled, seeded and diced

2 fresh jalapeño (hot green) chili peppers,
  seeded, if desired, and minced
  (see glossary)

6 cups (48 fl oz/1.5 l) fish stock or
  chicken stock (see page 295)

2 cups (10 oz/315 g) diced, peeled
  potatoes

1 cup (6 oz/185 g) fresh or thawed
  frozen corn kernels

1 cup (5 oz/155 g) fresh or thawed
  frozen baby lima beans

1 cup (8 fl oz/250 ml) half-and-half or
  heavy (double) cream, optional

2 lb (1 kg) assorted firm white fish
  fillets, cut into spoon-sized chunks, or
  a mixture of fish fillets and shellfish
  (see note above)

salt and freshly ground pepper

3 tablespoons chopped fresh cilantro
  (fresh coriander)

In a large, deep saucepan over medium heat, warm the olive oil. Add the onions and sauté, stirring, until tender and translucent, about 8 minutes. Add the garlic, ginger, lime or lemon zest and paprika and sauté for 2 minutes. Then add the celery, tomatoes and jalapeños and sauté for 2 minutes longer.

❧ Add the stock and potatoes and bring to a boil. Reduce the heat to medium and simmer, uncovered, until the potatoes are about half-cooked, 10–12 minutes.

❧ Add the corn, lima beans, half-and-half or cream (if using) and fish or fish and shellfish and simmer, uncovered, until just cooked, about 5 minutes; do not overcook or the seafood will toughen. Season to taste with salt and pepper and sprinkle with the cilantro. Serve at once.

CHICKEN CHOWDER

Omit the fish or fish and shellfish and use chicken stock instead of fish stock. Add 6 whole chicken breasts, skinned, boned and cut into 1-inch (2.5-cm) chunks, with the corn and lima beans. Simmer until the chicken is opaque and cooked through, 5–7 minutes.

Seafood Chowder

GREEN SALAD WITH CUCUMBERS, WALNUTS & MUSTARD-SHALLOT VINAIGRETTE

SERVES 6

This full-flavored vinaigrette coats the salad greens and adds a little zip to the crunchy but bland cucumbers. You can make the vinaigrette early in the day and toast the walnuts and wash and crisp the greens a few hours ahead of supper time. Then it's just toss and serve.

9 cups (9 oz/280 g) mixed torn salad greens, including romaine (cos), butter lettuces and watercress
2 cucumbers, peeled, seeded and diced (about 4 cups/1¼ lb/625 g)
1½ cups (6 oz/185 g) toasted walnuts (see glossary)
3 tablespoons chopped fresh dill, optional

FOR THE MUSTARD-SHALLOT VINAIGRETTE:

2 tablespoons Dijon mustard
3 tablespoons red wine vinegar
½ cup (4 fl oz/125 ml) mild olive oil
¼ cup (1¼ oz/37 g) minced shallots
salt and freshly ground pepper

In a large salad bowl, combine the salad greens, cucumbers, walnuts and the dill, if using.

❧ To make the vinaigrette, in a small bowl, whisk together the mustard and vinegar. Gradually whisk in the olive oil until the mixture emulsifies. Stir in the shallots and salt and pepper to taste. Drizzle the vinaigrette over the salad, toss well and serve at once.

For the best, most varied selection of cheeses in peak serving condition, seek out a good-quality food store cheese department, specialty cheese store or delicatessen. Shown here (clockwise from top left): blue cheese, sharp Cheddar, Danish Fontina, herb-coated goat cheese, striped Cheddar-and-blue Huntsman, and a black-peppercorn–flavored Havarti.

Green Salad with Cucumbers, Walnuts & Mustard-Shallot Vinaigrette

SESAME BREADSTICKS

MAKES ABOUT 1 DOZEN

These fat breadsticks are crisp on the outside and a little chewy on the inside. They can be made even stouter—sort of slim baguettes—and you will end up with only about half as many breadsticks. The dough can be mixed in an electric mixer with paddle and dough hook attachments or by hand. The breadsticks can be made 8 hours in advance and then warmed in a 350°F (180°C) oven just before serving. An equal amount of poppy seeds can be used in place of the sesame seeds.

4 teaspoons active dry yeast

2 tablespoons sugar

½ cup (4 fl oz/125 ml) lukewarm (110°F/43°C) water

⅔ cup (5 fl oz/160 ml) milk

2 tablespoons unsalted butter

3½ cups (17½ oz/545 g) all-purpose (plain) flour

1 teaspoon salt

1 egg

2–3 tablespoons cold water

¼ cup (1 oz/30 g) sesame seeds

In a small bowl, combine the yeast, sugar and the warm water and let stand until creamy, about 5 minutes.

❧ Meanwhile, in a small saucepan over medium heat, warm the milk until small bubbles appear along the edges of the pan. Add the butter to the milk, immediately remove from the heat and let cool to lukewarm.

❧ To make the dough in a heavy-duty electric mixer fitted with the paddle attachment, sift together the flour and salt into the mixer bowl. Add the yeast

A few basic ingredients—and a few leisurely hours for mixing, rising, shaping and baking— yield fresh-from-the-oven breadsticks.

mixture to the lukewarm milk, then gradually add the milk-yeast mixture to the flour mixture, beating with the paddle attachment just until a soft dough forms that pulls away from the sides of the bowl, about 5 minutes. Change to the dough hook and knead on medium speed until the dough is smooth and elastic, about 8 minutes.

❧ To make the dough by hand, prepare and combine the dry yeast and lukewarm milk as directed above. Meanwhile, sift together the flour and salt into a large bowl. Using a large wooden spoon, gradually beat the milk-yeast mixture into the flour mixture until a soft dough forms that pulls away from the sides of the bowl. Turn the bread dough out onto a floured work surface and knead until dough feels smooth and elastic, about 7–10 minutes.

❧ Shape the dough into a ball, place in a lightly oiled bowl and turn the dough to coat all surfaces with the oil. Cover with a dampened towel or plastic wrap and let stand in a warm, draft-free place until doubled in size, about 1½ hours.

❧ Preheat an oven to 425°F (220°C). Line 2 baking sheets with parchment paper or oil the sheets.

❧ Punch down the dough and turn out onto a floured work surface. Divide the dough into 12 equal pieces. Flour your hands and, using your palms, roll each piece on the work surface into a log about 10 inches (25 cm) long. Transfer the shaped breadsticks to the prepared baking sheets. Cover with a dampened towel and let rise in a warm, draft-free place until doubled in size, about 30 minutes.

❧ In a small bowl, lightly beat the egg with the cold water. Brush the egg mixture on the breadsticks, then sprinkle with the sesame seeds.

❧ Slip the baking sheets into the oven and mist the breadsticks with a spray mister. Bake until the breadsticks just begin to color, 7–10 minutes, misting the breadsticks about 5 more times during this period. Then reduce the oven temperature to 350°F (180°C) and continue to bake the breadsticks until they are golden brown and sound hollow when tapped on the bottom, about 20 minutes longer. Transfer to wire racks to cool.

Sesame Breadsticks

BAKED APPLES

SERVES 6

Few other desserts fill the house with such a wonderful fragrance as they cook. Look for Rome Beauty apples at your market, as they are the best for baking. The apples will hold their shape but will also become nice and custardy inside. If you like, serve them with a dollop of cream, crème fraîche, sweetened yogurt or vanilla ice cream. They can be baked up to 8 hours before serving and served at room temperature. Or, if you prefer, warm them in a 350°F (180°C) oven for 15 minutes.

6 large Rome Beauty apples
finely grated zest of 1 orange
    (see glossary)
6 tablespoons (2 oz/60 g) chopped
    raisins
¼ cup (2 oz/60 g) firmly packed
    brown sugar
¼ cup (2 oz/60 g) unsalted butter at
    room temperature
1 teaspoon ground cinnamon
¼ cup (3 oz/90 g) honey
½ cup (4 fl oz/125 ml) fresh orange
    juice or apple cider

Preheat an oven to 350°F (180°C).
❧ Core the apples to within ½ inch (12 mm) of the base. Then peel them only halfway down from the top. Place side by side in a baking dish.
❧ In a small bowl, stir together the orange zest, raisins, brown sugar, butter and cinnamon until well mixed. Divide this mixture evenly among the apples, pushing it down into the apple cavities.

❧ In a small saucepan over medium-low heat, combine the honey and orange juice or cider and heat just until the honey dissolves. Pour the honey mixture evenly over the apples and bake, basting often with the pan juices, until the apples are tender when pierced with a fork, about 45 minutes.
❧ To serve, let cool to room temperature. Place on individual plates and spoon the pan juices over the top.

GINGERSNAPS

MAKES ABOUT 4 DOZEN

Crisp ginger cookies are the ideal accompaniment to baked apples. They can be baked up to 2 days in advance of serving and stored in an airtight container at room temperature. Leftover cookies can then be stored for up to 2 days. Here the cookie dough is made with a hand-held mixer, but a stationary mixer fitted with a paddle attachment will make it go together even more easily. Or, of course, you can also beat together all the ingredients with a sturdy spoon.

1 cup minus 1 tablespoon (7½ oz/235 g)
    unsalted butter at room temperature
1¼ cups (10 oz/315 g) sugar
1 extra-large egg
½ cup (4 fl oz/125 ml) dark molasses
2½ cups (12½ oz/390 g) all-purpose
    (plain) flour
2½ teaspoons baking soda (sodium
    bicarbonate)
½ teaspoon salt
2 tablespoons ground ginger
2 tablespoons minced candied ginger
1¼ cups (5 oz/155 g) toasted pecan
    halves, coarsely chopped (see glossary)

In a large bowl, combine the butter and sugar. Using an electric mixer set on medium speed, beat until the mixture is fluffy and light. Add the egg and continue to beat on medium speed until fully incorporated, then beat in the molasses.
❧ In another, smaller bowl, sift together the flour, baking soda, salt and ground ginger. With the mixer set on low speed, beat the flour mixture into the butter mixture, one third at a time, beating well after each addition. Stir in the candied ginger and pecans.
❧ Turn the dough out onto a lightly floured work surface. Knead briefly, then divide into 2 equal portions. Using your palms, roll each dough portion into a log 1¼–1½ inches (3–4 cm) in diameter. Wrap each log separately in plastic wrap and refrigerate until well chilled, about 2 hours.
❧ Preheat an oven to 325°F (165°C). Line 2 baking sheets with standard parchment paper.
❧ On a lightly floured work surface, slice the dough logs crosswise ⅛ inch (3 mm) thick. Place the dough rounds 1 inch (2.5 cm) apart on the prepared baking sheets.
❧ Bake until golden, 8–10 minutes. Set on a wire rack to cool completely.

Baked Apples; Gingersnaps

Dinner with Dear Friends

WHEN BEST FRIENDS come to dinner, as we hope they often do, there's no need to prepare an elaborate feast. Whether you are celebrating a reunion, memories of a shared vacation or no occasion at all, a simple yet delicious meal offers the opportunity to relax a little and enjoy one another's company.

We decided to serve this sit-down dinner in an informal dining room setting. It would be equally appropriate to set it in a family room, or even in the kitchen, if large enough. We opted for everyday table accessories: a straw runner and mats, celadon dishware, bistro-style flatware and stemless glasses. Indeed, every item here might already be on your shelf, making this style of party ideal for a spontaneous get-together, whoever your guests might be.

Batik napkins add a touch of the tropics to casual dinnerware. Votive candles nestled within glass hurricane shades shed a soft, warm light.

Menu

OUR MENU FOR special friends features a main course that couldn't be more homey: beef stew, with potatoes and a big green salad, followed by an old-fashioned crisp made with seasonal fruit. Yet, you'll find sophisticated-but-easy touches in each of these recipes that make the cozy gathering feel extra special.

The first course is a variation on the Scandinavian-style, home-cured salmon known as gravlax. If you don't have the time to prepare this dish you can substitute good-quality, store-bought gravlax or smoked salmon, serving it with the mustard sauce, cucumber and pumpernickel suggested on page 131.

Let your friends help themselves from an old-fashioned dry bar arranged on a tray or side table. Provide assorted glasses, napkins, a bucket of ice, a pitcher of water and the spirits and mixers that you know from experience they'll like.

Gravlax with Mustard Sauce

Beef Stew

Creamless Potato Gratin

Green Salad with
Gruyère & Croutons

Fruit Crisp

PREPARATION LIST

◆ Four or five days before, make the gravlax and assemble and freeze the streusel topping for the crisp.

◆ Marinate the meat for the stew the night before you plan to cook it.

◆ The day before the dinner, cook the stew and make the mustard sauce.

◆ Four hours before, make the fruit crisp, vinaigrette and croutons; wash and crisp the lettuces and slice the potatoes for the gratin.

EACH RECIPE YIELDS 6 SERVINGS.

BEVERAGE IDEAS

Select a full-bodied American or Australian Chardonnay or an Alsatian white wine to accompany the gravlax. Pour an elegant Bordeaux, a Napa Valley Cabernet Sauvignon or a luscious Merlot from New York or Washington State to go with the stew. Open a tangy Italian Moscato or lush late-harvest wine to complement the fruit crisp.

For easy table decorations, group together any small, green houseplants you may have or buy some ferns or palms and repot them in containers, using a little Spanish moss to hide their soil.

GRAVLAX WITH MUSTARD SAUCE

SERVES 6, WITH LEFTOVERS

It is too difficult to cure a small piece of fish and then slice it neatly. Therefore, it is best to use a 2–3-pound (1–1.5-kg) whole salmon fillet and have some leftovers for sandwiches, brunch or a nice first course for another occasion. The salmon must be cured 4 or 5 days before you plan to serve it. The mustard sauce can be made 1 day in advance. Gin and mint create a particularly light and delicate gravlax with a bold pink color. If you like, for a more traditional gravlax, substitute aquavit (see glossary) for the gin and the mint.

1 whole salmon fillet, 2–3 lb (1–1.5 kg), with skin intact
¼ cup (2 oz/60 g) sugar
3 tablespoons kosher salt
½ teaspoon freshly ground pepper
1 tablespoon ground juniper berries
2 teaspoons ground coriander
½ teaspoon ground allspice
zest of 2 small lemons, cut into strips 2 inches (5 cm) long and ¼ inch (6 mm) wide (see glossary)
3 large fresh mint sprigs
3 tablespoons gin

FOR THE MUSTARD SAUCE:
¼ cup (2 oz/60 g) Dijon mustard
1 teaspoon dry mustard
3 tablespoons sugar
2 tablespoons white wine vinegar
½ cup (4 fl oz/125 ml) peanut oil
3 tablespoons chopped fresh mint

1 large English (hothouse) cucumber, peeled, halved lengthwise, seeded and thinly sliced
thinly sliced pumpernickel bread

Place the fish fillet skin-side down in a glass or plastic container. In a small bowl, stir together the sugar, salt, pepper, juniper, coriander and allspice. Rub this mixture evenly onto the flesh side of the fish. Cover the fish with the lemon zest strips and the mint. Sprinkle with gin.

❧ Cover the fish with plastic wrap. Place a board or tray directly on the fish and then weight the fish with 2 bricks or other heavy weights.

❧ Chill for 4 or 5 days, basting the fish daily with the juices that accumulate. Remove the weights on the last day.

❧ To make the sauce, in a food processor or blender, combine the Dijon mustard, dry mustard, sugar and vinegar. Pulse just to combine. Slowly add the peanut oil in a thin, steady stream, processing until the mixture thickens. Alternatively, in a small bowl, whisk together the mustards, sugar and vinegar. Then gradually whisk in the peanut oil until thickened. Fold in the mint.

❧ To serve, slice the gravlax across the grain at an angle and away from the skin into paper-thin slices. Arrange on a serving plate or individual plates, with the cucumber and pumpernickel. Pass the mustard sauce.

Gravlax takes its name from the Swedish "gravad lax," meaning "buried salmon," which describes the curing technique in its most primitive form. In modern kitchens, the salmon fillet is simply cured and weighted in a glass or plastic container.

Gravlax with Mustard Sauce

BEEF STEW

SERVES 6

This old-fashioned beef stew is cooked in the oven, but it can also be simmered on the stove top (see below). The choice of vegetables is also up to you. To give the stew a Greek accent, add currants and cinnamon (see below). Marinate the stew meat overnight (two nights before) and then cook the stew a day before serving. Put it on to cook slowly; the tantalizing aroma will tell you when it's done. Just before serving, reheat on the stove top.

3 lb (1.5 kg) boneless lean stewing beef, cut in 2-inch (5-cm) cubes

FOR THE MARINADE:
4 cups (32 fl oz/1 l) dry red wine
3 yellow onions, quartered
2 bay leaves
3 fresh thyme sprigs
1 fresh rosemary sprig
12 peppercorns
3 whole cloves
6 cloves garlic, smashed with the side of a knife
2 wide orange zest strips (see glossary)

1 can (28 oz/875 g) plum (Roma) tomatoes, seeded and chopped, with their juices
1 lb (500 g) carrots, peeled and cut into 2-inch (5-cm) lengths
1 lb (500 g) fresh mushrooms, halved if large
water or beef stock, as needed (see page 294)
1 cup (5 oz/155 g) black olives, pitted (optional)
salt and freshly ground pepper
chopped fresh flat-leaf (Italian) parsley

Beef Stew; Creamless Potato Gratin

Place the beef in a glass or plastic container. To make the marinade, in a bowl, stir together the red wine, onions, bay leaves, thyme and rosemary sprigs, peppercorns, cloves, garlic and orange zest. Pour the marinade evenly over the meat, turning the meat to coat well. Cover and refrigerate overnight.

❧ Preheat an oven to 400°F (200°C). Drain the beef, reserving the marinade, then strain the marinade through a sieve into a bowl. Remove the herbs, orange zest strips and spices from the sieve and place on a square of cheesecloth (muslin). Bring the corners together and tie to form a small bag. Retrieve the onions and garlic from the sieve and place in a large, heavy ovenproof pan with a tight-fitting lid. Add the beef, tomatoes, carrots and mushrooms.

❧ Add the strained marinade and the spice bag. If the meat is not covered completely by the wine, add water or stock to cover. Cover tightly and place in the oven. When the stew reaches a boil, reduce the heat to 275°–300°F (135°–150°C). Cook until the meat is very tender, about 3 hours.

❧ Remove from the oven and skim off any excess fat. If using the olives, stir them in and allow to heat through. Season to taste with salt and pepper and sprinkle with parsley.

STOVE-TOP VARIATION

To cook the stew on the stove top, drain the beef, strain the marinade, make a spice bag and reserve the marinade ingredients as directed. Dry the beef well. Coat with all-purpose (plain) flour that has been seasoned with salt and pepper. In a large sauté pan over medium-high heat, warm 1–2 tablespoons olive oil. Working in batches, brown the beef on all sides, about 10 minutes. Transfer it to a large, heavy pan with a tight-fitting lid. Add the onions, garlic, tomatoes, mushrooms, strained marinade, spice bag and additional water or stock as needed to cover the meat completely. Bring to a boil over high heat, cover, reduce the heat to low and simmer until tender, 2½–3 hours. Add the olives and heat through. Season with salt and pepper. Sprinkle with parsley and serve.

GREEK-STYLE BEEF STEW

Prepare the stew as directed, but omit the mushrooms and the olives. About 1 hour before the stew is ready, stir in 1 cup (6 oz/185 g) dried currants and 1 teaspoon ground cinnamon.

Marinating chunks of stewing beef overnight in red wine with onion, orange zest, herbs and spices gives them a rich flavor and tender texture.

CREAMLESS POTATO GRATIN

SERVES 6

You need not feel guilty when eating this flavorful low-calorie gratin. An alternative to the traditional gratin that is loaded with butter and cream, this gratin has such good flavor you may never make it the old way again. If you prefer to omit the broiler step, sprinkle the cheese over the potatoes before they go into the oven: it will melt and form a nicely browned crust. The potatoes can be sliced up to 4 hours before dinner and kept in water until you assemble the gratin.

3–4 cups (24–32 fl oz/750 ml–1 l) chicken stock or beef stock (see pages 294–5)
salt and freshly ground pepper
6 long white new potatoes, peeled and sliced crosswise ¼ inch (6 mm) thick
½ cup (2 oz/60 g) freshly grated Parmesan or Gruyère cheese

Preheat an oven to 375°F (190°C). Butter a 3-qt (3-l) shallow rectangular or oval baking dish.

❧ Pour the stock into a saucepan and bring to a boil. Season to taste with salt and pepper. Lay the potato slices in the prepared dish. Pour the hot stock evenly over the potatoes to barely cover. Cover tightly with aluminum foil.

❧ Bake until the liquid is absorbed and the potatoes are tender when pierced with a fork, about 40 minutes.

❧ Meanwhile, preheat a broiler (griller). Sprinkle the cheese evenly over the potatoes and slip under the broiler. Broil (grill) until the cheese melts, about 2 minutes. Serve at once.

Green Salad with Gruyère & Croutons

GREEN SALAD WITH GRUYÈRE & CROUTONS

SERVES 6

The vinaigrette, croutons and lettuces can be prepared about 4 hours before dinner.

FOR THE HERB VINAIGRETTE:

⅔ cup (5 fl oz/160 ml) mild olive oil
⅓ cup (3 fl oz/80 ml) fruity virgin olive oil
¼ cup (2 fl oz/60 ml) Champagne, white wine or sherry vinegar
salt and freshly ground pepper
1 teaspoon chopped fresh tarragon, chervil or chives

FOR THE CROUTONS:

18–24 baguette slices, each about ⅛ inch (3 mm) thick, about ½ loaf (see page 298)
mild olive oil
1–2 cloves garlic

FOR THE SALAD:

about 12 cups (1½ lb/750 g) torn mixed lettuces, carefully washed and dried
5 oz (155 g) Gruyère cheese, cut into thin strips 1½–2 inches (4–5 cm) long and ⅛ inch (3 mm) wide (about 1 cup)

Preheat an oven to 350°F (180°C).

❧ To make the vinaigrette, in a bowl, whisk together the mild and fruity olive oils, wine or vinegar, salt and pepper to taste and the tarragon, chervil or chives. Set aside.

❧ To make the croutons, place the baguette slices on a baking sheet. Brush them with olive oil and bake until crisp and golden, 10–15 minutes. Remove from the oven and, while still warm, rub each crouton with a garlic clove.

❧ To serve, place the lettuces in a large salad bowl. Add the cheese strips and croutons. Drizzle the vinaigrette over the top, toss well and serve at once.

FRUIT CRISP

SERVES 6

Bake the crisp 4 hours in advance. The streusel topping can be frozen for up to 5 days. Serve with vanilla ice cream.

FOR THE STREUSEL TOPPING:

1 cup (8 oz/250 g) unsalted butter, at
   room temperature
½ cup (3½ oz/105 g) firmly packed
   brown sugar
½ cup (4 oz/125 g) granulated sugar
1⅔ cups (8½ oz/265 g) all-purpose
   (plain) flour
⅔ teaspoon baking powder
½ teaspoon ground cinnamon
½ teaspoon ground ginger
1 cup (4 oz/125 g) chopped walnuts or
   almonds, lightly toasted (see glossary)

FOR THE FILLING:

½ cup (2½ oz/75 g) all-purpose
   (plain) flour
pinch of salt
1–1½ cups (7–10½ oz/220–330 g)
   firmly packed brown sugar
8 cups (2–3 lb/1–1.5 kg) sliced fruit or
   whole berries
1 tablespoon vanilla extract (essence)
2 tablespoons finely grated orange or
   lemon zest (see glossary)
2 tablespoons brandy, Calvados, kirsch
   or other complementary spirit

To make the streusel, in a bowl, beat the butter and sugars with an electric mixer set on medium until light and fluffy. Reduce the speed and gradually add the flour, baking powder and spices, beating until crumbly. Add the nuts and set aside.

☙ Preheat an oven to 350°F (180°C). Butter a 9-inch (23-cm) round baking dish or 2-qt (2-l) oval gratin dish.

☙ To make the filling, in a large bowl, combine the flour, salt and brown sugar, adjusting the amount of sugar depending upon the sweetness of the fruit. Add the fruit, vanilla, citrus zest and brandy or other spirit; toss to mix well. Transfer to the prepared dish.

☙ Scatter the streusel over the top. (If the streusel is frozen, place it in a food processor fitted with the metal blade and, using on-off pulses, process until the mixture is crumbly.)

☙ Bake until the top is golden brown and the fruit bubbles up along the edges of the dish, 25–40 minutes, depending upon the type of fruit.

Fruit Crisp

TREE-TRIMMING SUPPER

"IT'S TIME TO come and decorate the tree!" is an eagerly anticipated call when close family members are gathered together for the holiday celebration. Because trimming the tree can often be a major project, it makes sense to simplify the other elements of the gathering. We decided a meal served buffet style on the kitchen counter would be the easiest, letting family members help themselves and eat either in the kitchen or beside the tree.

To emphasize the spirit of the season, build a blazing fire. If your home lacks a fireplace, arrange large candles around the room, taking care, of course, to keep them clear of decorations and wrappings. We dressed our tree with natural ornaments, including pinecones and potpourri sachets, as well as fresh fruit, popcorn garlands and cookies.

A Douglas fir wears natural holiday adornments, such as pinecones and lemons tied on with long raffia strips and florist's wire. Cookies, iced to resemble stained-glass windows, make unusual ornaments.

Menu

THIS MENU FOR six can easily be doubled if you have a big family or if you want to invite guests to join in your celebration. The recipes allow much of the preparation to be done in advance. If you don't have time to bake the bread, buy a loaf from a good local bakery. Set out the pasta and salad in large bowls, with plates or bowls stacked alongside. The dessert can be served later on a tray by the fire.

BEVERAGE IDEAS

An herbaceous red wine, medium-full in body and rustic in style, is the perfect match for both the occasion and the dinner. Try an Australian Shiraz, California Merlot, tasty French Rhône or an Italian Chianti, Barbaresco or Valpolicella. A ruby port pairs perfectly with the *budino*.

*Pappardelle
with Mushroom Sauce*

Caesar Salad

Rosemary Bread

*Mascarpone Budino
with Sun-Dried Cranberry Compote*

Variegated holly, pine boughs and other evergreen foliage from the garden or the florist are bound together with florist's wire to make a casual holiday wreath in an unusual square shape.

PREPARATION LIST

◆ Two or three days before, cook the cranberry compote.

◆ One or two days before, make the starter for the rosemary bread.

◆ Toast the croutons for the Caesar salad and make the *budino* one day before.

◆ That day, bake the bread and make the pappardelle. Wash and crisp the lettuce.

◆ An hour before, make the mushroom sauce and the Caesar salad dressing.

EACH RECIPE YIELDS 6 SERVINGS.

An attractive wooden caddy holds casual cutlery for diners to help themselves.

139

PAPPARDELLE WITH MUSHROOM SAUCE

SERVES 6

Nothing is quite so satisfying as a bowl of steaming pasta cloaked in a delectable sauce. If you are making the pappardelle, which are ribbon noodles about 1 inch (2.5 cm) wide, the dough can be mixed and the noodles cut up to 8 hours in advance of cooking. If you do not have time to make the pasta, purchase good-quality fresh pappardelle. If you prefer a narrower noodle, make or purchase fresh fettuccine.

For the sauce, select an assortment of fresh mushrooms—chanterelles, porcini, crimini, portobellos and shiitakes. Even dried porcini can be used: Soak them first in hot water just to cover for about 1 hour, drain, squeeze dry and strain the soaking liquid through a sieve lined with cheesecloth (muslin). Chop the mushrooms and add them with the herbs; use the strained liquid in place of the stock. The sauce can be made up to 1 hour before serving and then re-heated while you cook the pasta.

homemade pasta (recipe on page 300)
 or 1½ lb (750 g) purchased fresh
 pappardelle or fettuccine
3 tablespoons unsalted butter
3 tablespoons olive oil
½ lb (250 g) pancetta, sliced ¼
 inch (6 mm) thick, then cut into long
 strips ¼ inch (6 mm) wide, optional
 (see glossary)
3 yellow onions, sliced ⅛ inch
 (3 mm) thick

2 lb (1 kg) mixed fresh mushrooms,
 sliced ¼ inch (6 mm) thick or left
 whole or halved if small (see note
 above)
about ½ cup (4 fl oz/125 ml) beef,
 chicken or vegetable stock, if needed
 (see pages 294–5)
2 tablespoons chopped fresh sage or
 thyme
1½ tablespoons minced garlic
salt and freshly ground pepper
freshly grated Parmesan cheese

If you are making the pasta, mix and roll out the dough as directed in the recipe and then cut into strips 1 inch (2.5 cm) wide to form pappardelle.

ੳ In a large sauté pan over medium heat, warm 1 tablespoon each of the butter and olive oil. If using the pancetta, add it to the pan and sauté, stirring occasionally, until lightly browned, 2–3 minutes. Add the onions and sauté, stirring occasionally, until almost tender, 7–8 minutes longer. Transfer to a bowl and set aside.

ੳ Add 1 tablespoon each butter and olive oil to the same pan over high heat. When the butter melts and is hot, add half of the mushrooms and sauté just until they begin to release their liquid and soften; the timing will depend upon the variety of mushrooms. Transfer to the bowl holding the onions.

ੳ Warm the remaining butter and oil in the same pan. Add the remaining mushrooms and sauté in the same manner. Return the mushroom-onion mixture to the sauté pan and reheat

A wide selection of mushrooms are now commercially grown and sold in good-quality produce shops (clockwise from top): shiitakes, crimini, chanterelles and portobellos.

over high heat. If the mixture seems dry, add as much of the stock as needed to moisten it. Then stir in the sage or thyme and the garlic and sauté, stirring often, for 2 minutes. Season to taste with salt and pepper. Keep warm.

ੳ Meanwhile, bring a large pot three-fourths full of salted water to a boil. When the sauce is ready, drop the pasta into the boiling water and cook, stirring to separate the strands, until al dente, 1–2 minutes. Drain and transfer to a warmed serving platter. Add the sauce, toss gently and serve immediately. Pass the Parmesan cheese.

Pappardelle with Mushroom Sauce

CAESAR SALAD

SERVES 6

This is probably the most popular salad in America after plain mixed greens. If possible, use salt-packed anchovies, as they have better flavor. Lightly rinse off the excess salt and remove any small bones before chopping. Buy young, tender romaine heads; reserve any large leaves for another purpose. A fruity olive oil and fresh lemon juice are necessary, as romaine is quite mild in flavor. If undercooked eggs are a concern, substitute 3 tablespoons plain low-fat yogurt. The croutons can be made the night before. The lettuce can be washed and chilled up to 8 hours in advance of serving. The dressing can be prepared 1 hour before the meal.

FOR THE CROUTONS:

18 baguette slices, each about ⅛ inch
   (3 mm) thick, about ½ loaf (see
   page 298)
olive oil
1–2 cloves garlic

FOR THE SALAD:

3 eggs
3–4 tablespoons finely chopped
   anchovy fillets (see note above)
6 tablespoons (3 fl oz/90 ml) fresh
   lemon juice
¾ cup (6 fl oz/180 ml) virgin olive oil
1 tablespoon minced garlic
4–6 tablespoons (1–1½ oz/30–45 g)
   freshly grated Parmesan cheese
freshly ground pepper
4–6 small heads romaine (cos) lettuce

To make the croutons, preheat an oven to 350°F (180°C). Arrange the bread in a single layer on a baking sheet. Brush the tops of the slices with olive oil. Bake until crisp and golden, 8–10 minutes.

Remove from the oven. Cut the garlic cloves in half. While the bread slices are still warm, rub the toasted slices with the cut side of a clove. Let cool. Alternatively, cut the baguette into ½-inch (12-mm) cubes instead of slices. Smash the garlic cloves. In a large sauté pan over medium heat, warm 4 tablespoons olive oil with the garlic. When the oil is hot, add the bread cubes and toss in the oil until crisp and golden, about 5 minutes.

❧ To make the salad, bring a small saucepan three-fourths full of water to a boil. Working quickly, lower each egg into the boiling water on a spoon. Allow the eggs to remain in the water for 1 minute, then transfer to a bowl of cold water to cool completely.

❧ In a bowl, mash the anchovies with the lemon juice. Break the eggs and add them to the bowl, along with the olive oil, minced garlic and 3 tablespoons of the Parmesan cheese. Whisk together until all the ingredients are fully incorporated. Season to taste with pepper.

❧ Tear the romaine leaves into large bite-sized pieces and place in a large salad bowl. Add the croutons and the dressing and toss to coat the leaves evenly.

❧ Transfer to individual plates and sprinkle with the remaining Parmesan cheese. Serve at once.

ROSEMARY BREAD

MAKES TWO 1½-LB (750-G) LOAVES

This rosemary-flecked loaf is a wonderful accompaniment to the pasta and salad. The recipe yields two loaves, more than you will need for dinner. Use the second loaf for sandwiches or serve at another meal. The starter must be made the night before you plan to bake the bread. It will impart
more flavor, however, if it is refrigerated for 1–2 days before using. This recipe yields more starter than you will need for the rosemary loaves. Use the leftover starter for making additional loaves or for other bread recipes, or discard it after 1 week.

FOR THE STARTER:

1 cup (8 fl oz/250 ml) tepid water
¼ teaspoon active dry yeast
2 cups (10 oz/315 g) unbleached all-
   purpose (plain) flour

FOR THE DOUGH:

2 tablespoons active dry yeast
½ cup (8 oz/250 g) starter
2 cups (16 fl oz/500 ml) warm
   (110°F/43°C) water
3 tablespoons olive oil
2–3 tablespoons chopped fresh
   rosemary
2 teaspoons salt
3–4 cups (15–20 oz/470–625 g)
   unbleached all-purpose (plain) flour

To make the starter, in the bowl of an electric mixer fitted with a paddle attachment, combine all the ingredients. Beat at medium speed until the mixture pulls away from the sides of the bowl, about 3 minutes. Alternatively, place all the starter ingredients in a bowl and beat with a wooden spoon until the mixture pulls away from the sides of the bowl. Transfer the starter to a 2-qt (2-l) plastic container that will allow the starter to triple in volume.

❧ Cover and leave at room temperature overnight or refrigerate for 1–2 days before using. You will have about 2½ cups (1¼ lb/625 g).

❧ To make the dough in a heavy-duty electric mixer fitted with the paddle attachment, combine the yeast, starter and warm water in the bowl. Beat until the water is chalky white and foamy, about 5 minutes. Change to the dough hook and add the olive oil, rosemary, salt and 3 cups (15 oz/470 g) of the flour. Beat on medium speed until the dough pulls away from the sides of the bowl, adding up to 1 cup (5 oz/155 g) additional flour if the dough is too soft. Continue to knead with the dough hook until the dough is smooth and elastic, about 10 minutes.

❧ To make the dough by hand, in a bowl and using a wooden spoon, beat together the yeast, starter and warm water until the water is chalky. Add the olive oil, rosemary, salt and 3 cups (15 oz/470 g) of the flour and beat until well combined and the dough pulls away from the sides of the bowl, adding more flour if the dough is too sticky. Turn out the dough onto a lightly floured board. Knead by hand until smooth and elastic, about 10 minutes, adding more flour as needed to prevent sticking.

❧ Shape the dough into a ball, place in a lightly oiled bowl, and turn the dough to coat all surfaces with the oil. Cover with a dampened kitchen towel or plastic wrap and let rise in a warm, draft-free place until tripled in size, 1½–2 hours.

❧ Punch down the dough and divide in half. Shape each half into a free-form loaf and place on a baking sheet. Cover with a towel and let rise until doubled in size, 45–60 minutes.

❧ Preheat an oven to 425°F (220°C). Make 4 shallow diagonal slashes in the top of each loaf. Bake until golden brown and the bottom of each loaf sounds hollow when tapped, about 45 minutes. Let cool on wire racks.

Caesar Salad; Rosemary Bread

MASCARPONE BUDINO WITH SUN-DRIED CRANBERRY COMPOTE

SERVES 6

Budino is the Italian term for pudding. This dessert is not only endearing, but it is also positively addictive. It is delicious eaten plain or topped with an orange-scented compote of sun-dried cranberries. Mascarpone, a buttery, creamy cheese, can be found in specialty-food shops and fine food stores. The compote can be made 2–3 days in advance and reheated over medium-low heat until warmed through. The budino can be made the day before serving.

FOR THE BUDINO:

1 lb (500 g) mascarpone cheese at room temperature

3 eggs

6 tablespoons (3 oz/90 g) sugar

¼ teaspoon almond extract (essence)

1 teaspoon finely grated orange zest (see glossary)

FOR THE COMPOTE:

1 cup (4 oz/125 g) sun-dried cranberries

1 teaspoon minced orange zest (see glossary)

1 cup (8 fl oz/250 g) fresh orange juice

½ cup (4 oz/125 g) sugar

Preheat an oven to 250°F (120°C).

꙳ To make the *budino*, in a bowl, whisk together the cheese, eggs, sugar, almond extract and zest until well mixed. Strain the mixture through a fine-mesh sieve into a pitcher to remove any lumps. Then divide the mixture among six ½-cup (4-fl oz/125-ml) ramekins. Place the ramekins in a large baking pan and pour in hot water to reach halfway up the sides of the ramekins. Cover the baking pan with aluminum foil.

꙳ Place in the oven and bake until the puddings are set along the edge but still quivery in the center, 35–40 minutes. Remove the puddings from the oven and then remove them from the baking pan. Let cool, cover and refrigerate until fully chilled.

꙳ To make the compote, in a small saucepan, combine the cranberries, orange zest and juice and sugar. Place over medium heat and bring to a simmer, stirring to dissolve the sugar.

꙳ Reduce the heat to very low and continue to simmer uncovered, stirring occasionally, until the juice reduces to a thin syrup and the cranberries are tender, about 1 hour.

꙳ Serve the chilled puddings with the warm compote spooned over the top.

An open area close to the tree, such as this French country bench, can be used to set out a selection of do-it-yourself tree decorations. A large grape-picker's basket holds an assortment of foliage ready to fashion into garlands and wreaths. A smaller basket holds freshly popped corn, to be strung into ropes. Small fresh fruits, preferably with stem and leaves attached, can be secured to the tree with lengths of florist's wire. Bow-shaped sachets filled with potpourri are tied on with raffia—a rustic counterpoint to their satiny fabric. To make the stained-glass cookies shown on these pages, prepare a favorite sugar cookie recipe, paint the dough in a pattern with beaten egg mixed with food coloring, then bake.

Mascarpone Budino with Sun-Dried Cranberry Compote

Holidays & Occasions

༄

When it comes to a major event—whether a romantic dinner for two, a garden buffet for a wedding, or a holiday open house—every host or hostess wants the party to be a smashing success. The menus that follow are expressly designed to produce just that.

Follow the individual menu and preparation guidelines to the letter, or improvise your own plan, mixing and matching ideas from a variety of menus as you like. Use the suggestions for centerpieces, table settings and other stylish effects to achieve the desired mood. Whatever approach you choose, you can count on a memorable party to celebrate that special moment. And you'll be able to enjoy the occasion along with your guests!

ROMANTIC DINNER FOR TWO

WHETHER YOU ARE MARKING Valentine's Day, a special anniversary or some other shared occasion, celebrate with this memorable menu for two. We show it served at a fireside table where the warmth and glow of the flames enhance the mood of romance, but it could just as well be set in a cozy window alcove, on a balcony with a view or by candlelight at the kitchen table.

For this intimate meal, we chose china with a whimsical gold pattern and favorite pieces of silver. Heart-shaped accessories play up the amorous theme, from vases to napkin rings to the salsa ramekin. White flowers such as tulips or roses are simple, yet elegant, and are easy to arrange. Candlelight adds atmosphere as well; a tray of votives fits the scale of a table for two. You could also set small candles in various spots around the room.

A color scheme of white and gold, with heart-shaped accents, creates a very romantic place setting.

Menu

SURPRISINGLY, a dinner for two often entails more advance planning than a larger party. Try to complete most of the preparation ahead of time so you are free to devote the maximum attention to your dinner guest once the evening begins. You can marinate the squabs and make the dessert the night before, then boil the lobster the next day. Check the preparation list on the facing page to help you plan.

If your schedule is tight, you could serve fewer courses: oysters followed by lobster, or the pear salad followed by the squab. If you are opening the oysters yourself, be sure to do this just before dressing up to avoid splattering your clothes.

Casually arranged in a crystal vase on a side table, the delicate white blossoms and curving stems of tulips add to the ambience.

Oysters with Tangerine Salsa

❧

*Roast Lobster
with Meyer Lemon Butter*

❧

Broiled Squabs in Honey Marinade

Wild Rice

Pear, Fennel & Frisée Salad

❧

*Chocolate Pots de Crème
with Candied Rose Petals*

PREPARATION LIST

◆ The night before, marinate the squabs; make and refrigerate the pots de crème.

◆ In the morning, boil the lobster, remove and cut up the meat, refill the shells and chill; make and refrigerate the lemon butter.

◆ Several hours before dining, make the salsa.

◆ About 30 minutes before, start cooking the wild rice; remove the lemon butter and lobster from the refrigerator. Assemble the salad.

◆ Before dining, preheat the oven for the lobster; take the dessert from the refrigerator.

◆ While eating the oysters, roast the lobster.

◆ While eating the lobster, preheat the broiler for the squabs; dress the salad.

EACH RECIPE YIELDS 2 SERVINGS.

*A tray of votive candles illuminates a side table on
which an intriguing present awaits opening.*

WINE RECOMMENDATIONS

Start the evening with a high-quality, lighter-style California sparkling wine or a French Champagne. Continue it with the lobster, or go on to a half-bottle of classic Chardonnay or Sauvignon Blanc, or even a soft Pinot Noir. With the squab, serve a distinctive red wine such as Merlot or Côtes du Rhône. With dessert, pour generous snifters of your favorite brandy.

OYSTERS WITH TANGERINE SALSA

SERVES 2

You can use more or less jalapeño to taste in this sweet, tart, spicy salsa, but don't make it so hot that it dominates the oysters' flavor. To shuck the shellfish, you need an oyster knife (available at a well-stocked cookware store), or have your fishmonger shuck the oysters and pack them to go on the half shell.

1 small jalapeño (hot green) chili
   pepper, seeded and minced (see
   glossary)
grated zest (see glossary) and juice of
   1 tangerine
freshly ground pepper to taste
12 oysters in the shell
rock salt

Combine the jalapeño, tangerine zest and juice. Add the pepper. Pour into a small ramekin or bowl.

➳ To open the oysters, hold each one in a heavy dish towel with the rounded side of the shell down. Work the tip of an oyster knife into the hinge near the narrow end of the shell; twist the knife to pop open the shell. Slide the knife along the inside of the upper shell to sever the muscle, then pull off the top shell and discard. Loosen the oyster from the bottom shell by sliding the knife under the oyster. Remove any bits of shell debris or sand.

➳ Spread some rock salt in a layer on a serving plate. Place the oysters in their shells on the plate and serve with the salsa. Spoon the salsa over the oysters to eat.

Oysters with Tangerine Salsa

ROAST LOBSTER WITH MEYER LEMON BUTTER

SERVES 2

If you can't find Meyer lemons, mix regular lemon juice and orange juice.

2 teaspoons minced shallot

2 teaspoons finely chopped
  fresh tarragon

2 tablespoons tarragon white
  wine vinegar

½ teaspoon grated Meyer lemon zest
  or regular lemon zest (see glossary)

1 tablespoon fresh Meyer lemon juice
  or 2 teaspoons fresh regular lemon
  juice plus 1 teaspoon orange juice

¼ cup (2 oz/60 g) unsalted butter
  at room temperature

salt and freshly ground pepper to taste

1 live Atlantic (Maine) lobster,
  about 1½ lb (750 g)

Place the shallot, tarragon and vinegar in a small saucepan and cook over high heat to reduce until the liquid is almost totally evaporated and syrupy. Stir in the lemon zest and juice. Let cool, then beat this mixture into the butter. Season to taste with salt and pepper. The butter may be made ahead and refrigerated, covered, up to 1 day.

❧ Bring a large pot of salted water to a boil, drop in the lobster and cook, covered, for 7–8 minutes. Plunge the lobster into cold water. Cut the lobster in half lengthwise and remove the meat from the body and claws as directed in the glossary; clean and reserve the body shell halves. Cut all the lobster meat into bite-sized pieces and replace it in the body shell halves. Cover tightly and refrigerate up to 8 hours.

❧ To roast, let the lobsters and the lemon butter come to room temperature; preheat an oven to 350°F (180°C). Spread the butter over the lobster meat, cover loosely with aluminum foil and bake until heated through, about 8 minutes. Serve at once.

Roast Lobster with Meyer Lemon Butter

BROILED SQUABS IN HONEY MARINADE

SERVES 2

The marinade adds delicate flavor and helps the skin turn a burnished mahogany when cooked. Eat rare for the best flavor.

2 squabs, about 1 lb (500 g) each
1 star anise
2 whole cloves
seeds from 1 cardamom pod
one 2-inch (5-cm) piece fresh ginger,
    smashed with the side of a knife
⅔ cup (5 fl oz/160 ml) light soy sauce
⅓ cup (3 fl oz/90 ml) Scotch
    or bourbon
⅓ cup (4 oz/125 g) honey
salt, freshly ground pepper, ground
    ginger and ground cinnamon to taste

To prepare the squabs, insert a sharp knife through the neck cavity of each bird and cut through the back, leaving the breast intact. Remove the backbone, breastbone, cartilage and ribs. Cut the birds in half through the breast. Place the squabs in a glass or plastic container.
ᴥ Combine the star anise, cloves, cardamom seeds, fresh ginger and soy sauce in a small saucepan over moderate heat. Simmer for 5 minutes, remove from the heat and let steep for 30 minutes. Strain, reserving the liquid. Stir the Scotch or bourbon and honey into the liquid. Pour over the squabs, cover and refrigerate overnight, turning once.
ᴥ To cook, let the squabs come to room temperature. Preheat a broiler (griller). Lightly sprinkle the squabs with salt, pepper, ground ginger and ground cinnamon. Broil skin-side down for 3–4 minutes, then turn and broil 3–4 minutes on the other side for rare, or cook slightly longer if desired.

WILD RICE

SERVES 2

The nutlike taste of wild rice is the perfect foil for the sweetly marinated squab.

1½ cups (12 fl oz/375 ml) water
salt to taste
½ cup (3 oz/90 g) wild rice
2 tablespoons minced green part of
    a green (spring) onion
¼ cup (1 oz/30 g) toasted sliced
    almonds (see glossary)

In a medium saucepan, bring the water to a boil, add the salt and wild rice and reduce heat to a simmer. Cover and cook the wild rice until tender, about 1 hour.
ᴥ Stir in the green onion. Spoon the wild rice onto individual plates and garnish with the sliced almonds.

What could be more romantic than love letters? Perhaps this is the night to pull out those treasured reminders and read them again together.

PEAR, FENNEL & FRISÉE SALAD

SERVES 2

This simple salad is served on the same plate as the squab and wild rice, but it could also be served as a first course.

1 firm ripe Comice or other winter
    pear
1 small fennel bulb
1 small head frisée or 1 bunch
    watercress
¼ cup (2 fl oz/60 ml) white
    wine vinegar
2 teaspoons grated fresh ginger
½ teaspoon sugar
½ cup (4 fl oz/125 ml) olive oil
salt and freshly ground pepper to taste

Cut the pear in half lengthwise, remove the stem, core and seeds, then slice thin. Remove the tubular stems from the fennel, reserving any attractive fronds for a garnish, if you like. Cut the bulb into quarters lengthwise and remove the hard center core and any discolored outer portions. Slice thin. Trim the tough stems from the frisée or the watercress.
ᴥ In a small bowl, stir together the vinegar and grated ginger. Let stand for 5 minutes, then whisk in the sugar and the oil. Season with salt and pepper. Toss the frisée or watercress with half of the vinaigrette and divide between 2 plates. Arrange the pear and fennel slices over the greens and drizzle the rest of the vinaigrette on top. Garnish with the reserved fennel fronds, if using.

*Broiled Squabs in Honey Marinade;
Wild Rice; Pear, Fennel & Frisée Salad*

CHOCOLATE POTS DE CRÈME WITH CANDIED ROSE PETALS

SERVES 2

You can find candied rose petals in gourmet shops, but making your own is quite easy. Be sure to use only unsprayed roses.

FOR THE POTS DE CRÈME:
⅔ cup (5 fl oz/160 ml) heavy
   (double) cream
2 oz (60 g) bittersweet chocolate, grated
2 teaspoons light brown sugar, packed
pinch of salt
2 egg yolks
½ teaspoon vanilla extract (essence)

FOR THE CANDIED ROSE PETALS:
unsprayed rose petals
1 egg white, lightly beaten
½ cup (4 oz/125 g) superfine
   (caster) sugar

To make the pots de crème, place the cream, chocolate, sugar and salt in the top of a double boiler and cook until scalding. Whisk the egg yolks lightly in a small bowl, then whisk in a bit of the hot chocolate cream to warm them. Gradually stir this mixture back into the cream in the double boiler and cook, stirring, over simmering water until thickened, about 10 minutes.

☙ Remove from the heat, stir in the vanilla and pour into pot de crème cups or small custard cups. Let cool uncovered, then chill until cold, about 2 hours or overnight. Remove from the refrigerator about 30 minutes before serving.

☙ Meanwhile, to make the candied rose petals, gently brush each flower petal with egg white, then sprinkle it with sugar. Place the petals on a cake rack and let dry, then use them to garnish the pots de crème.

Chocolate Pots de Crème with Candied Rose Petals

After dinner, retire to a comfy spot and toast each other with a final sip of brandy. Generously sized snifters are perfect for swirling the spirit to develop its aroma. If you are fond of the best, look for Cognac, the classic French brandy. It's labeled according to its age, with the oldest (those that are aged more than 6½ years) bearing the X.O. designation. Each brand has its own characteristics that result from the blender's art.

RITE-OF-SPRING BRUNCH

AS DAYS GROW LONGER and warmer, the advent of spring brings with it a desire to celebrate. This is a good time to enjoy some of nature's finest produce with family and friends at a weekend party. Mother's Day, Easter or any other special event is a good reason for a rite-of-spring brunch.

The season suggests a fresh, simple decorative approach, so we selected dishware in pastel colors for this festive table. For a no-fuss centerpiece, we filled an assortment of clear glass vases and colored mineral-water bottles with colorful blossoms such as tulips, jonquils, Gerbera daisies and anemones. To take advantage of the morning light, this brunch could be set in a sun room or patio, or beside a window with a garden view. If the weather is warm, you might want to move the party outdoors.

THE BRUNCH MENU that follows features ingredients that reflect a blend of seasons: spring's tender young asparagus and peas, late-winter pears and last summer's preserved vine-ripened tomatoes. Each dish is easily prepared and presented, suiting the relaxed pace of a Saturday or Sunday morning.

The best strategy for a weekend meal is to serve it with a minimum of effort. For that reason, we set the table casually, letting guests help themselves to the first-course salad from a platter placed on a side table. Freshly cooked spaghetti may be presented on individual warm plates, with the asparagus and toasts passed alongside. Dessert also may be offered buffet-style, along with coffee and tea.

Menu

Pastel-colored plates highlight the tones of the salad. The folded napkins are rolled like scrolls so that their pointed ends echo the star-shaped napkin rings.

WINE RECOMMENDATIONS

With the salad, offer a light-bodied, herbaceous white wine: Sauvignon Blanc or Riesling. For the spaghetti, pour a medium-bodied Italian Chianti or, from California, a slightly peppery Zinfandel. For dessert, try an Italian Vin Santo or sweet Marsala.

Avocado, Grapefruit & Endive Salad

*Toast with
Sun-dried Tomato Purée*

*Spaghetti alla Carbonara
with Peas*

*Asparagus with
Toasted Almonds & Balsamic Vinaigrette*

Polenta Pound Cake

Red Wine–poached Pears

Handwritten postcards double as clever invitations and serve to remind guests of the exact date and time.

PREPARATION LIST

◆ Up to 2 days before, prepare the sun-dried tomato purée; poach the pears.

◆ The day before, make the pound cake.

◆ The night before, prepare the grapefruit segments and vinaigrette for the salad.

◆ About 2 hours ahead, dice the pancetta and blanch the peas for the spaghetti.

◆ Up to 1 hour before eating, prepare the asparagus; boil the water for the spaghetti.

◆ Just before serving, cook the spaghetti; assemble and dress the salad.

EACH RECIPE YIELDS 6 SERVINGS.

Small glass vases bring blossoms close to each place setting.

AVOCADO, GRAPEFRUIT & ENDIVE SALAD

SERVES 6

Have this simple, refreshing salad ready to be served to guests as they are seated.

FOR THE VINAIGRETTE:

¼ cup (⅜ oz/10 g) chopped fresh mint, lightly packed

¼ cup (2 fl oz/60 ml) fresh lemon juice

½ cup (4 fl oz/125 ml) fresh grapefruit juice

1 cup (8 fl oz/250 ml) olive oil

3 tablespoons honey

1 tablespoon grated grapefruit zest (see glossary)

salt and freshly ground pepper to taste

FOR THE SALAD:

3 ripe avocados

3 pink grapefruits

4 small heads Belgian endive (chicory/witloof)

1 cup (1½ oz/40 g) fresh whole mint leaves

¼ cup (⅜ oz/10 g) chopped fresh mint

To make the vinaigrette, place the chopped mint and lemon juice in a small saucepan and bring to a boil. Remove from the heat and let steep for 10 minutes. Strain into a medium bowl. Add the grapefruit juice, olive oil, honey and zest and whisk together. Season with salt and pepper and adjust the sweet and tart ratio.

☙ To make the salad, cut the avocados in half, remove the pit, scoop from the shell with a large spoon and cut into long, thin slices. Peel the grapefruits, remove all the white pith and cut between the membranes to release the

Avocado, Grapefruit & Endive Salad

grapefruit segments. Trim the ends from the endive and separate the leaves. Thinly slice the endive leaves lengthwise. ❧ Combine the endive and mint leaves in a salad bowl and dress with half the vinaigrette. Place on a serving platter or divide among 6 individual plates. Alternate the grapefruit segments and avocado slices atop the greens. Drizzle with the remaining vinaigrette and top with the chopped mint.

TOAST WITH SUN-DRIED TOMATO PURÉE

SERVES 6

Sun-drying is a traditional Italian way to preserve tomatoes. Spread this classic purée on slices of the best-quality bread you can make (see page 298) or buy. A variation of this recipe appears on page 296.

1 cup (6 oz/185 g) oil-packed
   sun-dried tomatoes
1–2 cloves garlic, minced
½ cup (2½ oz/75 g) pitted
   black olives, such as Kalamata
olive oil as needed
½ cup (¾ oz/20 g) chopped fresh
   basil leaves, lightly packed
1 small baguette, sliced, or 12 slices
   fine-grained white bread, halved

Place some of the oil from the sun-dried tomatoes in a small saucepan. Add the minced garlic and warm over medium heat for about 2 minutes. Combine the tomatoes, olives, garlic and a little olive oil in a food processor or blender. Pulse to combine to a smooth paste. Stir in the basil. Transfer the purée to a small bowl. Cover and store in the refrigerator for up to 2 days. ❧ Toast the bread slices. Spread with purée and serve, or offer the toasts in a basket with the purée alongside.

SPAGHETTI ALLA CARBONARA WITH PEAS

SERVES 6

This classic Roman "charcoal-maker's" pasta is a fitting brunch dish. Fresh peas add a touch of spring.

¾ lb (375 g) lean pancetta (see glossary)
   or bacon
2 cups (8 oz/250 g) fresh shelled peas
   or thawed frozen peas
4 eggs
½ cup (2 oz/60 g) freshly grated
   Parmesan cheese or half pecorino
   romano and half Parmesan cheese
1 tablespoon freshly ground pepper
1 tablespoon salt
1 lb (500 g) spaghetti
2 tablespoons olive oil
additional grated Parmesan cheese and
   freshly ground pepper, optional

Unroll the pancetta and cut it crosswise into ¼-inch-wide (6-mm) strips; set aside. Blanch the peas in boiling salted water until tender-firm, about 1–2 minutes. Plunge into cold water, then drain and set aside. Beat together the eggs, cheese and pepper in a large serving bowl. Keep in a warm place near the stove or on a warming shelf. ❧ Bring a large pot of water to a boil. Add the salt, drop in the pasta and cook until al dente, 7–9 minutes. ❧ Meanwhile, heat the oil in a large sauté pan and add the pancetta. Cook, stirring occasionally, until the pancetta is cooked but not crisp, about 5 minutes. Set aside. ❧ When the pasta is al dente, drop the peas into the pasta pot to heat them through quickly. Drain the pasta and peas, add them to the bowl with the eggs, then add the pancetta and most of the drippings. Toss very quickly to combine. The sauce should be a thick liquid. Serve at once. Pass additional cheese and pepper if desired.

Spaghetti alla Carbonara with Peas; Toast with Sun-dried Tomato Purée

ASPARAGUS WITH TOASTED ALMONDS & BALSAMIC VINAIGRETTE

SERVES 6

You can serve the asparagus either hot or at room temperature, allowing you flexibility in make-ahead preparations.

2 lb (1 kg) fresh asparagus
¼ cup (2 oz/60 g) unsalted butter
¼ cup (2 fl oz/60 ml) olive oil
¾ cup (3 oz/90 g) toasted slivered almonds or pine nuts (see glossary)
⅓ cup (3 fl oz/90 ml) balsamic vinegar or to taste
salt and freshly ground pepper to taste

Trim the asparagus stalks to the same length. Bring about 2 inches (5 cm) salted water to a boil in a large frying pan; lay the asparagus in the pan and cook, uncovered, until tender-crisp, 3–5 minutes. Remove asparagus and plunge into cold water, then drain and pat dry. Let cool to room temperature, then prepare the vinaigrette, or prepare the vinaigrette and serve at once.

To prepare the vinaigrette, heat the butter and oil in a large sauté pan. Add the nuts and stir until hot. Add the balsamic vinegar and, when bubbly, pour over the asparagus. Season with salt and pepper and serve.

POLENTA POUND CAKE

MAKES ONE 9- BY 5- BY 3-INCH (23- BY 13- BY 7.5-CM) LOAF

During baking, this dense loaf cake fills the kitchen with the sweet smell of corn. If you make it in advance, wrap it well in plastic until ready to serve.

1¼ cups (6 oz/185 g) all-purpose (plain) flour
2 teaspoons baking powder
½ teaspoon salt
¼ teaspoon ground nutmeg
1 cup (8 oz/250 g) unsalted butter at room temperature
1 cup (8 oz/250 g) sugar
6 eggs
1 teaspoon vanilla extract (essence)
½ teaspoon almond extract (essence)
grated zest of 1 lemon (see glossary)
¾ cup (4 oz/125 g) sifted yellow cornmeal

Butter and flour a 9- by 5- by 3-inch (23- by 13- by 7.5-cm) loaf pan. Preheat an oven to 350°F (180°C).

Sift the flour, baking powder, salt and nutmeg together; set aside. In a large bowl, beat the butter and sugar together until fluffy. Add the eggs, vanilla, almond extract and lemon zest; beat well. Stir in the flour mixture and the cornmeal and combine well.

Pour into the prepared loaf pan and bake until a toothpick inserted in the center of the loaf comes out clean, about 1 hour. Let cool in the pan for 15 minutes, then unmold onto a rack to finish cooling. Serve sliced.

Asparagus with Toasted Almonds & Balsamic Vinaigrette

Polenta Pound Cake; Red Wine-poached Pears

On a side table, a coffee and tea service is framed by casual bouquets of tulips.

RED WINE–POACHED PEARS

SERVES 6

Excellent with polenta pound cake, these are also good on their own, topped with whipped cream or zabaglione. Try the recipe with apples, too.

6 small, firm-ripe Bosc, Winter Nellis or Bartlett pears

juice of 1 lemon

grated zest of 1 lemon and 1 orange (see glossary)

1 cinnamon stick

1 star anise

3 whole cloves

1 cup (8 oz/250 g) sugar

½ cup (4 fl oz/125 ml) water

3 cups (24 fl oz/750 ml) dry red wine

Peel the pears and remove the cores from the bottom with a corer, or cut them in half and remove the cores. Set the pears aside in a bowl of water (to cover) mixed with the lemon juice until ready to use.

&~ In a large saucepan or pot, stir together the grated zests, cinnamon, star anise, cloves, sugar, water and wine; bring to a boil. Add the pears, reduce heat to a simmer and poach, uncovered, until a skewer penetrates a pear easily, about 35 minutes for whole pears, 25 minutes for halves. Transfer the pears to a bowl with a slotted spoon. Let the poaching liquid cool, then pour it over the pears. Refrigerate overnight, or up to 2 days. Bring to room temperature, or warm slightly, before serving.

MEDITERRANEAN EASTER

EASTER IS A JOYOUS HOLIDAY in the Mediterranean, where it is usually celebrated with a midday or evening feast laden with symbols of the birth of a new season. Crisp greens, fresh seafood, tender spring lamb, fragrant herbs, plump eggplants and artichokes, sweet honey and rich nuts and cheese—each is a gift from the reawakening earth and each finds its way onto the Mediterranean Easter table.

For our holiday meal, we chose the dining room of a charming home with views of the surrounding hillsides. We set the table with handmade glazed pottery to complement the earthy food. To bring springtime sights and scents indoors, we decorated the room with bundles and bouquets of herbs and terra-cotta pots of fresh oregano, thyme and rosemary. Look for these in vegetable shops, farmer's markets and garden nurseries.

Small pots of Mediterranean herbs surround a place setting with fragrances of the new season.

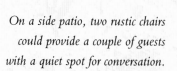

Menu

YOU DON'T HAVE TO OBSERVE the holiday to enjoy this Easter repast; it requires only a desire to celebrate the season. The food for this meal is perfect for family-style serving, with everything passed informally on platters at the table. Accompanying wines may be placed on a nearby sideboard, ready to open and share as the meal progresses.

For a traditional Easter symbol, try dyeing eggs using a natural, old-fashioned method. First, bring yellow onion skins to a boil in a saucepan of water to make a russet-colored dye; let the liquid cool. Then, form a pattern on the egg shells with thin strips of masking tape. Dip the eggs into the dye and let them dry on a rack before peeling off the tape to reveal the pattern. Or display small, mottled quail eggs, found in specialty food shops.

On a side patio, two rustic chairs could provide a couple of guests with a quiet spot for conversation.

Gypsy Spinach Pie

❧

Salmon Dolmas with Avgolemono

❧

*Rack of Spring Lamb Marinated in
Garlic, Allspice, Cumin & Thyme*

*Artichoke Hearts with
Tomatoes & Currants*

Stuffed Eggplant

*Asparagus & Potatoes
with Almonds & Mint*

❧

*Citrus & Honey Cheesecake
with Nut Crust*

PREPARATION LIST

◆ Up to 2 days ahead, start marinating the lamb.

◆ The day before, make the artichokes and the eggplant; re-warm the artichokes on the stovetop and the eggplant in the oven just before serving.

◆ The morning of the party, bake the cheesecake.

◆ Up to 4 hours ahead, make the spinach pie; roast the potatoes and blanch the asparagus.

◆ Two to 3 hours in advance, assemble the dolmas; bake them and prepare the sauce just before serving.

EACH RECIPE YIELDS 6 SERVINGS AND CAN EASILY BE DOUBLED TO SERVE 12 AS SHOWN.

Early strawberries add their sweet blush to glasses of Spanish sherry.

WINE RECOMMENDATIONS

With the spinach pie, serve a Sauvignon Blanc from Chile, France or California, or a moderately rich Italian Soave. With the salmon, pour a dry Chenin Blanc or a Washington State Riesling. For the lamb, offer a hearty, rich Italian red such as Barolo, or an American Merlot. With dessert, a Spanish cream or brown sherry.

GYPSY SPINACH PIE

MAKES ONE 9-INCH (23-CM) PIE (6 SERVINGS)

*This robust two-crust pie also makes a nice
lunch on its own. To serve twelve, make
two pies as shown.*

basic pie pastry for a double-crust pie
   shell (recipe on page 299)
2 lb (1 kg) spinach (about 4 bunches),
   washed well and stemmed; or a
   mixture of spinach, beet (beetroot)
   greens, sorrel and Swiss chard
   (silverbeet), about 8–9 cups; or two
   10-oz (315 g) packages frozen
   chopped spinach, thawed
¼ cup (2 oz/60 g) unsalted butter or
   olive oil (2 fl oz/60 ml)
2 bunches green (spring) onions, chopped
2 tablespoons all-purpose (plain) flour
salt and pepper to taste
¼ teaspoon ground nutmeg, or
   to taste
⅛ teaspoon cayenne pepper
¼ cup (1 oz/30 g) toasted pine nuts
   (see glossary)
½ cup (3 oz/90 g) dried currants,
   soaked in warm water for 10 minutes
½ cup (¾ oz/20 g) chopped
   fresh parsley
½ cup (¾ oz/20 g) chopped
   fresh dill
4 hard-cooked eggs
¼ cup (1 oz/30 g) toasted bread crumbs
olive oil for brushing

Preheat an oven to 375°F (190°C).
Roll out the pastry for the bottom crust
and use it to line a 9-inch (23-cm) pie
pan. Roll out the pastry for the top
crust and set it aside.
🌢 Place the spinach or greens with the
water clinging to the leaves in a large
frying pan and stir over medium heat

Gypsy Spinach Pie

until wilted, about 3 minutes. Drain well, chop coarsely and squeeze as dry as possible.

❧ Heat the butter or oil in a small sauté pan. Add the green onions and cook until soft, about 3 minutes. Stir in the flour and cook 2–3 minutes longer. Add this mixture to the chopped greens and season well with salt, pepper, nutmeg and cayenne. Fold in the pine nuts, drained currants, parsley and dill. Slice the hard-cooked eggs.

❧ Sprinkle the bread crumbs in a layer in the bottom of the pastry-lined pie pan, then add the greens mixture. Top with the sliced eggs. Brush the edge of the bottom crust with water, place the top crust on the pie and trim the excess dough, then crimp the edges together. Cut a steam hole in the center of the top crust and decorate the top with the pastry trimmings. Brush the crust top with olive oil and bake on the middle rack of the oven until golden, about 40 minutes. Remove from the oven and let rest for 10 minutes before slicing.

SALMON DOLMAS WITH AVGOLEMONO

SERVES 6

In traditional dolmas, a rice filling is wrapped in the grape leaves and fresh lemon juice is squeezed over the top.

1⅛ lb (560 g) salmon fillet, skinned
12 bottled grape leaves, rinsed of brine and stemmed (see glossary)
1 cup (8 fl oz/250 ml) fish stock or chicken stock (see page 295)
2 eggs, separated
2 tablespoons fresh lemon juice
freshly ground pepper to taste
chopped fresh dill
lemon wedges

Preheat an oven to 450°F (230°C). Cut the salmon into twelve 1½-oz (45-g) strips, each about 2½ inches (6 cm) long and 1½ inches (4 cm) wide. Wrap each piece in a grape leaf. Place the dolmas seam-side down in a shallow baking pan. Drizzle the fish stock or chicken stock over the dolmas and bake until the fish is firm but not mushy, about 4–5 minutes.

❧ Meanwhile, in a bowl, beat the egg yolks and lemon juice together until frothy. In a separate bowl, beat the egg whites until soft peaks form and fold them into the yolks.

❧ Remove the dolmas to warm individual plates. Pour the stock into a small sauté pan. Add the egg mixture to the warm stock, whisking constantly until thickened, 1–2 minutes. Pour the sauce over the dolmas, sprinkle with pepper and the chopped dill and serve at once, garnished with lemon wedges.

Salmon Dolmas with Avgolemono

Rack of Spring Lamb Marinated in Garlic, Allspice, Cumin & Thyme; Stuffed Eggplant; Artichoke Hearts with Tomatoes & Currants; Asparagus & Potatoes with Almonds & Mint (page 174)

RACK OF SPRING LAMB MARINATED IN GARLIC, ALLSPICE, CUMIN & THYME

SERVES 6

The marinade combines Greek, Turkish and North African flavors. For twelve guests, double the recipe as shown.

FOR THE MARINADE:

1 onion, grated
2 tablespoons minced garlic
3 tablespoons fresh lemon juice
grated zest of 1 lemon and 1 orange
 (see glossary)
1 tablespoon Dijon mustard
1 teaspoon ground allspice
2 teaspoons ground cumin
½ teaspoon cayenne pepper
2 tablespoons chopped fresh thyme
 leaves, or 2 teaspoons dried thyme
1 teaspoon freshly ground pepper
½ cup (4 fl oz/125 ml) olive oil

FOR THE LAMB:

2 racks of lamb, trimmed, or 12
 lamb chops
oil for brushing chops
salt to taste for chops

To make the marinade, combine the onion, garlic, lemon juice, zests, mustard, allspice, cumin, cayenne, thyme and ground pepper in a food processor or blender; purée. Gradually add the olive oil until the mixture is blended.
&❧ Place the lamb in a glass or plastic container and coat the meat with the marinade. Cover and refrigerate for at least 6 hours or up to 2 days.
&❧ To cook the racks, preheat an oven to 350°F (180°C). Sear the racks in a cast-iron frying pan over high heat or on a hot griddle until browned on all sides, then transfer to a roasting pan and roast in the oven until a meat thermometer inserted in the center of a rack

reads 125°F (52°C), about 10–12 minutes. Let the lamb rest for 10 minutes on a carving board, covered with aluminum foil, before slicing; meat will be medium rare.

❧ To cook the chops instead, preheat a broiler (griller). Or, prepare a fire in a grill and position the oiled grill rack 4–6 inches (10–15 cm) above the fire. Brush the chops with oil, sprinkle with salt and broil or grill them for 3 minutes on each side for rare, or 4 minutes on each side for medium rare.

ARTICHOKE HEARTS WITH TOMATOES & CURRANTS

SERVES 6

Sweet-sour artichoke preparations such as this one are common in the Mediterranean.

6 large (about 4-inch/10-cm diameter) artichokes
1 lemon half
2 tablespoons fresh lemon juice
¼ cup (2 fl oz/60 ml) olive oil
1 cup (8 fl oz/250 ml) water, stock or dry white wine
2 cups (12 oz/375 g) peeled, diced tomatoes or drained and chopped canned plum tomatoes
½ cup (3 oz/90 g) dried currants, soaked in warm water to cover for 10 minutes
2 tablespoons honey
salt and freshly ground pepper to taste

Cut the stems and tops off of the artichokes, break off and discard most of the outer leaves and remove all the rest with a sharp knife. Scoop out the fuzzy chokes with a small sharp spoon. Rub the cut surfaces with the lemon half and float the artichoke hearts in a bowl of cold water mixed with the lemon juice until all the artichokes

are prepared. Drain and pat dry just before cooking.

❧ Pour the olive oil into a large sauté pan and place over medium-high heat. Add the artichoke hearts and toss them to coat with the oil and add the water, stock or wine. Cover the pan and steam until the artichoke hearts are tender-crisp, about 12–15 minutes (most of the liquid will have been absorbed). Add the tomatoes, drained currants and honey; stir well and simmer, uncovered, until the artichokes are tender when pierced with a knife and the pan juices have reduced, about 10 minutes longer. Season with salt and pepper and add more honey or lemon juice if desired. Transfer the artichoke hearts to a platter and spoon the sauce on top.

STUFFED EGGPLANT

SERVES 6

Be sure to precook the eggplant shells to make them tender and completely edible.

3 baby globe eggplants (aubergines) or 6 slender (Asian) eggplants (aubergines)
salt
½ cup (4 fl oz/125 ml) plus 2 tablespoons olive oil
1 large onion, chopped
4 large cloves garlic, minced
1 tablespoon dried oregano
1½ cups (9 oz/280 g) peeled, diced tomatoes
¼ cup (⅜ oz/10 g) chopped fresh parsley
freshly ground pepper to taste
½ cup (4 fl oz/125 ml) water

Cut the eggplants in half lengthwise. With a sharp knife, carefully score the flesh and remove most of the eggplant pulp, leaving a shell that is ¼ inch (6 mm) thick. Dice the pulp and set aside. Salt the eggplant shells and let

sit, flesh sides down, in a colander for 1 hour, then rinse and pat dry.

❧ Preheat an oven to 350°F (180°C). Warm 2 tablespoons of the olive oil in a large sauté pan. Add the onion and cook until tender and translucent, about 10 minutes. Set aside in a bowl. In the same pan, heat 6 tablespoons (3 fl oz/ 90 ml) of the olive oil, add the diced eggplant and cook until softened, about 5 minutes. Stir in the garlic, oregano and tomatoes and simmer for about 3 minutes. Add the onion and parsley to this mixture. Season to taste with salt and pepper and set aside.

❧ Heat the remaining 2 tablespoons of the oil in a large sauté pan and cook the eggplant shells, turning once or twice, for a few minutes to soften them. Then place them side by side in an oiled baking dish and stuff with the reserved filling. Add the water to the pan, cover and bake until very tender, about 45 minutes.

Plant a selection of Mediterranean herbs in terra-cotta pots. They make beautiful table displays and the leaves can be used in myriad recipes.

Speckled quail eggs, home-dyed
hens' eggs and globes of bay leaves
connote Easter's earthly splendors.
To make the herb globes, attach
bay laurel or other leaves to
a Styrofoam ball with a hot-glue gun.
If desired, gird each sphere
with wire for extra holding.

ASPARAGUS & POTATOES WITH ALMONDS & MINT

SERVES 6

In this quickly assembled vegetable combination, pine nuts would also go well with the mint and fresh basil with the almonds.

24 small new red potatoes (about
  3 lb/1.5 kg)
about 2 tablespoons olive oil for coating
  plus ¼ cup (2 fl oz/60 ml)
salt and freshly ground pepper to taste
2 lb (1 kg) fresh asparagus
1 cup (8 fl oz/250 ml) chicken stock
  (see page 295)
2 cloves garlic, minced
½ cup (2 oz/60 g) toasted sliced or
  slivered almonds (see glossary)
½ cup (¾ oz/20 g) chopped fresh
  mint or basil

Preheat an oven to 400°F (200°C).
Place the potatoes in a baking pan, coat
them with about 2 tablespoons of the
olive oil and sprinkle with salt and
pepper. Roast until the potatoes are
cooked through but firm, about 25–35
minutes. Remove from the oven and let
sit until cool enough to handle.
∾ Meanwhile, prepare the asparagus.
Snap off the tough end of each stalk. If
the stalks are thick, peel the bottom
2–3 inches (5–7.5 cm) with a vegetable
peeler. Bring about 2 inches (5 cm) of
salted water to a boil in a frying pan.
Lay the asparagus in the pan and cook
until tender-crisp, 3–5 minutes. Remove
the asparagus and plunge them into ice
water, then drain and pat dry. Cut the
asparagus into 2-inch (5-cm) lengths.
∾ Cut the cooled potatoes into quarters.
Warm the ¼ cup (2 fl oz/60 ml) olive oil
in a very large sauté pan. Add the potatoes and heat them through. Add the
asparagus, chicken stock and garlic and
simmer a few minutes to heat through.
Season with salt and pepper, then add
the almonds and mint or basil and serve.

Asparagus & Potatoes
with Almonds & Mint

CITRUS & HONEY CHEESECAKE WITH NUT CRUST

MAKES ONE 9-INCH (23-CM) CHEESECAKE

Use dark honey for a fuller-bodied, more intense flavor. The cheesecake is best served slightly warm or at room temperature.

FOR THE CRUST:

2 cups (8 oz/250 g) hazelnuts, toasted and skinned (see glossary)

⅓ cup (3 oz/90 g) sugar

½ teaspoon ground cinnamon

4–5 tablespoons (2–2½ oz/60–80 g) unsalted butter, melted

FOR THE CHEESE FILLING:

1½ lb (750 g) cream cheese at room temperature

½ cup (4 fl oz/125 ml) sour cream at room temperature

¾ cup (9 oz/280 g) full-flavored honey

6 eggs, separated, at room temperature

1 tablespoon each grated lemon zest and grated orange zest (see glossary)

1 teaspoon vanilla extract (essence)

3 tablespoons chopped candied orange peel, optional

¼ cup (2 oz/60 g) sugar

FOR THE GARNISH:

chopped toasted and skinned hazelnuts (see glossary)

fresh strawberries, optional

Citrus & Honey Cheesecake with Nut Crust

To make the crust, in a food processor, chop the nuts with the sugar and cinnamon as finely as possible; do not let it turn to paste. Add enough butter to hold the mixture together. Press into the bottom and partially up the sides of a 9-inch (23-cm) spring-form pan. Set aside.

❧ To make the filling, preheat an oven to 350°F (180°C). Place the cream cheese and sour cream in the bowl of an electric mixer. Beat until smooth with the paddle attachment or beaters. Add the honey and beat until there are no lumps. Add the egg yolks, lemon and orange zests, vanilla and, if using, candied orange peel; mix well.

❧ In a large bowl, beat the egg whites until frothy. Gradually beat in the sugar until the peaks are almost stiff. Stir one third of the egg whites into the cheese mixture, then fold in the rest. Pour into the prepared cake pan. Bake on the middle rack of the oven until set just on the edges, about 45–50 minutes; gently shake the pan to test. Turn off the oven and leave the cheesecake inside with the door ajar for 2 hours.

❧ Remove the sides from the pan and slide the cheesecake onto a plate. Top with chopped hazelnuts and, if desired, arrange berries around the cheesecake.

TEATIME FÊTE

A TEATIME GATHERING in a garden, on a porch or in a sunroom can be both lighthearted and serene. Lighthearted because it may celebrate an engagement, a bridal or baby shower, the birthday of a special friend or a family member. Serene because tea is steeped in tradition, evoking an era past.

To complement the freshness of this menu, we used crisp linen tablecloths and napkins, floral-patterned dishware and an abundance of colorful roses and tulips. To encourage guests to mingle and to promote easy conversation, we arranged a variety of seating areas and separate serving tables for the assorted foods and beverages. The cakes, cookies and peaches could be arranged in one area while the sandwiches and their accompaniments could be set on another table, or even in a nearby room. Be sure to provide enough comfortable chairs and cushions for every guest to have a seat.

THE TEATIME MENU for twelve that follows is purposefully light, combining contemporary tastes and old-fashioned dishes. You could offer guests a choice of teas, such as Orange Pekoe or smoky Lapsang souchong to go with the sandwiches, and a scented Earl Grey or herbal teas with the sweets. Lemonade and wine spritzers are good alternatives for guests who prefer other drinks.

These recipes are readily adaptable for other meals, too. The sandwiches, cookies and madeleines are excellent at lunchtime or in a picnic basket. Try the conserve and tea bread at breakfast or brunch and the peaches for dessert at any time.

Strewn rose petals add a lovely, festive touch to the tea table. Arrange teaspoons in a small vase or sugar bowl.

Menu

WINE RECOMMENDATIONS

While freshly brewed tea will be poured, wine may also be offered in some form. Spritzers composed of equal parts wine and sparkling water, served over ice with a citrus slice, make a very refreshing drink; try using a slightly sweet wine such as Chenin Blanc or white Zinfandel. With the sandwiches, offer a simple white wine of light to medium body, such as French Mâcon-Villages or a Sancerre.

*Lemon Saffron Tea Bread
with Spiced Blueberry Conserve*

*Tomato, Tapenade &
Mozzarella Sandwiches*

*Tuna Pâté
with Sun-dried Tomatoes*

Pitas with Feta, Walnuts & Aïoli

❧

Jennifer's Chocolate Dream Cookies

Ginger-Orange Madeleines

Peaches in Wine

Long-stemmed Strawberries

If presents are brought for a guest of honor, display them prominently on a nearby chair or table.

PREPARATION LIST

♦ Several months to 1 day ahead, make the blueberry conserve.

♦ Up to a week ahead, make the tapenade.

♦ The day before, make the tea bread, the madeleines and the cookies.

♦ The night before, prepare the tuna pâté.

♦ Up to 4 hours ahead, prepare the pita sandwiches.

♦ One hour ahead, prepare the peaches.

THIS MENU SERVES 12. FOR A SMALLER GROUP, SERVE FEWER DISHES.

Lace-cap hydrangeas, their pots decorated with pretty ribbon bows, make charming host or hostess gifts.

LEMON SAFFRON TEA BREAD

MAKES ONE 9- BY 5- BY 3-INCH
(23- BY 13- BY 7.5-CM) LOAF

Crushed saffron gives this bread an intense yellow color and subtle perfume. See the glossary for directions on how to crush it.

2 cups (10 oz/315 g) all-purpose (plain) flour
2 teaspoons baking powder
1 teaspoon salt
¼ teaspoon baking soda (bicarbonate of soda)
½ cup (4 oz/125 g) unsalted butter at room temperature
¾ cup (6 oz/185 g) sugar
2 eggs
1 tablespoon grated lemon zest
¼ teaspoon saffron threads crushed and steeped in 2 tablespoons fresh lemon juice
¾ cup (6 fl oz/180 ml) milk
½ cup (2 oz/60 g) coarsely chopped walnuts (see glossary)

Preheat an oven to 350°F (180°C). Butter and flour a 9- by 5- by 3-inch (23- by 13- by 7.5-cm) loaf pan.
ໄ Sift together the flour, baking powder, salt and baking soda. In a large bowl, beat the butter and sugar together until fluffy. Beat in the eggs, lemon zest and saffron mixture. With a rubber spatula, fold in a third of the dry ingredients, then half the milk. Repeat, then add remaining dry ingredients. Mix in the walnuts; pour into the prepared loaf pan.
ໄ Bake on the middle rack of the oven until a skewer inserted in the center of the loaf comes out clean, about 1 hour. Cool in the pan on a rack for 10 minutes, then turn out onto the rack to cool completely. Wrap the bread in plastic; let sit overnight. Serve thinly sliced.

A doll-size tea set is displayed as a fitting decoration on a side table.

SPICED BLUEBERRY CONSERVE

MAKES ABOUT 5 CUPS (40 OZ/1.2 KG)

Sweet spices, citrus zest and a splash of cider vinegar contribute extra flavor and tang to this thick-textured preserve. For directions on grating citrus zest, see the glossary.

4 cups (1 lb/500 g) fresh or thawed frozen whole blueberries
3 cups (1½ lb/750 g) sugar
½ teaspoon ground cinnamon
¼ teaspoon ground allspice
¼ cup (2 fl oz/60 ml) cider vinegar
¼ cup (2 fl oz/60 ml) fresh lemon juice
grated zest of 1 lemon
grated zest of 1 orange, optional

In a large, heavy enameled or stainless-steel pot, combine all of the ingredients and bring to a boil. Reduce the heat and simmer, uncovered and stirring occasionally, until thickened, about 25 minutes. This jam sets up fast; it is done when a teaspoonful is still a little runny when dropped on a chilled plate.
ໄ Pour into 5 hot sterilized 1-cup (8–fl oz/250-ml) canning jars, leaving about ½ inch (12 mm) of head space, then seal the jars. Process in a hot-water bath for 10 minutes (see glossary), or store in the refrigerator for up to 3 months.

Lemon Saffron Tea Bread;
Spiced Blueberry Conserve

TOMATO, TAPENADE & MOZZARELLA SANDWICHES

MAKES 24 SMALL SANDWICHES

Tapenade, a pungent niçoise olive spread, can be made ahead and refrigerated for up to 1 week. A recipe for homemade baguettes appears on page 298. See the glossary for information on plum tomatoes, mozzarella cheese and arugula.

1 long baguette (about 1 lb/500 g)
tapenade (recipe on page 296)
6–8 plum (Roma) tomatoes, sliced
two 8-ounce (250-g) balls fresh
  mozzarella cheese, sliced
24 arugula leaves

Cut the baguette in half lengthwise, then cut each half into 12 diagonal slices. Spread each slice with tapenade. Top each piece equally with sliced tomatoes, sliced mozzarella cheese and an arugula leaf. Serve the sandwiches open-faced.

TUNA PÂTÉ WITH SUN-DRIED TOMATOES

MAKES ABOUT 24 OPEN-FACED SANDWICHES

Sun-dried tomatoes, red onion and fresh basil brighten the taste and color of this simple spread. If you wish to make your own country bread, see the recipe on page 298.

FOR THE TUNA PÂTÉ:

1 lb (500 g) fresh tuna, cut about 1 inch
  (2.5 cm) thick, or canned solid-pack
  tuna in oil or water, drained
¼ cup (2 fl oz/60 ml) fresh lemon juice
⅔ cup (3 oz/90 g) finely chopped red
  (Spanish) onion
about 1 cup (8 fl oz/250 ml) mayonnaise
½ cup (4 oz/125 g) finely chopped
  sun-dried tomatoes
¼ cup (⅜ oz/10 g) chopped
  fresh basil
salt and freshly ground pepper to taste

FOR THE SANDWICHES:

1 cup (1½ oz/40 g) lightly packed
  fresh basil leaves
¼ cup (1 oz/30 g) freshly grated
  Parmesan cheese
3 tablespoons pine nuts
2 cloves garlic
½ cup (4 fl oz/125 ml) olive oil
12 large slices focaccia or country bread
paper-thin lemon slices

To make the pâté: If using fresh tuna, place the fillet in an oiled baking dish, cover tightly with aluminum foil and bake in a preheated 450°F (230°C) oven until it is barely pink and still moist in the center, about 8–10 minutes. Remove and let cool. Mash the cooked or canned tuna with a fork or pulse briefly in a food processor. Transfer to a bowl and add the lemon juice, red

onion, mayonnaise, sun-dried tomatoes and chopped basil. Mix until you have a spreadable consistency. Season with salt and pepper. Cover and refrigerate until ready to use, up to 8 hours.

❧ To make the sandwiches, process the basil leaves, cheese, pine nuts, garlic and oil in a blender or food processor until smooth. Cut the focaccia or country bread slices into small squares, then top with the basil mixture and the tuna pâté. Serve open-faced. Garnish with lemon.

PITAS WITH FETA, WALNUTS & AÏOLI

MAKES 12 PITA SANDWICH HALVES,
OR 24 MINI PITAS

A vivid combination of tastes, textures and colors goes into these sandwiches. If made ahead, cover them with a clean, damp cloth to keep the pita moist.

6 pita bread rounds, or 24 mini pitas
about ½ cup (4 fl oz/125 ml) aïoli
  (recipe on page 295)
24 large watercress sprigs
36 large fresh mint leaves
1 lb (500 g) feta cheese, cut into 12
  thin slices
1½ cups (6 oz/185 g) chopped walnuts
  (see glossary)
6 red bell peppers (capsicums), roasted,
  peeled and chopped (see glossary)

Cut the pita rounds in half and carefully open the pockets (for mini pitas, slice off the top third of the pita rounds and open the pocket). Spread the aïoli inside the pitas. Into each sandwich, tuck even amounts of watercress, mint, feta, walnuts and bell peppers. If desired, cover and refrigerate the sandwiches until ready to serve, up to 4 hours.

JENNIFER'S CHOCOLATE DREAM COOKIES

MAKES 48 COOKIES

Light and crackly on the outside, soft and chewy within, these cookies are reminiscent of good chocolate fudge.

2 cups (10 oz/315 g) all-purpose (plain) flour
¾ cup (3 oz/90 g) sifted cocoa
2 teaspoons baking powder
1 teaspoon salt
1 cup (8 oz/250 g) unsalted butter at room temperature
1 cup (7 oz/220 g) dark brown sugar, packed
1 cup (8 oz/250 g) granulated sugar
2 teaspoons vanilla extract (essence)
2 eggs
6 oz (185 g) bittersweet chocolate, coarsely chopped, or bittersweet chocolate chips

Preheat an oven to 325°F (170°C). Line 2 baking sheets with baking parchment. Sift the flour, cocoa, baking powder and salt together into a medium bowl.
෨ In a large bowl, beat the butter, brown sugar and granulated sugar together until fluffy. Add the vanilla and eggs and beat well. Stir in the flour-cocoa mixture, then fold in the chocolate chunks.
෨ Drop the cookie dough by the tablespoonful onto the prepared baking sheets. Bake until the cookies are puffed and set but still chewy in the middle, about 8–10 minutes. Let cool on racks. If made ahead, store in a plastic container until ready to use.

GINGER-ORANGE MADELEINES

MAKES 36 MADELEINES

These delicate little sponge cakes gain subtle flavor from orange zest and candied ginger. If you don't have enough madeleine pans, bake them in batches.

3 eggs
2 egg yolks
pinch of salt
¾ cup (6 oz/185 g) granulated sugar
2 tablespoons grated orange zest (see glossary) soaked in 3 tablespoons orange juice
1¼ cups (5 oz/155 g) sifted all-purpose (plain) flour
¼ cup (1 oz/30 g) finely chopped candied ginger
½ cup (4 oz/125 g) plus 2 tablespoons unsalted butter, clarified (see glossary)
confectioners' (icing) sugar for sprinkling

Preheat an oven to 350°F (180°C). Butter and lightly flour 4 standard madeleine pans (or fewer, if necessary).
෨ Combine the whole eggs, egg yolks and granulated sugar in the bowl of an electric mixer, set the bowl over hot water and whisk for a few minutes until warm to the touch. Remove from the hot water, add the salt and beat on high speed until the mixture is very thick and pale. Add the orange zest and juice and beat well. Sift the flour over the batter and fold it in, then fold in the ginger. Fold in the butter a little at a time. Fill the molds two-thirds of the way full with batter, then bake until golden, about 15 minutes.
෨ Gently loosen the sides of the madeleines from the molds and turn them out onto a rack. Sprinkle the ribbed sides with confectioners' sugar while still warm.

If you want to offer a selection of teas, provide a few individual pots and tea strainers so that a guest can pour his or her own cupful.

Ginger-Orange Madeleines;
Jennifer's Chocolate Dream Cookies

PEACHES IN WINE

SERVES 12

For such elegant results, the preparation of this light dessert could not be simpler. Nectarines also work well.

12 ripe peaches
4 cups (32 fl oz/1 l) fruity white wine
  such as Asti Spumante, Moscato or
  Riesling, or a light, fruity red wine
  such as Lambrusco or Beaujolais
1 cup (8 oz/250 g) sugar

Bring a large pot of water to a boil.
Drop in a few peaches at a time for
5 seconds to loosen the skin. Lift out
with a slotted spoon, let cool briefly,
then peel. Cut the peaches in half and
remove the pits.
≥ Combine the wine and sugar in
an attractive glass bowl; stir until the
sugar dissolves. Slice the peaches and
place them in the wine. Chill for
1 hour, then serve.

*Refreshing lemonade, served
in tall glasses over ice,
is a delicious beverage to offer
in addition to tea.*

Peaches in Wine

AL FRESCO LUNCH

WARM WEATHER BRINGS the irresistible urge to eat outdoors. While that usually means a casual barbecue or picnic, you might want to try a sit-down, open-air lunch. You'll find plenty of reasons to serve this menu: summer holidays, birthdays, end-of-the-weekend send-offs.

A beachside getaway is an ideal location, with the table set up in or near the sand, but this menu is equally appropriate served on a deck or even in a sunny room at home. To contrast with the casual outdoor setting, we dressed the table with good china, silver, crystal and linens, and folded the napkins into bishop's hats (page 311). Director's chairs provided informal seating. Taking advantage of the seaside locale, we scattered shells and sand dollars on the table and placed sea grass in vases filled with sand and smooth stones; if you're not at the beach, other greenery will do.

Package extra shortcake biscuits in decorated bags as gifts for guests.

Menu

INSPIRED BY NEW ENGLAND cuisine, our al fresco lunch features summertime favorites such as lobster, sweet corn, maple syrup and fresh blueberries. All the recipes are easily prepared, since much of the work may be done in advance and the last-minute cooking is limited primarily to the main course. With a few substitutions, these recipes can be made anywhere and at any time of year.

To mark this unique occasion, you might want to bake an extra batch of dessert short-cakes and package them in paper bags tied with raffia or twine for guests to take home. Try knotting shells onto the ties as a reminder of the seaside theme.

A tray holds small glasses of chilled ruby port to accompany the shortcakes for dessert.

*Lobster, Potato & Green Bean Salad
with Pesto Vinaigrette*

❧

Maple Syrup– & Mustard-glazed Poussins

Fresh Corn & Polenta Cakes

*Honey-baked Tomatoes
with Crusty Topping*

Spiced Peaches

❧

Warm Blueberry Shortcakes

PREPARATION LIST

◆ Up to a week or more ahead of time, prepare the spiced peaches.

◆ The night before, cook and refrigerate the lobsters in their shells. Coat the poussins; cook and refrigerate the polenta to be cut into triangles the next day.

◆ The morning of the party, bake the short-cake biscuits, to be gently rewarmed in the oven before serving.

◆ One hour ahead, cook the potatoes and green beans for the salad.

EACH RECIPE YIELDS 6 SERVINGS.

Trophy cups or an assortment of other unique containers make ideal vases for displaying sea grass. Fill with sand and smooth stones to weight them down in case of sudden gusts.

WINE RECOMMENDATIONS

With the lobster salad, sip a rich white with herbal accents, ample body and acidity: a Sauvignon Blanc or a northern Italian white wine. With the main course, try a spicy white Riesling or an off-dry blush wine. For dessert, a chilled ruby port or a black Muscat.

Lobster, Potato & Green Bean Salad with Pesto Vinaigrette

SERVES 6

A relative of salade niçoise, this extravagant first course is also delicious made with shrimp or fresh tuna. Try the dressing on grilled fish or chicken.

salt

3 live Atlantic (Maine) lobsters, 1–1¼ lb (500–625 g) each

12–18 small red new potatoes (creamers) or yellow Finnish potatoes, about 2 lb (1 kg) total

1½ lb (750 g) green beans, trimmed and cut into 2-inch (5-cm) lengths

1 cup (1½ oz/45 g) tightly packed fresh basil leaves

1 teaspoon minced garlic

2 tablespoons toasted pine nuts or walnuts (see glossary)

about ¾ cup (6 fl oz/180 ml) olive oil

¼ cup (2 fl oz/60 ml) red wine vinegar

freshly ground pepper

butter lettuce

cherry tomatoes

Bring a very large pot of salted water to a boil. Drop in the lobsters and cook, covered, for 10 minutes. Remove the lobsters from the pot and drop them into a sinkful of ice water. (If desired, refrigerate the lobsters overnight.) Cut each lobster in half lengthwise and remove the meat from the body and claws as directed in the glossary; discard the shells. Cut the meat into bite-sized pieces, place in a bowl, cover and refrigerate until serving.

❧ Place the potatoes in a saucepan, cover them with cold water and add salt. Bring to a boil, then reduce heat and simmer, uncovered, until the potatoes

are cooked through but still firm, about 10–20 minutes. Drain and refrigerate to stop further cooking.

❧ Bring a large pot of salted water to a boil. Drop in the green beans and cook until tender-crisp, about 2–4 minutes. Drain the beans and plunge them into ice water. Drain, pat dry and set aside.

❧ Combine the basil leaves, garlic and nuts in a food processor or blender. Pulse to combine. Add about ½ cup (4 fl oz/125 ml) of the olive oil and process to a coarse purée. Transfer the pesto to a bowl and stir in the vinegar and enough of the remaining oil to make a spoonable vinaigrette. Season with salt and pepper.

❧ To serve, cut the potatoes into ¼-inch (6-mm) slices. In a large bowl, toss the potatoes and green beans with half the vinaigrette. Divide among 6 salad plates lined with lettuce leaves; top with lobster pieces and drizzle with the remaining vinaigrette. Garnish with cherry tomatoes.

Large and small seashells and brightly colored coral accent the table.

Lobster, Potato & Green Bean Salad with Pesto Vinaigrette

MAPLE SYRUP– & MUSTARD-GLAZED POUSSINS

SERVES 6

Take care not to overcook the poussins: When done, their flesh is slightly pink.

6 poussins or Cornish hens, about
    1 lb (500 g) each, or 12 quail
2 teaspoons dry mustard
½ teaspoon ground cinnamon
2 tablespoons cider vinegar
⅔ cup (5 fl oz/160 ml) maple syrup
3 tablespoons prepared Dijon mustard
2 tablespoons soy sauce
salt and freshly ground pepper to taste
oil for brushing

Butterfly the poussins or Cornish hens: Insert a sharp knife through the neck cavity of each bird and carefully cut down one side of the backbone. Cut along the other side of the backbone and remove it. Press on the breastbone to flatten it. (Leave the quail whole.)
☙ In a bowl, combine the dry mustard, cinnamon and vinegar and mix into a paste. Add the maple syrup, prepared mustard and soy sauce and adjust the seasoning; it should be spicy but sweet. Spread half of this mixture evenly over the birds, cover and let sit at room temperature for 1 hour or refrigerate for up to 8 hours. Reserve the remaining half of the paste for basting.
☙ Preheat a broiler (griller). Or, prepare a fire in a grill; position the oiled grill rack 4–6 inches (10–15 cm) above the fire. Sprinkle the birds with salt and pepper and brush with a little oil. Broil the poussins or hens, or grill them over medium-hot coals, flesh-side down for 5 minutes, then brush with the glaze, turn and cook for 5 minutes longer. (Cook quail for 3–4 minutes on each side.)

FRESH CORN & POLENTA CAKES

SERVES 6

Look for polenta in a well-stocked food shop or an Italian grocer. When cooked and cooled, it can be cut into any shape.

4 ears corn or 3 cups (1¼ lb/625 g)
    thawed frozen corn kernels
1½ cups (9 oz/280 g) polenta or
    coarse yellow cornmeal
6 cups (48 fl oz/1.5 l) cold water or
    more as needed
salt and freshly ground pepper to taste
about ½ cup (4 fl oz/125 ml) olive oil
    or vegetable oil
minced fresh chives

If using ears of corn, cut the kernels off the ears with a large knife. Drop the corn kernels into boiling salted water and cook for 1–2 minutes. Drain the corn and rinse in cold water. Dry very well on paper towels.
☙ Combine the polenta or cornmeal and cold water in a large saucepan. Cook over low heat, stirring often, until thick and no longer grainy on the tongue, 20–30 minutes. Add more water gradually if the polenta is thick but still grainy. When the polenta is done, stir in the corn kernels. Season with salt and pepper and spread in an even layer in an oiled baking sheet with sides; the polenta should be about ¾ inch (2 cm) thick. Cover with plastic wrap and refrigerate until firm.
☙ To serve, cut the polenta into circles, triangles or rectangles. Heat the oil in a frying pan to a depth of ¼ inch (6 mm) and sauté the polenta pieces until pale gold on both sides, about 5 minutes total. Transfer to plates and sprinkle with chives.

HONEY-BAKED TOMATOES WITH CRUSTY TOPPING

SERVES 6

Basting with honey highlights the natural sweetness of these baked tomatoes. If desired, place each tomato on a plate with a handful of fresh watercress or arugula sprigs for a refreshingly bitter contrast.

1½ cups (3 oz/90 g) fresh bread crumbs
½ cup (4 fl oz/125 ml) olive oil
1 teaspoon salt
½ teaspoon freshly ground pepper
6 tablespoons (4 oz/125 g) honey
pinch of ground nutmeg
6 ripe tomatoes

Preheat an oven to 350°F (180°C). Spread the bread crumbs on a baking sheet, toss with 6 tablespoons (3 fl oz/ 90 ml) of the oil and sprinkle with ½ teaspoon of the salt and the pepper. Bake, stirring often, until golden and slightly crunchy but not hard, about 20 minutes. Set aside, leaving the oven on.
☙ In a small saucepan over low heat, warm the honey, remaining 2 tablespoons of oil and the nutmeg.
☙ Cut a slice off the stem end of each tomato. Place the tomatoes in a baking dish. Sprinkle with the remaining ½ teaspoon salt, brush the top of each tomato with a little of the honey mixture and top each tomato with some of the bread crumbs, pressing them into the tomato. Bake the tomatoes until soft and lightly browned on top, basting with the honey mixture several times, about 15–20 minutes.

Maple Syrup– & Mustard-glazed Poussins;
Fresh Corn & Polenta Cakes;
Honey-baked Tomatoes with Crusty Topping

SPICED PEACHES

MAKES 12 PEACHES

A classic American conserve, these keep for up to a month in the refrigerator or up to a year when canned. Serve them with the main course, cut in half, pitted and garnished with watercress.

1½ cups (12 fl oz/375 ml) cider
   vinegar
1½ cups (12 fl oz/375 ml) water
2 cups (1 lb/500 g) sugar
3 sticks cinnamon
10–12 whole cloves
1 teaspoon black peppercorns
2 strips lemon zest (see glossary)
12 firm ripe peaches

Combine the vinegar, water, sugar, cinnamon, cloves, peppercorns and lemon zest in a large, deep enameled or stainless-steel saucepan. Bring to a boil and stir until the sugar dissolves. Reduce the heat and simmer the syrup for 10 minutes.

☞ Meanwhile, drop a few peaches at a time into a large pot of boiling water for 1–2 minutes to loosen the skin. Lift out with a slotted spoon, let cool briefly, then peel. Add the peaches to the hot syrup and poach for 2 minutes, then remove them with a slotted spoon and place in 2 sterilized 4-cup (32–fl oz/1-l) canning jars. Spoon the syrup over the peaches to within ½ inch (12 mm) of the top and seal the jars. Process in a hot-water bath for 25–30 minutes (see glossary), or store in the refrigerator for up to 1 month.

Spiced Peaches

Cluster sea treasures in a half shell.

WARM BLUEBERRY SHORTCAKES

SERVES 6

Classic cream biscuits accompany this variation on strawberry shortcake.

FOR THE SHORTCAKES:

1¾ cups (9 oz/280 g) all-purpose (plain) flour

½ teaspoon salt

1 tablespoon baking powder

2 teaspoons sugar

6 tablespoons (3 oz/90 g) unsalted butter or vegetable shortening (vegetable lard), chilled

1 cup (8 fl oz/250 ml) milk or heavy (double) cream

grated zest of 1 orange or 2 lemons

about 3 tablespoons unsalted butter, melted, or heavy (double) cream

FOR THE BLUEBERRY COMPOTE:

6 cups (1½ lb/750 g) fresh or thawed frozen whole blueberries

2 tablespoons fresh lemon juice

1 teaspoon ground cinnamon

1½ cups (12 oz/375 g) sugar

grated zest of 1 lemon or 1 orange

FOR THE MAPLE WHIPPED CREAM:

1 cup (8 fl oz/250 ml) heavy (double) cream

2 tablespoons maple syrup

¼ teaspoon vanilla extract (essence)

Preheat an oven to 450°F (230°C). To make the shortcakes, combine the flour, salt, baking powder and sugar in a medium bowl. Cut the butter or shortening into bits, then blend into the flour mixture with a pastry cutter or 2 knives until the mixture resembles cornmeal. Make a well in the center and add the milk or cream and zest. Stir quickly until the dough comes free from the sides of the bowl, about 1 minute. Turn the dough out onto a lightly floured board and knead gently and quickly, turning it about 12 times, or until the dough is no longer sticky. Pat into a ½-inch-thick (12-mm) square.

❧ Dipping a 2¼-inch (5.5-cm) cutter into flour each time, cut the dough into 12 round or square biscuits. Place on an ungreased baking sheet, brush the tops with the melted butter or the cream and bake on the middle rack of the oven until pale gold, 12–15 minutes.

❧ Meanwhile, to make the compote, combine 4 cups (1 lb/500 g) of the blueberries with the lemon juice, cinnamon, sugar and zest in a heavy saucepan over moderate heat. Simmer until thickened and hot, about 5 minutes. Stir in the remaining blueberries and set aside.

❧ To make the maple whipped cream, in a bowl beat the cream, maple syrup and vanilla until it forms soft peaks.

❧ To serve, split the warm biscuits in half crosswise. Place 2 bottoms on each of 6 individual plates. Spoon half of the blueberry compote on the biscuits, add a dollop of whipped cream and a little more compote to each, then top with the remaining biscuit halves. Spoon on remaining compote and serve at once.

Warm Blueberry Shortcakes

GALA BUFFET

ON A WARM SPRING OR SUMMER DAY, what could be better than a sunny setting for celebrating an engagement, wedding, anniversary or graduation? A lawn, garden, patio or one or more bright rooms provides ample space for a large-scale gathering. For any of these important occasions, the food, decorations and setting should be both elegant and welcoming. To achieve this, we show one long rented table for seating guests, although of course you could seat guests at two or more smaller tables. For china, we selected blue and white heirloom plates. Flowers may be placed everywhere, in containers of all shapes and sizes.

To make an unforgettable place card, use an instant camera to snap photos of guests as they arrive, slipping the pictures into frames and placing them at each setting. At the party's end, they become charming keepsakes of the event.

Use an instant photo for a place card that's also a keepsake.

Menu

WITH THIS PARTY for twenty-four, a buffet allows guests a greater opportunity to mingle. It is also the most logical way to serve a maximum number of people with minimal effort. The variety of recipes guarantees that there will be something to suit each person's taste. But you could prepare fewer dishes for a smaller gathering, or add recipes from other menus in this book for a larger group.

To make sure that all the buffet items are ready to serve at the same time, read through the preparation list and recipe introductions well ahead of the party. A caterer, friend or family member could provide help if your time is limited, but since all the food is served at room temperature, this menu is not difficult to assemble in advance.

Experiment with a variety of containers for your flowers: bowls, champagne buckets, silver teapots, egg cups, Chinese teacups and porcelain tumblers all stand in as vases.

Cheese Platter

Shrimp with Oregano & Garlic

Celery, Mushroom & Endive Salad

*Fillet of Beef with Paprika,
Coriander & Cumin*

Rice & Wild Rice Salad

Tuna with Peppers & Olives

Berry Tiramisù

PREPARATION LIST

◆ Four days ahead, start marinating the beef.

◆ The day before, sprinkle the beef with salt.

◆ The night before, prepare the tiramisù.

◆ Up to 4 hours ahead, make the rice salad.

◆ Three hours before, prepare the tuna.

◆ Up to 2 hours before, marinate the shrimp; make the celery salad.

◆ One hour before, grill the shrimp and roast the beef fillet.

EACH RECIPE YIELDS 6 OR MORE REGULAR-SIZE SERVINGS. FOR A BUFFET PARTY FOR 24 GUESTS, AS SHOWN, MULTIPLY EACH RECIPE BY THE QUANTITY INDICATED.

Set up a liquor bar where guests can serve themselves; a separate bar for wine and water could be set up on the lawn.

WINE RECOMMENDATIONS

Offer both white and red wines. Choose a medium-bodied white with fresh green flavors, such as a light Chardonnay or a French Chablis; for the red, try a Pinot Noir or a Cabernet Sauvignon. With the tiramisù, pour sparkling wine flavored with a little berry liqueur or crème de cassis if desired.

SHRIMP WITH OREGANO & GARLIC

SERVES 6 (MULTIPLY BY 2 FOR BUFFET)

Classic paella-style flavorings season these grilled shrimp. Make extra marinade to offer as a sauce, or simply garnish with lemon. If using wooden skewers, soak them first in warm water for 20 minutes.

36 large shrimp (prawns)
3 tablespoons dried oregano
1 tablespoon minced garlic
1 cup (8 fl oz/250 ml) olive oil
⅓ cup (3 fl oz/90 ml) sherry vinegar
salt and freshly ground pepper to taste
lemon wedges

Shell and devein the shrimp (see glossary); set aside. Warm the oregano and garlic in a small saucepan over medium heat with about 2 tablespoons of the olive oil for about 2 minutes to remove the bite. Remove from the heat and stir in the vinegar and the remaining oil. Season with salt and pepper. Let cool, then pour over the shrimp and marinate for up to 2 hours in the refrigerator.
ê Prepare a fire in a grill. Position the oiled grill rack 4–6 inches (10–15 cm) above the fire. Or, preheat a broiler (griller). Lift the shrimp from the marinade and thread 3 shrimp on each of 12 skewers. Grill over hot coals or broil until pink, about 2 minutes on each side. Serve with lemon wedges.

CELERY, MUSHROOM & ENDIVE SALAD

SERVES 6 (MULTIPLY BY 2 FOR BUFFET)

A piquant dressing complements the endive's mild bitterness. The dressed salad stays crisp for up to 2 hours.

½ cup (4 fl oz/125 ml) olive oil
¼ cup (2 fl oz/60 ml) toasted walnut oil
¼ cup (2 fl oz/60 ml) fresh lemon juice
¼ cup (2 fl oz/60 ml) heavy (double) cream
2 teaspoons Dijon mustard
salt and freshly ground pepper to taste
2 cups (8 oz/250 g) thinly sliced celery
½ lb (250 g) fresh mushrooms, thinly sliced
5 oz (155 g) Gruyère cheese, cut into long, thin strips
3–4 heads Belgian endive (chicory/witloof)
1 cup (4 oz/125 g) walnuts, toasted and coarsely chopped (see glossary)

In a small bowl, whisk together the olive oil, walnut oil, lemon juice, cream and mustard until smooth. Season with salt and pepper.
ê Combine the celery, mushrooms and cheese in a large bowl. Add the vinaigrette and toss. Trim the ends from the endive and separate the leaves. Line a large platter with the endive leaves and top with the celery mixture. Or, pour the vinaigrette over the celery, mushrooms and cheese, toss well and use this mixture to fill the endive leaves. Place the filled leaves on a platter and top them with the chopped walnuts.

As an hors d'oeuvre, present a variety of cheeses, breads and crackers. Balance flavors and textures by offering creamy, hard and fresh cheeses such as (clockwise from top right): double-cream Brie, layered Gorgonzola and Cheddar, peppered goat cheese, dry jack, and two varieties of Port Salut. For easy service, place the cheese board near your wine bar.

Shrimp with Oregano & Garlic; Celery, Mushroom & Endive Salad

FILLET OF BEEF WITH PAPRIKA, CORIANDER & CUMIN

SERVES 6 (MULTIPLY BY 2 FOR BUFFET)

The beef, which gets an aromatic flavor from the spice rub, requires 4 days of marination. Serve it rare, leaving the end slices for those who like their meat well done.

1 fillet of beef, about 3½ lb (1.75 kg)
3 tablespoons paprika
2 teaspoons ground cumin
1 tablespoon ground coriander
2 tablespoons freshly ground pepper
1 teaspoon ground nutmeg
¼ teaspoon cayenne pepper
1 tablespoon salt
hot-sweet mustard

Trim the fillet of any visible fat and silverskin. Mix together the paprika, cumin, coriander, ground pepper, nutmeg and cayenne. Spread this spice mixture evenly over the beef. Place the meat in a large glass or plastic dish and cover. Let sit in the refrigerator for 4 days. On the third day, sprinkle the meat with the salt.

Tuna with Peppers & Olives; Fillet of Beef with Paprika, Coriander & Cumin; Rice & Wild Rice Salad

❧ To cook, let the meat sit at room temperature for about 1 hour. Preheat a stove-top griddle or a large cast-iron frying pan and preheat an oven to 350°F (180°C). Sear the fillet on the griddle, or in the pan, until brown on all sides, about 6–8 minutes. Transfer the meat to a roasting pan and roast in the oven until a meat thermometer inserted in the center of the fillet registers 120°F (50°C), about 10–15 minutes. Let the meat rest on a carving board, covered with aluminum foil, for 15 minutes, then slice thin. Serve with the hot-sweet mustard.

RICE & WILD RICE SALAD

SERVES 6 (MULTIPLY BY 3 FOR BUFFET)

Subtly perfumed basmati rice and nutlike wild rice combine with a sweetly spiced dressing for this flavorful salad.

FOR THE RICE:

4 cups (32 fl oz/1 l) cold water
4 teaspoons salt
½ cup (3 oz/90 g) wild rice
1½ cups (10 oz/ 315 g) basmati rice
one 2-inch (5-cm) piece fresh ginger

FOR THE VINAIGRETTE:

½ teaspoon ground nutmeg
½ teaspoon ground cumin
2–3 tablespoons fresh lemon juice
½ cup (4 fl oz/125 ml) olive oil or
   peanut oil
salt and freshly ground pepper to taste

TO FINISH THE SALAD:

½ cup (1½ oz/45 g) chopped green
   (spring) onions
½ cup (3 oz/90 g) dried currants,
   soaked in ½ cup (4 fl oz/125 ml)
   Marsala until soft (10–20 minutes)
⅓ cup (2 oz/60 g) toasted pine
   nuts or slivered almonds (see glossary)

To cook the rice, bring 1½ cups (12 fl oz/375 ml) of the water and 2 teaspoons of the salt to a boil in a medium saucepan. Add the wild rice, reduce heat to low, cover and simmer until the rice is tender, about 1 hour.
❧ Combine the basmati rice and the remaining 2½ cups (20 fl oz/625 ml) water in a medium saucepan. Let sit for 1 hour. Then bring to a boil, add the remaining 2 teaspoons salt and the ginger, reduce heat to low, cover and simmer until the rice has absorbed all of the water and is tender, about 15 minutes. Discard the ginger.
❧ To make the vinaigrette, combine the nutmeg and cumin in a small bowl and whisk in the lemon juice. Add the oil and season with salt and pepper.
❧ To finish the salad, combine the wild rice and basmati rice while still warm in a large bowl. Toss the vinaigrette with the rice, then stir in the green onions, currants and any remaining Marsala, and nuts. Adjust the seasoning. Serve at room temperature.

*Serve any extra rice salad in
a bowl alongside the beef.*

TUNA WITH PEPPERS & OLIVES

SERVES 6 (MULTIPLY BY 2 FOR BUFFET)

Make this easy Mediterranean-style salad up to 3 hours ahead to let the flavors mingle.

1 lb (500 g) fresh tuna, cut about 1 inch
   (2.5 cm) thick, or canned solid-pack
   tuna in oil or water, drained
2 red bell peppers (capsicums)
2 yellow bell peppers (capsicums)
¾ cup (6 fl oz/180 ml) olive oil
¼ cup (2 fl oz/60 ml) red wine
   vinegar or more to taste
1 tablespoon minced garlic
2 tablespoons minced anchovy
⅓ cup (2 oz/60 g) capers, rinsed and
   coarsely chopped
freshly ground pepper to taste
arugula for lining plate, optional
½ cup (2½ oz/75 g) pitted black olives,
   such as Kalamata, halved
⅓ cup (½ oz/15 g) chopped fresh
   flat-leaf (Italian) parsley

If using fresh tuna, place the fillet in an oiled baking dish, cover tightly with aluminum foil and bake in a preheated 450°F (230°C) oven until it is barely pink and still moist in the center, about 8–10 minutes. Remove and let cool. Meanwhile, roast, peel and derib the peppers as directed in the glossary. Slice the peppers into thin strips.
❧ Break the cooked or canned tuna into chunks and place in a bowl. In a separate bowl, combine the oil, vinegar, garlic, anchovy and capers. Season with pepper and pour half of this over the tuna. Toss well. Toss the peppers with the remaining vinaigrette. Spread the peppers on a platter lined with arugula, if using, and top the peppers with the tuna; garnish with the olives and parsley.

BERRY TIRAMISÙ

SERVES 12 (MAKE 2 CAKES FOR BUFFET)

*This popular Italian dessert gains fresh
new flavor from ripe berries. For easier
slicing, make and weight the tiramisù the
night before. Serve the berry sauce alongside.*

FOR THE GÉNOISE:

6 eggs

1 cup (8 oz/250 g) granulated sugar

1 teaspoon vanilla extract (essence)

1 teaspoon grated lemon zest

1 cup (4 oz/125 g) cake (soft-wheat)
   flour, sifted

6 tablespoons (3 oz/90 g) unsalted
   butter, melted

FOR THE CUSTARD FILLING:

5 eggs, separated

⅓ cup (3 oz/90 g) granulated sugar

1 lb (500 g) mascarpone cheese at
   room temperature

2 tablespoons dark rum or Marsala

1 teaspoon vanilla extract (essence)

FOR THE BERRY FILLING:

4 cups (1 lb/500 g) raspberries or
   sliced strawberries

¼ cup (2 fl oz/60 ml) dark rum
   or Marsala

2 tablespoons granulated sugar

FOR THE BERRY SAUCE:

1 cup (4 oz/125 g) raspberries or
   strawberries

¼ cup (2 oz/60 g) granulated sugar

1 teaspoon vanilla extract (essence)

FOR THE GARNISH:

confectioners' (icing) sugar

12 whole raspberries or strawberries

To make the génoise, preheat an oven
to 350°F (180°C). Butter a 9-inch
(23-cm) cake pan and line the bottom
with baking parchment.

❧ Place the eggs and sugar in the bowl
of an electric mixer, set the bowl over
hot water and whisk for a few minutes
until warm to the touch. Remove from
the hot water and beat on high speed
with the whisk attachment until very
thick and pale and a small amount trailed
from the whisk forms a ribbon on the
surface of the mixture, about 8 minutes.
Stir in the vanilla and lemon zest. With
a spatula, gently fold in half the sifted
flour, then the melted butter, then the
remaining flour. Pour into the prepared
pan, tap the pan lightly on the counter
to level the batter and bake on the
middle rack of the oven until a toothpick inserted in the center of the cake
comes out clean, about 30 minutes.
Turn the cake out onto a rack to cool.
When cool, cut the génoise into 3
layers with a serrated knife.

❧ To make the custard filling, in the
bowl of an electric mixer whisk the egg
yolks and half the sugar over hot water
for a few minutes until warm to the
touch. Remove from the hot water and
beat on high speed with the whisk
attachment until thick, pale and fluffy,
about 8–10 minutes.

❧ Mix the mascarpone with a fork to
make sure it is smooth. Fold the
mascarpone into the yolks and sugar,
then fold in the rum or Marsala and the
vanilla. In a large bowl, beat the egg
whites for a few minutes until foamy.
Gradually beat in the remaining sugar
until soft peaks form, about 1 minute
longer. Do not overbeat. Fold the
whites into the mascarpone mixture.

❧ To make the berry filling, mix the
berries with the dark rum or Marsala and
the sugar and let stand for 10 minutes.

❧ To assemble, place 1 layer of the
génoise in the bottom of a 9-inch (23-
cm) springform pan. Top evenly with

half of the berry filling. Spoon half
of the custard over the berries. Place
another third of the génoise over the
custard and add the remaining filling,
then the remaining custard, then the
remaining génoise. Wrap the pan with
aluminum foil. Weight the cake with
several plates and refrigerate overnight.

❧ To prepare the berry sauce, purée
the berries, sugar and vanilla in a food
processor or blender. Strain out the
berry seeds and chill the sauce until
serving time.

❧ Immediately before serving, remove
the sides from the springform pan
and place the cake on a serving plate.
Sprinkle the top with confectioners'
sugar, garnish with the whole berries
and serve with the berry sauce.

*For serving the sparkling wine that
accompanies the dessert, your most
elegant Champagne flutes and a silver
cooler add festivity to the celebration.*

Berry Tiramisù

HARVEST LUNCH

IN VINEYARDS AND ON FARMS everywhere, family, friends and co-workers stop harvesting at midday to share a simple feast that highlights nature's bounty. We chose a vineyard location for our harvest lunch, but you don't need to live or work in the countryside to enjoy this autumnal celebration. Whether you set your table beneath trees, on a patio or near a sunny window, what matters is an abundance of seasonal food and a spirit of fellowship.

We aimed to capture the feel of the harvest by using a rustic, weather-beaten table, setting it with ceramic dishes and simple cutlery. For the centerpiece, we gathered wildflowers from a nearby garden; any mixed seasonal blooms from a flower vendor do just as well. Fresh fruit or grape clusters, bunches of autumn leaves and vine trimmings are also fitting tokens of the harvest to add to your decorations.

Wildflowers and vine trimmings are casually arranged in a large vase or pitcher to form the centerpiece.

THE MENU THAT FOLLOWS features seasonal fare that's abundant, yet simple to prepare. While the ingredients are readily available in food stores, the best fruits and vegetables—especially figs and blue plums—will probably be found at your local farmer's market. And be sure to take advantage of this occasion to offer one or more of your favorite vintage or varietal wines.

This menu doesn't have to be limited by the seasons, however. With the substitutions suggested in the recipe introductions, you'll find that these dishes can be reliable standbys at lunches and dinners throughout the year.

Menu

A watering can becomes an impromptu vase for seasonal blossoms for a side table. Clusters of just-picked grapes, hung by their stems from the side of the can or draped alongside it, are an edible embellishment.

*Grilled Peppered Figs
with Grilled Goat Cheese in Grape Leaves*

Walnut Focaccia

❧

*Butterflied Leg of Lamb
in Middle Eastern Yogurt Marinade*

Spiced Apricot Chutney

*Grilled Eggplant
with Sweet Cherry Tomato Sauce*

Lentil Salad

❧

Blue Plum Tart

PREPARATION LIST

♦ Several months ahead, prepare the chutney (commercial chutney may be substituted).

♦ Up to 1 week ahead, make the cherry tomato sauce for the eggplant.

♦ The day before, wrap and oil the cheese.

♦ The night before, marinate the lamb.

♦ The morning of the lunch, bake the focaccia; make the lentil salad and the plum tart.

♦ One hour before, let the lamb come to room temperature before grilling.

EACH RECIPE YIELDS 6 SERVINGS.

Bottles of a favorite vintage, adorned with flowers and homemade name tags, make ideal gifts for guests.

PHOTOGRAPH BY PETER JOHNSON

WINE RECOMMENDATIONS

Celebrate the harvest with a choice of flavorful young white and red wines. Choose a white with generous flavor and fruit that echoes the menu's sweet-sour contrasts: a rich Chardonnay from Australia or America or a dry Gewürztraminer. The red wine should be full-bodied, but not heady: a fresh Pinot Noir or a Cabernet blend. With dessert, offer chilled plum brandy.

GRILLED PEPPERED FIGS WITH GRILLED GOAT CHEESE IN GRAPE LEAVES

SERVES 6

The sweetest figs of all are often the cracked, homely looking ones. When figs are not in season, substitute peaches or good, juicy pears.

six 1-inch-thick (2.5-cm) slices mild
    fresh goat cheese
6 bottled grape leaves, rinsed of brine
    and stemmed (see glossary)
6 large ripe figs
6 thin slices prosciutto
olive oil for brushing
freshly ground pepper to taste
6 lime wedges

Wrap each slice of goat cheese in a grape leaf, folding in the ends and sides so it resembles a neat packet. If made ahead, cover and refrigerate overnight.
∾ Prepare a fire in a grill. Position the oiled rack 4–6 inches (10–15 cm) above the fire. Or, preheat a broiler (griller).
∾ Cut each fig in half lengthwise. Cut the prosciutto slices in half lengthwise. Wrap each fig half with a piece of prosciutto and thread 2 halves on each of 6 skewers. Brush the wrapped figs and cheese lightly with olive oil and sprinkle with pepper.
∾ Cook the figs and cheese on the grill over medium-hot coals or broil until figs are heated through (about 3 minutes) and the cheese is soft and warm (about 4 minutes), turning once. Divide the figs and cheese among 6 small plates and garnish each with a lime wedge.

WALNUT FOCACCIA

MAKES ONE 11- BY 18-INCH
(28- BY 46-CM) FOCACCIA

Add grapes to this hearty bread if you are not serving the figs in the same menu. Toasted walnut oil is richer in flavor than pale, untoasted varieties.

FOR THE DOUGH:
2 teaspoons active dry yeast
1¼ cups (10 fl oz/300 ml) warm
    (110°F/43°C) water
2 tablespoons sugar
3¾ cups (19 oz/595 g) unbleached
    all-purpose (plain) flour
3 tablespoons toasted walnut oil
1 teaspoon salt

FOR THE TOPPING:
toasted walnut oil
1 cup (4 oz/125 g) chopped toasted
    walnuts (see glossary)
2 tablespoons minced fresh rosemary
2 cups (10 oz/315 g) halved and seeded
    red grapes, optional
1–2 tablespoons sugar, optional

Newly harvested grapes, cut from the vines with a traditional knife, wait in a wooden lug to go to the winepress.

To make the dough, dissolve the yeast in ½ cup (8 fl oz/250 ml) of the warm water in the bowl of an electric mixer. Add the sugar and ½ cup (2½ oz/75 g) of the flour and mix to combine. Cover and let sit for about 30 minutes. Add the remaining flour, the remaining water, the walnut oil and the salt and mix well. Beat on low speed with the dough hook attached until the dough leaves the bowl cleanly, about 10 minutes. Or, mix the dough in a food processor until well combined. Then turn out onto a lightly floured board and knead until the dough is smooth and elastic, about 10 minutes, adding more flour if necessary to prevent sticking. Transfer the dough to an oiled bowl, cover with a kitchen towel and let rise in a warm place until doubled, about 1 hour.
∾ Preheat an oven to 475°F (240°C). Punch down the dough and turn it out on a lightly floured board. Form into an 11- by 18-inch (28- by 46-cm) rectangle and place in a sided baking pan of the same dimensions. Cover the dough loosely and allow it to rest until doubled, about 15–30 minutes.
∾ To make the topping, brush the dough lightly with walnut oil, then dimple the top with your fingers. Sprinkle with the walnuts and rosemary. (If using grapes, push them into the dough and sprinkle the focaccia with the sugar, then add the walnuts and rosemary.) Bake on the lower rack of the oven until golden brown on top, about 12–15 minutes.

Grilled Peppered Figs with Grilled Goat Cheese in Grape Leaves; Walnut Focaccia

BUTTERFLIED LEG OF LAMB IN MIDDLE EASTERN YOGURT MARINADE

SERVES 6

A butterflied leg of lamb has thick and thin portions, yielding both rare and medium meat. The very simple marinade produces spectacular results.

1 large leg of lamb, about 6 lb (3 kg), boned, butterflied and trimmed of fat and silverskin
1 large onion, chopped
2–3 cloves garlic, minced
½ teaspoon ground cinnamon
½ teaspoon ground cardamom
¼ teaspoon saffron threads, crushed (see glossary)
1 teaspoon ground ginger or 1 tablespoon grated fresh ginger
1 tablespoon ground coriander
½ teaspoon freshly ground pepper
2 cups (1 lb/500 g) plain lowfat or nonfat yogurt
3 tablespoons fresh lemon juice
½ cup (¾ oz/20 g) chopped fresh mint
oil for brushing
salt and freshly ground pepper to taste

Place the butterflied lamb leg in a glass or plastic container large enough to hold it in one layer. Set aside.

❧ Place the onion and garlic in a food processor or blender and pulse until coarsely chopped. Add the cinnamon, cardamom, saffron, ginger, coriander, pepper, yogurt, lemon juice and mint and purée. Pour over the lamb, cover and marinate overnight in the refrigerator, turning occasionally.

Butterflied Leg of Lamb in Middle Eastern Yogurt Marinade; Spiced Apricot Chutney; Grilled Eggplant with Sweet Cherry Tomato Sauce

PHOTOGRAPH BY PETER JOHNSON

⮞ Prepare a fire in a grill. Position the oiled rack 4–6 inches (10–15 cm) above the fire. Or, preheat a broiler (griller).

⮞ Remove the lamb from the marinade. Brush with oil and sprinkle with salt and pepper. Grill over medium-hot coals or broil for 8–10 minutes on each side for rare, or 12 minutes for medium rare. The thicker section may take a few minutes longer. Slice across the grain to serve.

SPICED APRICOT CHUTNEY

MAKES ABOUT 6 CUPS (48 OZ/1.5 KG)

Sweet-tart apricots have an affinity for lamb. Make the chutney when the fruit is in season and let it sit in a cool, dark place for 2–3 weeks to mellow the flavors before using. Or, substitute commercial chutney.

6 cups (1½ lb/750 g) pitted and
    quartered fresh apricots
2 cups (1 lb/500 g) sugar
½ tablespoon salt
1 onion, chopped
one 4- by 1½-inch (10- by 4-cm)
    piece fresh ginger, peeled and sliced
3 cloves garlic
1 teaspoon ground cinnamon
½ teaspoon ground cloves
½ teaspoon cayenne pepper or 3–4
    jalapeño (hot green) chili peppers,
    minced
1½ cups (12 fl oz/375 ml)
    cider vinegar

Place the apricots in a large, heavy enameled or stainless-steel pot. Cover with the sugar and salt and let stand for at least 1 hour or up to 8 hours.

⮞ In a food processor or blender, pulse or blend the onion, ginger, garlic, cinnamon, cloves and cayenne or chilies until chopped. Add half of the vinegar and purée. Pour this mixture over the apricots and stir in the remaining vinegar. Bring to a boil, then reduce heat and simmer, uncovered and stirring often, until the mixture is thick and a teaspoonful sets up on a chilled plate, about 1 hour. Pour into 3 hot sterilized 2-cup (16–fl oz/500-ml) canning jars, leaving about ½ inch (12 mm) of head space, then seal the jars. Process in a hot-water bath for 10 minutes (see glossary) or store in the refrigerator for up to 3 months.

GRILLED EGGPLANT WITH SWEET CHERRY TOMATO SAUCE

SERVES 6

The sauce, more like a conserve, is also excellent on cream cheese, goat cheese or grilled chicken.

FOR THE CHERRY TOMATO SAUCE:
2 cups (12 oz/375 g) stemmed
    cherry tomatoes
½ cup (3½ oz/105 g) light brown
    sugar, packed
grated zest of 1 lemon (see glossary)
¼ cup (2 fl oz/60 ml) fresh
    lemon juice
1 tablespoon grated fresh ginger
3 tablespoons water
½ teaspoon ground cinnamon
½ teaspoon ground cumin
pinch of cayenne pepper
salt and freshly ground pepper to taste

FOR THE GRILLED EGGPLANT:
1 clove garlic, crushed
¼ cup (2 fl oz/60 ml) olive oil,
    slightly warmed
2 firm globe eggplants (aubergines),
    about ½–¾ lb (250–375 g) each, or
    6 slender (Asian) eggplants (aubergines)
salt and freshly ground pepper to taste

To make the sauce, combine the tomatoes, brown sugar, lemon zest, lemon juice, ginger, water, cinnamon, cumin and cayenne in a saucepan. Cook, uncovered, over moderate heat, stirring occasionally, until the tomatoes break down and the mixture becomes thick and syrupy, about 30 minutes. Season with salt and pepper and transfer to a bowl or jar. If desired, cover and refrigerate up to 1 week. Makes about 1 cup (8 fl oz/250 ml).

⮞ To make the grilled eggplant, steep the garlic in the warm olive oil for about 1 hour. Prepare a fire in a grill. Position the oiled rack 4–6 inches (10–15 cm) above the fire. Or, preheat a broiler (griller). Peel the globe eggplants and slice them 1 inch thick (2.5 cm) crosswise. If using slender eggplants, do not peel; cut each in half lengthwise and score the top with the point of a knife. Brush the eggplants with the garlic oil and sprinkle with salt and pepper. Grill or broil the eggplant, turning once, until soft but not too browned, about 3 minutes on each side.

⮞ Meanwhile, rewarm the tomato sauce over low heat. When the eggplants are done, divide the slices among 6 plates (or place 2 halves of slender eggplant on each), top with the tomato sauce and serve.

Lentil Salad

LENTIL SALAD

SERVES 6

For the best texture, make the salad no more than several hours in advance. If you make it ahead, fold in half the mint, adding the rest before serving.

2 cups (14 oz/440 g) green or
 brown lentils
1 bay leaf
1 teaspoon salt
½ cup (4 fl oz/125 ml) plus 3 tablespoons olive oil
¼ cup (2 fl oz/60 ml) fresh
 lemon juice
2 cups (8 oz/250 g) diced onions
1 teaspoon minced garlic
2 tablespoons ground cumin
1 teaspoon ground coriander
grated zest of 1 lemon (see glossary)
½ cup (¾ oz/20 g) chopped
 fresh mint
salt and freshly ground pepper to taste

Place the lentils and bay leaf in a deep saucepan and cover with cold water to a depth of 3 inches (7.5 cm) above the lentils. Bring to a boil over high heat, add the salt, reduce heat and simmer, covered, until the lentils are tender but still firm. Green lentils can take as long as 45 minutes, brown as few as 15, so keep testing. When the lentils are done, drain off any excess water, toss the lentils in the ½ cup (4 fl oz/125 ml) olive oil and the lemon juice and set aside.
❧ Heat the remaining 3 tablespoons oil in a large sauté pan, add the onions and cook until tender and translucent, about 10 minutes. Add the garlic, cumin, coriander and lemon zest and cook 2–3 minutes longer. Add the cooked onion mixture to the lentils. Fold in the mint and season with salt and pepper. Serve at room temperature.

Blue Plum Tart

PHOTOGRAPH BY PETER JOHNSON

BLUE PLUM TART

MAKES ONE 8- BY 11-INCH (20- BY 28-CM)
RECTANGULAR TART OR ONE 10-INCH
(25-CM) ROUND TART

*Plum and citrus flavors predominate in
this nutty tart. Substitute other varieties
of plums for the prune plums if necessary.*

basic pie pastry for a single-crust pie
    shell (recipe on page 299)
½ cup (2 oz/60 g) plus 2 tablespoons
    hazelnuts, toasted and skinned
    (see glossary)
½ cup (4 oz/125 g) plus 2
    tablespoons sugar
½ teaspoon ground cinnamon
½ teaspoon ground ginger
3 tablespoons unsalted butter at
    room temperature

16–20 Italian prune plums, halved
    and pitted
¾ cup (6 fl oz/180 ml) orange
    marmalade
whipped cream flavored with about 1
    teaspoon grated orange zest, optional

Preheat an oven to 400°F (200°C).
Roll out the pastry into a large rectangle
on a lightly floured surface. Use to
line an 8- by 11-inch (20- by 28-cm)
rectangular tart pan or a 10-inch
(25-cm) round tart pan. Set aside in the
freezer while you make the filling.
ॐ Finely chop the ½ cup (2 oz/60 g)
hazelnuts and coarsely chop the remaining 2 tablespoons hazelnuts. Combine
the finely chopped hazelnuts, the ½ cup
(4 oz/125 g) sugar, cinnamon, ginger
and butter in a food processor or a

medium bowl; pulse or cut in the butter
with a pastry cutter or 2 knives until
blended into a paste. Press onto the
bottom of the pastry-lined tart pan. Top
with the plums, arranged in overlapping
rows. Sprinkle with the remaining 2
tablespoons sugar and bake on the middle
rack of the oven for 10 minutes. Reduce
the heat to 350°F (180°C) and bake
until the plums are bubbly and the crust
is golden, about 20–30 minutes more.
ॐ Meanwhile, melt the orange marmalade in a small saucepan; strain and keep
warm. When the tart is done, brush the
marmalade over the plums and sprinkle
with the 2 tablespoons coarsely chopped
hazelnuts. If desired, top each serving of
the tart with a dollop of orange-flavored
whipped cream.

$\mathcal{P}$RE-THEATER COCKTAILS

WHEN GROUPS OF FRIENDS gather together to attend an evening event such as a play, opera or dance performance, dinner can pose a challenge. With curtain-up usually between 7 and 8 P.M., there is little time for a sit-down meal. That's why a cocktail party makes such perfect sense, not just before a show but for any occasion when you want to entertain guests without extending the party into a full night's event.

We set our cocktail party in a living room with a lovely city view, but a den or library anywhere is also appropriate. Because of the relaxed style of this gathering, we decorated the room simply by placing seasonal foliage and fruit in various spots. The owner's collection of personal memorabilia served as the ideal backdrop.

On a side table, an arrangement of wine bottles, glasses and cocktail napkins allows guests to serve themselves.

Menu

THE ARRAY OF FINGER FOODS and small dishes selected for this cocktail party for twelve offers something to please everyone. The portions are generous enough to keep appetites at bay all evening. Autumn flavors predominate, since fall is the time when many arts seasons begin, but you can make these recipes any time of year. Most dishes can be prepared at least partly in advance, with minimal cleanup.

Try placing platters of food with plenty of small plates, cutlery and cocktail napkins at various convenient spots around the room where guests can serve themselves. Likewise, you might want to arrange separate stations for a self-service wine bar and a full liquor bar with ready-to-mix cocktails and mineral water. In so doing, you'll establish different conversation areas and encourage guests to mingle.

Seasonal foliage and fruits, such as autumn leaves and persimmons, add a simple, elegant decorative flourish.

Greek Chicken Strudel

*Roasted Peppers
with Herbed Goat Cheese*

❧

Tomato Tart

Roasted Eggplant Salad

Crab Salad in Endive Leaves

❧

Baked Clams Oreganati

*Mushrooms
Stuffed with Sweet Sausage*

PREPARATION LIST

◆ The morning of the party, make the eggplant salad; stuff and refrigerate the mushrooms.

◆ Three to 4 hours ahead, assemble and slice the peppers with goat cheese and cover with plastic wrap; steam and open clams, top with bread crumbs, cover and refrigerate.

◆ One to 2 hours ahead, bake the tart, to be gently rewarmed at serving time or served at room temperature; prepare the crab in endive.

THE FOLLOWING MENU SERVES 12 GENEROUSLY FOR COCKTAILS. FOR A SMALLER GROUP, SERVE FEWER DISHES.

WINE RECOMMENDATIONS

Offer a choice of white and red wines. For the white, select one with a pronounced flavor to accent the sharper tastes of the food: a classic Sauvignon Blanc or a Pinot Gris from Oregon or Alsace. Choose a well-concentrated red with earthy overtones: a Cabernet Sauvignon or a high-quality Beaujolais, such as a Moulin à Vent or a Morgon.

An elegant silver tray with premium liquors, ice bucket, cocktail shaker and assorted glasses transforms a sideboard into a self-service bar.

GREEK CHICKEN STRUDEL

MAKES 3 STRUDELS

This recipe is also excellent as a light main course for supper. If you prefer, you could layer the filo and filling in lasagna pans, then slice into wedges to serve.

FOR THE FILLING:

about 3 cups (24 fl oz/750 ml)
   chicken stock (see page 295)
6 boneless, skinless chicken breast halves
6 cups (12 oz/375 g) loosely packed
   chopped spinach leaves, well washed
3 tablespoons olive oil
1½ cups (5 oz/155 g) minced green
   (spring) onions
⅓ cup (½ oz/15 g) chopped fresh dill
⅓ cup (½ oz/15 g) chopped fresh parsley
¾ lb (375 g) feta cheese, crumbled,
   about 2½ cups
5 oz (155 g) Monterey jack cheese,
   grated, about 1¼ cups
3 eggs
½ teaspoon freshly grated nutmeg
1 teaspoon ground coriander
¼ teaspoon cayenne pepper
¾ cup (3 oz/90 g) chopped toasted
   walnuts (see glossary)
salt and freshly ground pepper to taste

FOR ASSEMBLY:

12 sheets filo pastry
⅓–½ cup (3–4 oz/90–125 g)
   unsalted butter, melted, for brushing

To make the filling, bring enough stock to cover the chicken breasts to a boil in a wide sauté pan. Add the breasts, reduce the heat and poach, uncovered, until the chicken is cooked through, about 8–10 minutes. Lift out and let cool, then shred or chop the meat. Save the stock for another recipe.
❧ Place the spinach with the water clinging to it in a large frying pan and stir over medium heat until wilted, about 3 minutes. Drain well and squeeze dry.
❧ Heat the oil in a sauté pan, add the green onions and cook until soft, about 5 minutes. Place in a bowl with the chicken, spinach, dill, parsley, feta cheese, jack cheese, eggs, nutmeg, coriander, cayenne and walnuts; stir until well combined. Season liberally with salt and pepper.
❧ Preheat an oven to 325°F (170°C). To assemble the strudels, brush a sheet of filo with the melted butter. Place another sheet on top, brush again, repeat for 2 more layers, then place a thin row of chicken mixture along the long side. Tuck in the ends and roll up. Repeat until all the filling and filo are used up; you will have 3 strudels. Transfer to baking sheets and bake on the middle rack of the oven until golden brown, about 25–30 minutes. Allow to rest for 10 minutes, then cut into 1-inch (2.5-cm) slices crosswise with a serrated knife.

*A quiet corner provides
comfortable seating.*

ROASTED PEPPERS WITH HERBED GOAT CHEESE

MAKES ABOUT 72 APPETIZERS

Resembling colorful pinwheels, this simple hors d'oeuvre combines the rich, creamy tang of goat cheese with the sweetness of bell peppers.

6 large red bell peppers (capsicums) or
   pimiento peppers (capsicums)
1¼ lb (625 g) fresh mild goat cheese,
   crumbled, about 4 cups
¼ cup (⅜ oz/10 g) chopped
   fresh chives
¼ cup (⅜ oz/10 g) chopped
   fresh parsley
2 cloves garlic, minced
2 teaspoons chopped fresh thyme
3 tablespoons chopped fresh basil
grated zest of 1 lemon (see glossary)
½ teaspoon freshly ground pepper
pinch of cayenne pepper
heavy (double) cream, optional
fresh thyme sprigs, optional

Roast, peel and derib the peppers as directed in the glossary. Try to keep the peppers in unbroken halves.
❧ In a bowl, mix well the cheese, chives, parsley, garlic, thyme, basil, lemon zest and ground pepper; season to taste with cayenne. Add a bit of cream if the cheese mixture is very stiff and difficult to mix. Spread the cheese mixture onto the pepper halves and roll them into cylinders lengthwise. Refrigerate for a few hours to firm the filling.
❧ At serving time, cut each pepper roll crosswise into about 6 rounds. Arrange on a platter and garnish with the thyme sprigs, if using.

*Greek Chicken Strudel;
Roasted Peppers with Herbed Goat Cheese*

TOMATO TART

MAKES 12 SERVINGS

Similar to a quiche, this French-style tart could be given an Italian flair by substituting basil for the mint and mozzarella for the Gruyère.

basic pie pastry for a single-crust pie
    shell (recipe on page 299)
3 large tomatoes, cut into ½-inch-
    thick (12-mm) slices
salt to taste
2 tablespoons Dijon mustard
3 tablespoons chopped fresh mint
4 oz (125 g) Gruyère or Emmenthaler
    cheese, cut into 8 thin slices
2 eggs
1 cup (8 fl oz/250 ml) heavy
    (double) cream
freshly ground pepper to taste

Roll out the pastry and use it to line a 10-inch (25-cm) pie or tart pan. Set it aside in the freezer for 30 minutes.
❧ With your fingers, carefully push out the seeds and watery juices from the tomato slices. Sprinkle the sliced tomatoes with salt and place in a large colander to drain. After 30 minutes, remove the tomatoes from the colander and pat them dry.
❧ Preheat an oven to 350°F (180°C). With a rubber spatula, spread the mustard over the bottom of the tart shell and sprinkle the chopped mint over the mustard. Top with the cheese, then place the tomato slices over the cheese. In a small bowl, beat together the eggs and cream, season with salt and pepper and pour over the tomatoes. Bake until pale gold and the custard is set, about 30 minutes. Let rest for 10 minutes, then slice and serve.

ROASTED EGGPLANT SALAD

MAKES 12 SERVINGS

If you make this low-fat salad ahead of time, wait until just before serving to fold in the mint and almonds.

3 large globe eggplants (aubergines)
1 cup (8 oz/250 g) plain nonfat yogurt
2 tablespoons fresh lemon juice or
    to taste
1 tablespoon minced garlic
1 teaspoon minced jalapeño (hot green)
    chili pepper or more to taste
2 teaspoons ground cumin
salt and freshly ground pepper to taste
⅔ cup (3 oz/90 g) toasted almonds
    (see glossary), chopped
¼ cup (⅜ oz/10 g) chopped fresh mint
4 pita bread rounds, cut into 6
    wedges each

Preheat an oven to 400°F (200°C). Place the eggplants on a baking sheet and prick all over with a fork. Roast, turning occasionally for even cooking, until the eggplants are soft and tender, about 1 hour. Remove from the oven and let sit until cool enough to handle. Peel the eggplant and place the pulp in a colander to drain for about 30 minutes.
❧ Place the eggplant pulp in a food processor or blender and pulse to purée. Add the yogurt, lemon juice, garlic, jalapeño and cumin. Pulse quickly to mix. Add salt and pepper. Transfer the purée to a serving bowl. If desired, cover and refrigerate for up to 6 hours. Stir in the chopped toasted almonds and mint and serve with the pita wedges.

Tomato Tart; Roasted Eggplant Salad

CRAB SALAD IN ENDIVE LEAVES

MAKES 24 APPETIZERS

The crisp, slightly bitter endive contrasts nicely with the mild sweetness of the crab. Substitute small romaine leaves if you like.

grated zest of 1 lemon (see glossary)
2 tablespoons lemon juice
1 teaspoon chopped fresh tarragon
2 tablespoons chopped fresh chives
2 tablespoons chopped fresh parsley
1 tablespoon Dijon mustard
½ cup (4 fl oz/125 ml) mayonnaise or as needed to bind
1 lb (500 g) fresh crab meat, picked over and any cartilage removed
¾ cup (4 oz/125 g) diced celery
salt, freshly ground pepper and cayenne pepper to taste
24 Belgian endive (chicory/witloof) leaves

In a bowl, combine the lemon zest, lemon juice, tarragon, chives, parsley, mustard and mayonnaise; mix well. Stir in the crab and celery and season with salt, ground pepper and cayenne. Cover and refrigerate up to 6 hours. To serve, spoon the crab mixture into the endive leaves and chill for at least 30 minutes or up to 2 hours to firm the filling.

A slice of tomato tart, a glass of wine and an inviting chair await a guest.

BAKED CLAMS OREGANATI

MAKES 36 APPETIZERS

When preparing live clams, tap each one to be sure the shells close tightly.

36 Manila or littleneck clams, scrubbed
dry white wine
3 tablespoons olive oil
2 cloves garlic, minced
1 tablespoon dried oregano
½ cup (2 oz/60 g) dried bread crumbs
1 tablespoon chopped fresh parsley
3 tablespoons freshly grated Parmesan cheese, optional
salt and freshly ground pepper to taste
rock salt
lemon wedges

Place the clams in a large sauté pan with about 1 inch (2.5 cm) of white wine. Cover the pan and steam over high heat just until the clams open, 2–8 minutes. Remove from the heat immediately and, using a slotted spoon, transfer the clams to a platter; discard any unopened clams. Remove the top shells and discard. Loosen each clam from its bottom shell with a knife so that it can be picked up easily. Strain the juices in the pan and reserve.

ð Warm the olive oil in a small sauté pan, add the garlic and oregano and cook over low heat for 2 minutes. Remove from the heat and stir in the bread crumbs, parsley and Parmesan, if desired. Let cool. Sprinkle the bread crumbs over the clams and drizzle with a few drops of the reserved pan juices. Season with salt and pepper. Cover and refrigerate until serving time.

ð To serve, preheat a broiler (griller). Arrange the clams on a rock salt–lined baking pan that can fit under the broiler. Broil the clams until browned on top, about 5 minutes. Serve with lemons.

MUSHROOMS STUFFED WITH SWEET SAUSAGE

MAKES 24 APPETIZERS

You can stuff and refrigerate the mushroom caps the morning of the party.

24 large fresh mushrooms
4 tablespoons (2 fl oz/60 ml) oil
½ cup (2 oz/60 g) chopped onion
1 tablespoon minced garlic
½ lb (250 g) ground pork
½ teaspoon ground cinnamon
¼ teaspoon ground nutmeg
1 teaspoon toasted fennel seed, ground (see glossary)
1 tablespoon grated orange zest
¼ cup (1 oz/30 g) dried bread crumbs
salt and freshly ground pepper to taste
1 cup (8 fl oz/250 ml) chicken stock

Remove the stems from the mushrooms and chop them; reserve the caps. Heat 2 tablespoons of the oil in a large sauté pan. Add the chopped onion and cook until soft, about 5 minutes. Add the chopped stems and cook over high heat until they start to become dry, about 5 minutes. Stir in the garlic and cook for 1 minute. Transfer to a bowl and set the mixture aside.

ð Heat the remaining 2 tablespoons of oil in the same pan. Cook the pork, breaking it up with a fork, until it is no longer pink, about 5 minutes. Stir in the cinnamon, nutmeg, fennel seed and orange zest. Add the cooked mushroom and onion mixture and the bread crumbs; mix well. Season with salt and pepper and adjust the rest of the spices.

ð Preheat the oven to 350°F (180°C). Stuff the pork mixture into the mushroom caps. Place the mushrooms in a baking pan and drizzle the stock around them. Bake until cooked through, about 20–25 minutes. Serve warm.

Baked Clams Oreganati; Mushrooms Stuffed with Sweet Sausage; Crab Salad in Endive Leaves

TRADITIONAL THANKSGIVING

AMERICAN FAMILIES EVERYWHERE hold the national harvest celebration dear to their hearts. The Thanksgiving feast provides some of our most enduring holiday memories and features a roster of ingredients so ritualized that they have become almost sacred.

We presented our Thanksgiving menu in a classic American dining room featuring an extra-long table so it could accommodate not only the guests but also the roast turkey. Side dishes and other courses were placed close at hand on a sideboard. We also set up a separate children's table, a tradition in some families. Heirloom dishes and antique silver, glassware and linens were selected to reinforce a sense of family heritage. Wreaths, baskets, nuts, dried corn, wheat sheaves and game bird feathers helped to evoke the spirit of the American harvest.

AS OUR HOLIDAY MENU SHOWS, there is room for creativity within the traditional bounds of the Thanksgiving meal. Here butternut squash takes over for pumpkin in the first-course soup, while a vivid tangerine custard assumes the pumpkin's usual role as a pie filling. The turkey features a corn bread stuffing enriched with sweet Italian sausage and subtle spices perfume the cranberry sauce.

It takes advance planning to cook and serve such an extensive menu. We recommend that you carefully read through the preparation list and the recipes up to several weeks before Thanksgiving Day, allowing yourself ample time for shopping and advance cooking. By all means, mix and match this menu with your own favorites as you wish.

Keep place settings uncomplicated. Set the soup plate atop the dinner plate and provide only essential cutlery and glasses.

Menu

WINE RECOMMENDATIONS

The first choice to accompany Thanksgiving turkey is a just-released Beaujolais Nouveau. For white wine drinkers, pour a Riesling from Germany's Rhine or Mosel regions. With dessert, offer a late-harvest Semillon from Australia or America, or an outstanding Sauternes.

Spiced Squash & Apple Soup

*Roast Turkey
with Corn Bread Stuffing*

Cranberry Chutney

*Chanterelles, Chestnuts &
Pearl Onions with Thyme*

Celery Root & Potato Purée

Brussels Sprouts with Garlic & Parmesan

Tangerine Custard Tart

*A wooden cupboard opens to reveal a collection of glistening
Early American silver pieces for coffee and tea service.*

PREPARATION LIST

◆ Up to 1 week ahead, make the chutney.

◆ Up to 2 days ahead, make and refrigerate
the tangerine custard pie filling.

◆ The day before, make the soup; prepare
the stuffing (but do not stuff the turkey).

◆ On Thanksgiving morning, prepare and
bake the pie crust.

◆ Three hours before, fill and top the pie.

◆ Up to several hours ahead, prepare the
celery root and potato purée.

◆ Fifteen minutes before, bake the chanterelle
casserole; start cooking the Brussels sprouts.

EACH RECIPE YIELDS 12 SERVINGS.

*Baskets and bowls of nuts, dried Native
American corn and sheaves of wheat are
strong symbols of Thanksgiving's blessings.* ❧

*Along with the soup, serve
basketfuls of bakery breads.
Loaves with raised decorations in
the forms of wheat, hearts and
leaves are especially homey.*

SPICED SQUASH & APPLE SOUP

SERVES 12

*Butternut squash is similar to pumpkin in
taste and texture but is easier to peel and
dice. Apple lightens and sweetens the purée.*

4 tablespoons (2 oz/60 g) unsalted
   butter or olive oil
2 large onions, diced, about 4 cups
   (1¼ lb/625 g)
2 large green apples, peeled, cored and
   diced, about 2 cups (1 lb/500 g)
1 teaspoon ground nutmeg
½ teaspoon ground allspice
½ teaspoon ground cinnamon
10 cups (5 lb/2.4 kg) peeled and diced
   butternut squash (about 4 whole)
12 cups (3 qt/3 l) chicken stock (see
   page 295)
salt and freshly ground pepper to taste
thin slices of green apple for garnish

Melt the butter or heat the olive oil
in a large pot over moderate heat. Add
the diced onions and apples and cook
until tender, about 10 minutes. Stir in
the spices, cook for 1 minute, then add
the squash and chicken stock. Bring
to a boil, reduce the heat and simmer,
uncovered, until the squash is very
tender, about 20–30 minutes.

❧ Purée the vegetables in batches with
a little bit of the stock in a blender or
food processor. Transfer to a large bowl.
Add enough of the remaining stock to
make a medium-thick soup. Reserve
any leftover stock if not serving right
away, as the soup may thicken on
standing. Season with salt and pepper
and adjust the spices. This soup may
be made a day ahead, refrigerated uncovered until cold and then covered.

❧ To serve, in a large pot heat the soup
almost to scalding. Ladle into bowls and
top with thin slices of apple.

Spiced Squash & Apple Soup

ROAST TURKEY WITH CORN BREAD STUFFING

SERVES 12

While the turkey roasts, make the giblet stock; just before carving, make the gravy. For best results, always use fresh (not frozen) turkey. For chicken stock, see page 295.

FOR THE STUFFING:

2 tablespoons olive oil
1 lb (500 g) sweet Italian sausages, removed from casings and crumbled
6 tablespoons (3 oz/90 g) unsalted butter
2 onions, diced, about 1½ cups (8 oz/250 g)
1 cup (5 oz/155 g) diced celery
2 cloves garlic, minced
2 tablespoons finely chopped fresh marjoram or sage
2 teaspoons ground fennel seed
½ teaspoon ground nutmeg
½ teaspoon ground cinnamon
1 cup (8 fl oz/250 ml) chicken stock
4 cups (8 oz/250 g) packaged corn bread stuffing
salt and freshly ground pepper to taste

FOR THE TURKEY:

1 fresh turkey, 12–14 lb (6–7 kg), neck and giblets removed for gravy
1 lemon, cut in half
1 clove garlic
salt, freshly ground pepper and sweet paprika to taste

FOR THE GIBLET STOCK AND GRAVY:

turkey neck and giblets
8 cups (64 fl oz/2 l) water or chicken stock
2 sliced onions
2 sliced peeled carrots
1 or 2 celery ribs
1 fresh thyme sprig
1 clove garlic
2 tablespoons all-purpose (plain) flour
salt, freshly ground pepper and ground allspice to taste

To prepare the stuffing, heat the oil in a large sauté pan. Add the sausage and sauté until browned. Remove from the pan with a slotted spoon and set aside. Add the butter to the pan and cook the onions until translucent, about 10 minutes. Add the celery, garlic, marjoram or sage, fennel seed, nutmeg, cinnamon and the stock and cook 3 minutes longer. Transfer to a large bowl and add the sausage and corn bread. Season with salt and pepper and mix well. At this point, you can cover and refrigerate the stuffing overnight.

☙ To prepare the turkey, preheat an oven to 350°F (180°C). Wipe the turkey with a damp cloth and rub the body cavity with the cut lemon and garlic and salt. Sprinkle the outside with salt, pepper and paprika.

☙ Spoon the stuffing loosely into the body and neck cavities and sew or truss them closed. Place any extra stuffing in a buttered casserole, moisten with a little extra stock and cover. Place in the oven 1 hour before the turkey is done.

☙ To roast the turkey, place it breast-side down on a rack in a roasting pan. Tent with aluminum foil. Roast for 20 minutes per pound (4–4½ hours total). Uncover the turkey and turn it breast-side up for the last 45 minutes of baking.

☙ Meanwhile, to prepare the giblet stock, simmer the neck, gizzard and heart (do not use the liver) in a large pan with the water or stock, onions, carrots, celery, thyme and garlic. Bring to a boil, then reduce heat and simmer for 1½ hours, skimming the surface; add more stock as needed. Remove the neck and discard. Remove the giblets and chop fine. Discard the thyme. Transfer the cooked vegetables with a slotted spoon to a blender and purée. Reserve the giblets, giblet stock and the puréed vegetables to make the gravy.

☙ The turkey is done when a meat thermometer inserted in the thickest part of the thigh (away from the bone) registers 180°F (82°C). Remove from the oven and let rest at least 15 minutes before carving. Remove the stuffing.

☙ To make the gravy, pour off all but 3 tablespoons of drippings from the roasting pan. Place the pan over medium heat and stir in the 2 tablespoons flour until bubbly, then add 1 cup (8 fl oz/250 ml) of the reserved giblet stock. Bring to a boil. Stir in the vegetable purée and thin with additional stock. Add the chopped giblets. Season with salt, pepper and allspice. Carve the turkey (see page 302). Serve with the stuffing and gravy.

CRANBERRY CHUTNEY

MAKES ABOUT 6 CUPS (48 OZ/1.5 KG)

This sweetly spiced variation on traditional cranberry sauce may be made 1 week ahead.

2 cups (16 fl oz/500 ml) water
3 cups (1½ lb/750 g) sugar
2 unpeeled oranges, diced, seeded and finely chopped in a blender
two 2-inch (5-cm) pieces fresh ginger, peeled and cut into thin slices
4 cups (1 lb/500 g) cranberries
1 teaspoon ground cinnamon
½ teaspoon ground cloves
1 cup (6 oz/185 g) raisins

Combine the water and sugar in a deep saucepan and bring to a boil, stirring. Add the oranges and ginger; reduce heat and simmer, uncovered, for 20 minutes. Add the cranberries, cinnamon and cloves and cook, uncovered, until thickened, about 15 minutes. Stir in the raisins and cook until big bubbles appear, about 7 minutes. Pour into a bowl and let cool. Serve or cover and refrigerate for up to 1 week.

Roast Turkey with Corn Bread Stuffing; Cranberry Chutney

CHANTERELLES, CHESTNUTS & PEARL ONIONS WITH THYME

SERVES 12

Peeling fresh chestnuts is a painstaking task, but worth every minute of hot-fingered torture. See if you can talk someone into helping you. Or purchase canned peeled chestnuts instead.

1 lb (500 g) chestnuts
1 lb (500 g) cipolline (see glossary) or pearl onions
2 lb (1 kg) chanterelles or brown mushrooms
8 tablespoons (4 oz/125 g) unsalted butter
2 tablespoons chopped fresh thyme
½ cup (4 fl oz/125 ml) chicken stock, or as needed (see page 295)
salt and freshly ground pepper to taste

Cut a cross in the rounded side of each chestnut. Place in a single layer in one or more large saucepans, cover with water and bring to a boil. Reduce heat and simmer, uncovered, for 10 minutes. While the chestnuts are hot, remove the outer peel and the thin inner brown skin. Try to keep the chestnuts whole, if possible. (The chestnuts are done when the inside is the same color as the cooked outer parts. Cut one in half to check. If the center is whiter than the outside, the chestnuts are not cooked through; simmer them in additional water for about 8–10 minutes more.) Set the cooked chestnuts aside.

❧ Trim the roots of the onions carefully without cutting across the ends. Cut a cross on the bottom of each onion to prevent them from telescoping while cooking. Place the onions in a medium saucepan, cover with water and bring to a boil. Reduce heat and sim-

mer, uncovered, until tender-firm, about 8–10 minutes. Drain, let cool slightly, then remove the peels. Set the onions aside.

❧ Wipe the mushrooms clean with a damp paper towel or clean with a mushroom brush. Cut into thick slices. Or, if the mushrooms are small, leave them whole. Melt half of the butter in a large sauté pan and sauté half of the mushrooms over high heat until softened, 3–5 minutes. Repeat with the remaining butter and mushrooms.

❧ To serve, preheat an oven to 350°F (180°C). Combine the cooked chestnuts, onions and mushrooms in a large casserole. Toss with the thyme. Add enough chicken stock to moisten the mixture. Season with salt and pepper. Bake until heated through, about 15 minutes. Serve at once.

CELERY ROOT & POTATO PURÉE

SERVES 12

Celery root contributes a subtle edge of sweetness and lightness. It's best to purée the potatoes with a ricer or food mill since processors yield gummy results.

8 large baking potatoes
3 large celeriacs (celery roots)
3–4 cups (24–32 fl oz/750 ml–1 l) chicken stock (see page 295)
6 tablespoons (3 oz/90 g) unsalted butter
1 cup (8 fl oz/250 ml) heavy (double) cream
salt, freshly ground pepper and ground nutmeg to taste

Preheat an oven to 400°F (200°C). Poke the potatoes in several places with a fork and bake until very tender, about 1 hour. Cut in half, remove the pulp and pass it through a ricer or food mill.

❧ While the potatoes are baking, trim the leaves and roots from the celeriacs and peel. Cut into dice and simmer, uncovered, in enough chicken stock to cover until very tender, about 25 minutes. Drain and purée in a food processor or pass through a food mill.

❧ Combine the potato and celeriac purée in a large, heavy saucepan over moderate heat. Stir in the butter and cream; if necessary add more butter and cream or stock until a thick, smooth consistency is achieved. Season with salt, pepper and a little nutmeg.

BRUSSELS SPROUTS WITH GARLIC & PARMESAN

SERVES 12

The sprouts stand up well to the large quantity of garlic in this vivid green, quickly cooked side dish.

3 lb (1.5 kg) Brussels sprouts
¼ cup (2 oz/60 g) unsalted butter
¼ cup (2 fl oz/60 ml) olive oil
12 large cloves garlic, minced
1½–2 cups (12–16 fl oz/375–500 ml) chicken stock (see page 295)
salt and freshly ground pepper to taste
1½ cups (6 oz/185 g) freshly grated Parmesan cheese

Trim the ends from the Brussels sprouts and cut the sprouts in half lengthwise. Heat the butter and oil in 1 or 2 sauté pans large enough to hold all the Brussels sprouts in one layer. Add the garlic and cook over low heat to remove the bite, about 2 minutes. Add the Brussels sprouts and chicken stock to a depth of 1½ inches (4 cm) and cover the pan. Simmer until tender-crisp, stirring occasionally, about 5–8 minutes. Season with salt and pepper and top with the cheese. Serve at once.

Brussels Sprouts with Garlic & Parmesan; Celery Root & Potato Purée; Chanterelles, Chestnuts & Pearl Onions with Thyme

TANGERINE CUSTARD TART

MAKES TWO 10-INCH (25-CM) TARTS

Sweet-tart tangerines make an elegant curdlike filling for a festive dessert. Be sure to grate the tangerine zest (see glossary) for the topping before you juice the fruit for the filling.

FOR THE TARTS:

12 egg yolks

1 cup (8 fl oz/250 ml) fresh
  tangerine juice

½ cup (4 fl oz/125 ml) fresh
  lemon juice

1½ cups (12 oz/375 g) granulated
  sugar

8 tablespoons (4 oz/125 g) unsalted
  butter, cut into small bits

grated zest of 6 tangerines

2 tablespoons mandarin orange liqueur

basic pie pastry for a double-crust pie
  shell (recipe on page 299)

FOR THE TOPPING:

2 cups (16 fl oz/500 ml) heavy
  (double) cream

¼ cup (1½ oz/45 g) sifted confectioners' (icing) sugar

grated zest of 4 tangerines

mandarin orange liqueur to taste

To make the filling, combine the egg yolks, juices and sugar in a bowl. Strain into a heavy stainless-steel saucepan or the top part of a double boiler set over, but not touching, simmering water and whisk the mixture constantly until thick. Stir in the butter, zest and mandarin orange liqueur. Cover and chill for at least 3 hours or up to 2 days.

~ Roll out half of the pastry and use it to line a 10-inch (25-cm) tart pan. Repeat with the other half of the pastry. Set the shells aside in the freezer for 30 minutes. Fully bake the pie shells as directed on page 299. Cool completely, then spread equal amounts of tangerine filling in each pie shell.

~ To make the topping, in a bowl whip the cream until it holds soft peaks; beat in the confectioners' sugar, tangerine zest and mandarin orange liqueur. Spread the cream evenly over the top of each pie, filling almost to the edges.

Decorate the dessert table with fresh tangerines arranged with poetic simplicity in a wooden bowl.

Tangerine Custard Tart

Casual Hanukkah Buffet

HANUKKAH, THE FESTIVAL OF LIGHTS, commemorates the rededication of the Temple of Jerusalem some 2,100 years ago. For eight successive evenings in November or December, Jewish families light candles to mark that event. Especially on the first and last nights, they gather together to feast and give gifts.

Appropriate for any convivial get-together in late autumn or winter, our Hanukkah party takes place in a large kitchen, where everyone can savor the warmth and rich aromas. If your kitchen is big enough, by all means use it; at the very least, you can set dishes out on the counter for buffet-style service. We lit candles in a traditional Jewish menorah to mark the start of the meal, but any candlelight will add to the ambience. Displays of fruits and nuts are apt decorations to grace the entire kitchen.

The menorah displays one lighted candle for each night of Hanukkah and an additional candle to light the others.

THIS HEARTY WINTER BUFFET is made up of traditional Eastern European–style dishes that have become as synonymous with Hanukkah as turkey is with Thanksgiving. They belong to the category of comfort foods, excellent for a cold-weather meal any time.

In observation of Jewish dietary laws, we kept the menu free of dairy ingredients. But if you don't keep kosher, feel free to garnish the borscht and latkes with sour cream and the pecan torte with whipped cream.

Once the candles have been lit, you could start the meal by ladling the soup at the table, then ask guests to join you in the kitchen to cook the latkes. Let guests help themselves from the buffet for the main course and dessert.

Menu

Everyday items, such as baskets, pitchers, dried wildflowers and pretty containers, adorn a kitchen counter.

Beet, Cabbage & Mushroom Borscht

Potato Latkes

Chunky Applesauce

Spiced Brisket of Beef

Carrot Tsimmes

Pecan Torte

Tangerine Sorbet

PREPARATION LIST

◆ Two to 3 days ahead, coat the brisket with the spices.

◆ Up to 2 days ahead, make and refrigerate the applesauce to be rewarmed before serving.

◆ The day before, prepare the borscht and make and freeze the sorbet.

◆ The morning of the party, make the torte.

◆ Just before dinner, start the potato latkes.

EACH RECIPE YIELDS 12 SERVINGS.

Potted narcissus, a simple basket of pears and softly glowing candles symbolize the winter season in a dramatic still-life composition.

WINE RECOMMENDATIONS

Many high-quality kosher wines are made today in Israel, France, New York and California. Select one red wine for the meal that is light to medium in body and both spicy and earthy in flavor: a supple Cabernet Sauvignon or an herbal Merlot would work well. With dessert, sip a tawny port or a cream sherry.

BEET, CABBAGE & MUSHROOM BORSCHT

SERVES 12

An Eastern European favorite, this tastes best if made the day before. Supplement any leftovers with extra brisket for the next day's meal.

8–10 large beets (beetroots)
3 tablespoons olive oil
2 large red (Spanish) onions, chopped
6 large carrots, peeled and sliced
2 heads cabbage, shredded
4 cups (12 oz/375 g) sliced
   fresh mushrooms
1 lemon, pricked with a fork in
   several places
10 cups (2½ qt/2.5 l) beef (see page
   294) or vegetable stock
salt and freshly ground pepper to taste
sugar to taste
fresh lemon juice if needed
½ cup (¾ oz/20 g) chopped
   fresh dill

Cut the greens from the beets, leaving about 2 inches (5 cm) of stems attached. Wash the beets well, place them in a pot and cover with cold water. Bring to a boil, then reduce the heat and simmer, uncovered, until tender, about 30–50 minutes, depending on the size of the beets. Drain. Cover the beets with lukewarm water. When cool, slip off the skins and dice the beets. Set aside.

ৡ In a stockpot, warm the olive oil over moderate heat. Add the onions and carrots and cook for about 10 minutes, stirring occasionally. Add the cabbage, beets, mushrooms, lemon and stock; bring to a boil. Reduce the heat and simmer, uncovered, until the soup is red and the flavors are blended, about 30 minutes. Remove the lemon. Season with salt and pepper; adjust the seasoning with sugar and lemon juice if necessary. Sprinkle with chopped dill before serving.

Beet, Cabbage & Mushroom Borscht

POTATO LATKES

MAKES ABOUT 24 POTATO PANCAKES

Grate the potatoes and onions for more robust potato pancakes; dice and purée them for finer-textured results.

2 small onions
6–7 large russet potatoes, peeled
2 large eggs, beaten
2 teaspoons salt
1 teaspoon freshly ground pepper
¾–1 cup (4–5 oz/125–155 g)
   all-purpose (plain) flour
vegetable shortening or oil for frying

Grate the onions and potatoes and place them in a large bowl. Using paper towels, blot up any liquid they might have released and stir in the eggs, salt, pepper and enough flour to bind the mixture.

❧ Heat 2 inches (5 cm) of melted shortening or oil in a large frying pan and drop in spoonfuls of batter. Cook until golden brown, about 3 minutes on each side. Drain on paper towels and keep warm in a 350°F (180°C) oven while cooking the remaining batter. Serve as soon as the last batch is cooked; latkes will stay crisp for only a few minutes.

❧ Alternately, dice the onions and potatoes. Place half of the diced onions and 1 egg in the container of a blender. Purée until liquified. Add half of the diced potatoes and purée until smooth, but not liquified. Transfer the mixture to a bowl. Repeat with the remaining onions, egg and potatoes. Combine the 2 batches in a bowl, add the salt and pepper and blot up any excess liquid with paper towels. Fold in the flour. Cook as directed above.

Potato Latkes; Chunky Applesauce

CHUNKY APPLESAUCE

MAKES 4–5 CUPS (32–40 FL OZ/1–1.2 L)

A traditional companion to potato latkes, this applesauce has a bracing tartness. If you wish, add a little more sugar to taste.

8–10 apples, peeled, cored and cut into
   1-inch (2.5-cm) chunks
juice of 2–3 oranges, about 1 cup
   (8 fl oz/250 ml)
½ cup (4 oz/125 g) sugar or to taste
2 teaspoons grated lemon zest
½ teaspoon ground cinnamon

Place the apples and orange juice in a heavy sauté pan. Cook over moderate heat, stirring often, until the apples start to soften, about 10 minutes. Stir in the sugar, lemon zest and cinnamon and cook, uncovered, until tender but still chunky, about 20–25 minutes. Adjust the seasoning and serve warm. Or cool, cover and refrigerate for up to 2 days. Rewarm before serving.

SPICED BRISKET OF BEEF

SERVES 12

A blend of Middle Eastern spices adds an exotic touch to the classic Jewish braised brisket.

1 brisket of beef, about 10 lb (5 kg)
½ cup (4 oz/125 g) sugar
1 teaspoon ground nutmeg
1 teaspoon ground cloves
1 teaspoon ground allspice
2 tablespoons ground pepper
1 teaspoon ground ginger
6 tablespoons (3 fl oz/90 ml) olive oil
    or chicken fat
salt to taste
12 cups (3 lb/1.5 kg) diced onions
2 cups (16 fl oz/500 ml) beef stock, or
    as needed (see page 294)
2 cups (16 fl oz/500 ml) tomato purée
    (see glossary)

Place the meat in a large glass or plastic container. Combine the sugar, nutmeg, cloves, allspice, pepper and ginger and sprinkle them over the meat. Cover and refrigerate for 2 days, turning once each day. Lift the meat from the marinade and pat dry.

↣ Heat 3 tablespoons of the oil or fat in a large heavy frying pan or on a griddle. Sprinkle the meat with salt and brown on both sides. Set aside.

↣ In a heavy pot large enough to hold the brisket, heat the remaining 3 tablespoons oil or fat and cook the onions until tender and translucent, about 10 minutes. Place the beef atop the onions and cover the pot. Reduce the heat and simmer the brisket for 2 hours. Add the beef stock if the onions and beef haven't exuded enough juices;

you will need about 3 cups (24 fl oz/ 750 ml) of liquid. Add the tomato purée and cook until the meat is tender, about 1 hour longer.

↣ Remove the brisket to a carving board and let rest, covered with aluminum foil, for 10 minutes. Cook the pan juices over medium heat to reduce them if they are too thin or lack flavor. Adjust the seasoning. Slice the meat across the grain and serve with the pan juices.

CARROT TSIMMES

SERVES 12

In Yiddish, the term tsimmes *often describes a messy situation. Add sweet potatoes or dried fruit, if you like, to this flavorful mess.*

1 cup (6 oz/185 g) raisins
3 tablespoons vegetable oil or
    chicken fat
2 onions, sliced thin
24 carrots, peeled and cut into ¼-inch
    (6-mm) slices
6 tablespoons (4 oz/125 g) honey
grated zest of 2 lemons (see glossary)
chicken stock or wine
salt and freshly ground pepper to taste

Soak the raisins in hot water to cover for 10 minutes; drain, reserving the raisin water to use in the tsimmes.

↣ Heat the oil or fat in a large saucepan. Add the sliced onions and cook until tender, about 5 minutes. Add the carrots, honey, lemon zest, raisin water and enough stock or wine to cover the carrots. Bring to a boil, reduce heat, cover and simmer until the carrots are tender, about 10–15 minutes. You may need to add a bit more liquid from time to time. Add the raisins in the last 5 minutes. Season with salt and pepper.

Foil-wrapped chocolate coins, known as gelt, are a traditional Hanukkah party favor, usually given to the children as tokens of prosperity and goodwill. You can set the coins out in a small basket or a net bag, or strew them festively around the table.

Spiced Brisket of Beef; Carrot Tsimmes

*If your plan for this
Hanukkah Buffet includes giving
a small gift, homemade preserves
are a loving reminder of the fruits of
your kitchen. Dress each jar with
an illustrated label showing the
fruit used in the preserve, if possible.
A soft-colored ribbon is all the
wrapping you need. Of course,
top-quality purchased jams are a
delicious present as well.*

PECAN TORTE

MAKES ONE 10-INCH (25-CM) TORTE

*The torte includes tangerine zest to link
it to its accompanying sorbet. At a non-
kosher meal, top it with whipped cream.*

3 cups (12 oz/375 g) chopped pecans
  (see glossary)
1½ cups (12 oz/375 g) sugar
10 eggs, separated
½ cup (4 fl oz/125 ml) fresh
  tangerine juice
grated zest of 3 tangerines (see glossary)
½ cup (2 oz/60 g) sifted all-purpose
  (plain) flour
½ teaspoon salt
1 teaspoon ground cinnamon
chopped candied tangerine peel,
  optional

Preheat an oven to 350°F (180°C).
Oil and flour a 10-inch (25-cm) tube
pan or angel food cake pan and set aside.
❧ Chop the nuts with ½ cup (4 oz/
125 g) of the sugar in a food processor
as finely as possible; do not let it turn
to paste. Set aside.
❧ In the bowl of an electric mixer,
combine the egg yolks and ½ cup
(4 oz/125 g) of the remaining sugar, set
the bowl over hot water and whisk for
a few minutes until warm. Remove
from the hot water and beat on high
speed with the whisk attachment until
the mixture is very thick and pale and
a small amount trailed from the whisk
forms a ribbon on the surface of the
mixture, about 8 minutes. Stir in the
tangerine juice and zest.
❧ In a bowl, toss the nut mixture
with the flour, salt and cinnamon, then

gradually fold these dry ingredients
into the yolks with a rubber spatula.
❧ In a large bowl, beat the egg whites
until soft peaks form. Gradually beat
in the remaining ½ cup (4 oz/125 g)
sugar. Fold the whites into the batter.
Fold in the optional candied peel. Pour
the batter into the prepared pan and
bake until a toothpick inserted in the
center of the cake comes out clean,
about 45 minutes. Let cool in the pan,
then invert onto a plate; slice to serve.

TANGERINE SORBET

MAKES ABOUT 4 CUPS (32 FL OZ/1 L)

*Whole tangerines, at their peak during the
holidays, are traditionally given as gifts to
children at the Hanukkah feast. Be sure
to grate the zest before juicing the fruit.*

4 cups (32 fl oz/1 l) fresh tangerine juice
1½ cups (12 oz/375 g) sugar
1 tablespoon fresh lemon juice
2 tablespoons grated tangerine zest
  (see glossary)

Combine 2 cups (16 fl oz/500 ml) of
the tangerine juice and the sugar in
small saucepan. Cook, stirring occasionally, until the sugar dissolves and the
mixture is clear. Set aside and let cool.
Stir in the remaining tangerine juice
and lemon juice. Add the zest. Freeze in
an ice cream maker according to the
manufacturer's instructions.

Pecan Torte; Tangerine Sorbet

CHRISTMAS SEASON OPEN HOUSE

AT NO OTHER TIME OF YEAR are we more likely to invite friends and family to drop by than during December. Holiday gatherings, whether for traditional gift exchanges or simply to share good cheer, call for a menu that can be prepared in advance and served buffet-style.

Our Christmas season open house takes place in a living room, where guests can comfortably mingle around the tree and beside the hearth. Traditional ornaments play the major role in setting the party's scene. You'll probably want to supplement yours with an abundance of seasonal touches; pine cones, boughs of holly and sprigs of mistletoe, wreaths of various sizes and myriad glowing candles fill the room with warmth and merriment. If you have a fireplace and the weather is cold, keep the flames roaring all day long.

THIS CHRISTMAS BUFFET menu for eighteen is as robust and warming as the season itself. There are light dishes for guests who just want to nibble, as well as hearty recipes for those who want a complete meal.

To arrange separate stations for serving the different dishes, clear coffee tables, side tables and other surfaces in a living room, dining room or den. Present the biscotti, cheese and pâté arranged on platters to welcome newcomers. The pizza, blintzes and duck may be replenished hot from the oven as the afternoon or evening progresses. A variety of other beverages, including a favorite hot cider or cocoa, may be served as well as the wine.

Menu

A punch bowl of cider mulled with citrus zests, sugar and sweet spices offers holiday warmth to guests on arrival.

WINE RECOMMENDATIONS

Offer both white and red. For the white, pour a medium-to-full-bodied assertive wine with notes of spice and earth: a rustic Pinot Blanc or a flinty Chardonnay. For the red, try an Australian Shiraz or a simple French country wine such as Madiran or Corbières. With dessert, offer a Malmsey Madeira or a brown or cream sherry from Spain.

Savory Biscotti

Herbed Cheese Spread

Country Pâté

❧

Potato & Onion Pizza

Mushroom Blintzes

Duck with Lentils

❧

*Chestnut Torte with Chocolate
Mocha Butter Cream*

An ensemble of natural decorations, including pine cones, oranges, fir boughs and cranberries, flanks a log birdhouse to create a miniature winter scene. Finch eggs fill the tiny bird's nest.

PREPARATION LIST

◆ Up to 2 weeks ahead, prepare the pâté.

◆ Up to 2 days ahead, make the biscotti and store them in an airtight container; make and refrigerate the cheese spread.

◆ The day before, roast and cut up the ducks; make the lentils. Refrigerate them separately.

◆ The morning of the party, make and refrigerate the crêpes. Make and refrigerate the torte.

◆ Several hours ahead, make the pizza dough and toppings, to be assembled and baked just before serving.

THE FOLLOWING MENU SERVES 18 GUESTS; FOR A SMALLER PARTY, OFFER FEWER DISHES.

Napkins in a plaid pattern of traditional holiday colors are folded as buffet servers to hold knives and forks.

SAVORY BISCOTTI

MAKES 48 BISCOTTI

Make a double batch so you'll have extra throughout the holidays. Recrisp them on a baking sheet in a 350°F (180°C) oven for 5 minutes.

1 cup (8 oz/250 g) unsalted butter at
    room temperature
1 cup (8 oz/250 g) sugar
6 eggs
2 tablespoons aquavit (see glossary)
4½ cups (1⅓ lb/665 g) all-purpose
    (plain) flour
2 teaspoons salt
1 tablespoon baking powder
¼ cup (2 oz/60 g) toasted cumin
    seeds, crushed (see glossary)
3 tablespoons toasted caraway seeds,
    crushed (see glossary)
2 cups (8 oz/250 g) ground toasted
    walnuts (see glossary)

Preheat an oven to 350°F (180°C). In a large bowl, beat the butter and sugar until fluffy. Add the eggs and aquavit and beat well. Add the flour, salt, baking powder, cumin seeds, caraway seeds and walnuts and mix until blended. Form into 4 oval logs and place on 2 ungreased baking sheets. Bake until golden brown and firm to the touch, about 30 minutes. Remove from the oven and let cool on a rack for about 10 minutes.

☙ Reduce the oven temperature to 250°F (120°C). Cut the logs diagonally into ½-inch (12-mm) slices and lay the slices flat on the baking sheets. Bake until dried, about 8–10 minutes longer. Let cool, then store in an airtight container for up to 2 days, or freeze for longer storage.

HERBED CHEESE SPREAD

MAKES ABOUT 5 CUPS (40 OZ/1.25 KG)

Influenced by Italian, French and Romanian dishes, this creamy spread is also good on pumpernickel bread with watercress and cucumber. It can be made up to 2 days in advance.

3 tablespoons olive oil or unsalted
    butter
1 tablespoon minced garlic
3 cups (15 oz/470 g) crumbled mild
    fresh goat cheese or feta cheese
1–2 cups (8–16 oz/250–500 g) ricotta
¼ cup (⅜ oz/10 g) chopped
    fresh parsley
¼ cup (⅜ oz/10 g) minced
    fresh chives
2 tablespoons finely chopped
    fresh thyme
2 teaspoons freshly ground pepper

In a small frying pan, heat the oil or melt the butter over moderate heat, add the garlic and cook until tender but not colored, about 3 minutes. Transfer to a food processor or blender and add the goat or feta cheese, 1 cup of the ricotta, the parsley, chives, thyme and pepper. Process to combine. Taste and add more ricotta if goat cheese flavor is too strong. Transfer to a small crock or serving dish. Cover and refrigerate until serving time.

Everybody loves crunchy fresh vegetables, especially when served along with rich holiday fare. Present spears of cucumbers and carrots, endive leaves, crisp scallions and cherry tomatoes near the biscotti and herbed cheese spread for guests to snack on. Use double old-fashioned glasses or French confiture jars to hold each kind of crudité upright.

Savory Biscotti; Herbed Cheese Spread

COUNTRY PÂTÉ

MAKES THREE 9- BY 5- BY 3-INCH
(23- BY 13- BY 7.5-CM) PÂTÉS

Weighting is essential to compact these pâtés. Use another loaf pan or a flat object that fits inside the rim, topped with kitchen weights, heavy cans or bricks. Children's building blocks work in a pinch, too.

1 lb (500 g) finely ground veal
2 lb (1 kg) finely ground pork shoulder
½ lb (250 g) pork fat, coarsely ground
2 lb (1 kg) chicken livers
¼ cup (2 fl oz/60 ml) heavy
  (double) cream
½ cup (3 oz/90 g) all-purpose
  (plain) flour
3 eggs
½ cup (4 fl oz/125 ml) Cognac
  or Armagnac
8 large cloves garlic
1 teaspoon ground nutmeg
½ teaspoon ground allspice
½ teaspoon ground ginger
½ teaspoon ground cinnamon

Country Pâté

4 teaspoons salt
2 teaspoons freshly ground pepper
9–12 bay leaves
6 thin sheets pork fat (2 combined should
  be large enough to cover each loaf)
3 large baguettes, sliced (see page 298)
cornichons (see glossary)

Preheat an oven to 400°F (200°C). Oil three 9- by 5- by 3-inch (23- by 13- by 7.5-cm) loaf pans and set aside. Combine the ground veal, ground pork and fat in a large bowl. Combine the livers, cream, flour, eggs, Cognac or Armagnac, garlic, nutmeg, allspice, ginger, cinnamon, salt and pepper in a large food processor (or in a blender, in batches) and purée. Combine with the ground meat and mix until well blended.
❧ Pour the mixture into the prepared loaf pans. Top each loaf with a few bay leaves and 2 sheets of fat cut to fit the pan. Cover the loaf pans with a double thickness of aluminum foil. Place the loaf pans in a large baking pan and add hot water to come halfway up the sides.

❧ Bake for 2 hours. Remove and reserve the aluminum foil. Continue baking until lightly browned, about 20 minutes longer. Remove from the oven and re-cover with the foil. Place another loaf pan on top of each pâté and weight it with heavy tins. Let the pâtés sit until cool. Chill well. These pâtés will keep for about 2 weeks under refrigeration. To serve, unmold the pâtés, slice and offer with baguettes and cornichons.

POTATO & ONION PIZZA

SERVES 18

Instead of mixing prosciutto strips with the onions, thin slices of the ham may be draped over the pizza after baking.

FOR THE CRUST:

1 tablespoon active dry yeast
1¼ cups (10 fl oz/300 ml) warm
  (110°F/43°C) water
3½ cups (1⅛ lb/560 g) unbleached
  all-purpose (plain) flour
⅓ cup (1½ oz/45 g) rye or buckwheat
  flour or an additional ⅓ cup
  (2 oz/60 g) all-purpose (plain) flour
3 tablespoons olive oil
1 teaspoon salt
3 tablespoons finely chopped
  fresh rosemary

FOR THE TOPPING:

8 small red new potatoes
6 tablespoons (3 fl oz/90 ml) olive oil
salt and freshly ground pepper to taste
4 large onions, sliced thin
1 cup (4 oz/125 g) long, thin prosciutto
  strips, optional
cornmeal for sprinkling
1 tablespoon minced garlic
1–1½ cups (4–6 oz/125–185 g)
  grated mozzarella
2 tablespoons chopped fresh sage
  or rosemary
½ cup (2 oz/60 g) freshly grated Parmesan

Potato & Onion Pizza

To make the crust, dissolve the yeast in ½ cup (4 fl oz/125 ml) of the warm water in the bowl of an electric mixer. Add ½ cup (2½ oz/75 g) of the all-purpose (plain) flour and mix to combine. Cover and let sit for about 30 minutes.

❧ Add the remaining all-purpose flour, buckwheat flour, remaining water, olive oil, salt and rosemary and mix well. Beat on low speed with the dough hook attached until the dough leaves the sides of the bowl cleanly, about 10 minutes. Or, to make by hand, knead on a lightly floured board for about 10 minutes, or until the dough is no longer sticky. Transfer the dough to an oiled bowl,

cover with a towel and let rise in a warm place until doubled, about 1 hour.

❧ Meanwhile, to make the topping, preheat an oven to 400°F (200°C). Place the potatoes in a small baking pan. Brush the potatoes with 1 tablespoon of the olive oil, sprinkle with salt and pepper and roast for 25–30 minutes, or until cooked through but firm. Let cool, then cut into ¼-inch-thick (6-mm) slices.

❧ Heat 3 more tablespoons of the oil in a large sauté pan, add the onions and cook, stirring occasionally, until tender and translucent, about 10 minutes. If desired, caramelize the onions (cook them until golden). Season with salt and pepper; stir in the prosciutto, if using.

❧ Turn the dough out onto a lightly floured board. Shape into a ball. Cover and allow to rest in the refrigerator for 30 minutes. Meanwhile, preheat an oven to 475°F (240°C).

❧ Roll and stretch the dough into 1 large rectangle; place on a baking sheet sprinkled with cornmeal. Mix the garlic and the remaining 2 tablespoons oil and spread over the dough. Top with the mozzarella, then with the cooked onions and potatoes. Sprinkle with the chopped sage or rosemary and the Parmesan. Bake until the edges are golden brown and puffed, about 12–15 minutes. Brush the edges of the pizza with additional olive oil to add a shine, if desired.

MUSHROOM BLINTZES

MAKES 36 BLINTZES

In this Russian-inspired dish, thin crêpes, or blini, are folded around a mushroom filling in neat parcels resembling Jewish deli blintzes.

FOR THE CRÊPES:

1 cup (8 fl oz/250 ml) cold water

1 cup (8 fl oz/250 ml) cold milk

4 eggs

½ teaspoon salt

2 cups (8 oz/250 g) sifted all-purpose (plain) flour

¼ cup (2 oz/60 g) unsalted butter, melted

FOR THE FILLING:

8 tablespoons (4 oz/125 g) unsalted butter, plus additional for cooking blintzes

2 cups (10 oz/315 g) finely chopped onions

1½ lb (750 g) fresh mushrooms, chopped coarsely

2 teaspoons minced garlic

4 teaspoons chopped fresh thyme or 5 tablespoons (½ oz/15 g) chopped fresh dill

3–4 tablespoons all-purpose (plain) flour

⅓ cup (3 fl oz/90 ml) Madeira or sherry

½ cup (4 fl oz/125 ml) chicken stock, if needed (see page 295)

salt and freshly ground pepper to taste

TO COOK AND SERVE THE BLINTZES:

12 tablespoons (6 oz/180 g) unsalted butter

sour cream, optional

To make the crêpes, put the water, milk, eggs and salt in a blender or food processor. Add the flour and melted butter and blend until smooth. Cover and let the batter rest in the refrigerator for about 2 hours.

❧ Lightly butter a small (about 7-in/18-cm) crêpe pan or small nonstick sauté pan and place it over moderate heat. Ladle 2 tablespoons of batter into the pan and swirl it around until it coats the bottom of the pan. Let cook for a minute or two until set and not shiny. Loosen the crêpe with a spatula, then flip it or turn it with both hands and cook for 30 seconds on the other side. Slide the crêpe out of the pan. Repeat until all the batter is used, stacking the cooked crêpes.

❧ To make the filling, melt 3 tablespoons of the butter in a sauté pan over moderate heat and cook the onions until tender and translucent, about 10 minutes. Lift out and set aside. Melt the remaining 5 tablespoons (2½ oz/80 g) butter in the pan as needed and cook the mushrooms in batches over very high heat so they don't give off too much liquid, about 5 minutes. Place all the cooked mushrooms in the pan and add the garlic. Cook for 1 minute, return the onions to the pan, add the thyme or dill and flour and cook for 3 minutes, stirring constantly. Add the Madeira or sherry and cook until the mixture holds together, 3–4 minutes; if too dry, add enough stock to moisten. Season with salt and pepper.

❧ To assemble the blintzes, place 2 generous tablespoons of filling in the center of each crêpe. Tuck in the sides and fold the top over the bottom edge to make a neat packet. Repeat until all the filling is used. Melt about 2 tablespoons of the butter in a sauté pan and fry the blintzes in batches of 6 until golden on both sides. Keep warm, covered with aluminum foil. Repeat, adding the remaining butter as needed, until all the blintzes are cooked. Serve with dollops of sour cream, if desired.

DUCK WITH LENTILS

SERVES 18

Based on traditional French and Italian winter fare, this recipe extracts more fat from the ducks by roasting instead of braising them. If you have only one small oven, roast the ducks two at a time.

FOR THE DUCKS:

6 ducks, about 5 lb (2.5 kg) each, necks and wing tips removed and reserved, and excess fat removed

12 cloves garlic, minced

grated zest of 6 large lemons (see glossary)

2 tablespoons salt

2 tablespoons freshly ground pepper

12 fresh thyme or marjoram sprigs

3 lemons, cut into quarters

FOR THE LENTILS:

6 cups (2½ lb/1.25 kg) lentils, preferably French green lentils

14 cups (3½ qt/3.5 l) water

½ cup (4 oz/125 g) unsalted butter

6 large onions, diced, about 6 cups (1½ lb/750 g)

6 large carrots, peeled and cut into ¼-inch (6-mm) dice

3 ribs celery, cut into ¼-inch (6-mm) dice

2 tablespoons minced garlic

1 teaspoon ground cinnamon

2 teaspoons ground cumin

4 pippin or other tart green apples, peeled, cored and diced

2 cups (16 fl oz/500 ml) chicken stock (see page 295)

½ cup (¾ oz/20 g) chopped fresh parsley

3 tablespoons chopped fresh thyme or marjoram

2 tablespoons grated lemon zest (see glossary)

salt and freshly ground pepper to taste

To prepare the ducks, preheat an oven or ovens to 475°F (240°C). Place 2 ducks on a rack in each of 3 large roasting pans. Prick the ducks evenly all over with a fork. Mash together the garlic, lemon zest, salt and pepper and spread this over the inside and outside of the birds. Place the herbs and lemon quarters inside the ducks. Roast until they are tender and well browned and the juices run clear when the thighs are pierced with a knife, about 1 hour. Let sit until cool enough to handle, then cut the ducks into quarters with shears, cutting off and discarding the backbones. Set aside.

❧ Meanwhile, to make the lentils, combine them with the water in a large pot and bring to a boil. Reduce the heat and simmer, covered, until the lentils are tender but still firm to the bite, about 20 minutes for brown lentils, or up to 25–40 minutes for green lentils. Test them every 5–10 minutes for doneness. Remove from the heat and set aside.

❧ Melt the butter in a large sauté pan with high sides and cook the onions, carrots and celery over moderate heat, stirring occasionally, until they are tender, about 15 minutes. Add the garlic, cinnamon, cumin and apples and cook for 1–2 minutes. Add the lentils and their cooking liquid, stock, herbs and lemon zest; cover and simmer until all the flavors are blended, about 5 minutes. Season to taste with salt and pepper and adjust the spices to taste. The duck and the lentils can be cooked to this point up to 1 day ahead and refrigerated separately.

❧ To serve, combine the duck pieces and lentils in a large heatproof casserole, cover with aluminum foil and place in a preheated 400°F (200°C) oven until bubbly and hot, about 25 minutes.

Mushroom Blintzes; Duck with Lentils

CHESTNUT TORTE WITH CHOCOLATE MOCHA BUTTER CREAM

SERVES 12

You could have mugs of cocoa and gingerbread men from the bakery on hand as a dessert snack if you are expecting children at your party.

Chestnuts, synonymous with winter holidays, combine with a chocolate mocha butter cream for an intensely rich dessert. Look for glacéed chestnuts in specialty food shops or an Italian market.

FOR THE TORTE:

6 large eggs, separated
1½ cups (12 oz/375 g) sugar
1 tablespoon vanilla extract (essence)
2 cups (1 lb/500 g) chestnut purée, pushed through a sieve
1 cup (4 oz/125 g) almonds, finely ground

FOR THE CHOCOLATE MOCHA BUTTER CREAM:

8 oz (250 g) bittersweet chocolate
¼ cup (2 fl oz/60 ml) strong coffee
4 egg yolks
1 cup (8 oz/250 g) sugar
⅓ cup (3 fl oz/90 ml) water
1½ cups (12 oz/375 g) unsalted butter, cut into pieces
3 tablespoons dark rum

FOR THE GARNISH:

whole glacéed chestnuts

Preheat an oven to 350°F (180°C). Butter and flour two 8-inch (20-cm) springform pans.

&❧ To prepare the torte, place the egg yolks and 1 cup (8 oz/250 g) of the sugar in the bowl of an electric mixer, set the bowl over hot water and whisk for a few minutes until warm. Remove from the hot water and beat on high speed with the whisk attachment until the mixture is very thick and pale and a small amount trailed from the whisk forms a ribbon on the surface of the mixture, about 8 minutes. Beat in the vanilla, then fold in the chestnut purée and the ground almonds.

&❧ Beat the egg whites until soft peaks form, then gradually beat in the remaining ½ cup (4 oz/125 g) sugar until the mixture is stiff but not dry. Stir one third of the whites into the chestnut mixture, then fold in the rest. Divide the batter between the 2 prepared pans and bake until the cakes are pale gold and pull away from the sides of the pans, about 40–50 minutes. Let cool in the pans on racks. Loosen the edges with a knife and then remove the pan sides.

&❧ To make the butter cream, combine the chocolate and coffee in the top of a double boiler and melt over simmering water. Set aside and keep warm. Place the egg yolks in the bowl of an electric mixer, set the bowl over hot water and whisk for a few minutes until warm. Remove from the hot water and beat on high speed with the whisk attachment until thick and pale.

&❧ Meanwhile, combine the sugar and water in a small saucepan and bring to a boil over high heat, stirring until the sugar dissolves. Boil rapidly until the sugar reaches 236°F (113°C) on a candy thermometer. With the mixer on low speed, gradually beat the hot syrup into the beaten yolks. Fold in the chocolate mixture. Beat in the butter a little at a time. Add the dark rum. Chill until thick enough to spread.

&❧ To assemble, place 1 cake on a serving plate, frost it, then place the second cake on top. Frost the top and sides. Refrigerate until the frosting is set, then bring to room temperature for serving. Top with glacéed chestnuts.

Chestnut Torte with Chocolate Mocha Butter Cream

HERITAGE CHRISTMAS DINNER

MOST OF US LAVISH MORE attention on the Yuletide dinner than on any other meal of the year. Whether celebrated on Christmas Eve or Christmas Day, or both, the occasion brings back memories of holidays past and we usually turn faithfully to family traditions when planning the meal.

We set our Christmas dinner in a formal dining room alongside a roaring fire. Rather than conceal the table's beautiful wood surface, we placed an ornate fabric runner down its center; an extra-wide ribbon would work as well. We decked the mantel and table with wreaths, bouquets of pine and lilies, silver bowls filled with cranberries and strands of colored beads. Our Christmas tree centerpiece is a variation on the easy-to-make Holiday Tree (see page 314). You could make a large one for the main table and smaller ones to go alongside, as shown on these pages.

China accented in gold gleams at a holiday place setting decorated with fresh cranberries and golden beads.

FOR CHRISTMAS MENU INSPIRATION, we looked to the Old World, including dishes that have been handed down to us through the generations. The recipes that follow reflect a diversity of European cuisines, with an appetizer and dessert from France, an Italian-inspired salad and side dishes and a traditional English roast beef.

During this busy time of year, careful organization is essential to enjoying the holidays. It's a good idea to begin planning Christmas dinner at least several weeks in advance by reading through the preparation list and recipes. To ensure that you get the best prime or choice beef roast, order it well ahead of time from a quality butcher shop.

Menu

Achieve lavish results with little effort by attaching gold ornaments to calla lilies and holiday greens.

Onion Tart

Radicchio, Fennel & Walnut Salad

Rib-Eye Roast
with Mustard & Black Pepper

Winter Greens
with Pancetta & Mint

Potato & Sage Gratin

Apple Charlotte
with Brandied Whipped Cream
& Apricot Sauce

PREPARATION LIST

♦ The day before, make the tart crust.

♦ The morning of the dinner, make the charlotte, to be rewarmed and unmolded before serving.

♦ Up to 3 hours before dinner, coat the roast with its seasoning spread; prepare the salad ingredients and the dressing.

♦ Up to 2 hours ahead, assemble the gratin.

♦ Just before serving, cook the winter greens and toss the salad.

EACH RECIPE YIELDS 6 SERVINGS.

Baby pears, lady apples, artichokes and seasonal berries and greens are affixed to an artificial base for this variation on the Holiday Tree (page 314).

WINE RECOMMENDATIONS

Begin with a white from the Pacific Northwest, such as an Oregon Pinot Gris or, if you prefer red wine, a Pinot Noir. With the beef, pour an elegant, full-bodied Bordeaux, or an aged Rhône such as Châteauneuf-du-Pape. After dessert, pass quality Calvados or Cognac.

ONION TART

MAKES ONE 9-INCH (23-CM) TART

Serve slices of this classic French quiche as a first course with the radicchio and fennel salad.

basic pie pastry for a single-crust pie
   shell (recipe on page 299)
1½ lb (750 g) large onions
¼ cup (2 oz/60 g) unsalted butter
2 tablespoons oil
salt, freshly ground pepper and ground
   nutmeg to taste
4 eggs
1½ cups (12 fl oz/375 ml) heavy
   (double) cream

Roll out the pastry dough and use it
to line a 9-inch (23-cm) pie pan. Flute
the edges and set the shell aside in
the freezer for 30 minutes or overnight.
↋ Peel the onions, cut them into
quarters and slice thin. Heat the butter
and oil in a large sauté pan over
moderate-low heat. Add the onions and
cook, stirring occasionally, until they are
golden brown and starting to caramelize,
about 30 minutes. Season the onions with
salt, pepper and nutmeg.
↋ Preheat an oven to 375°F (190°C).
Place the onions in the bottom of the
pie shell. In a bowl, beat together the
eggs and cream and season with salt and
pepper. Pour the mixture over the
onions and bake the tart on the middle
rack of the oven until set and golden,
30–40 minutes. Let sit for 10 minutes,
then slice and serve.

RADICCHIO, FENNEL & WALNUT SALAD

SERVES 6

Italian in style, this pretty salad combines mildly bitter and sweet tastes that nicely counterpoint the onion tart.

3 heads radicchio
3 small fennel bulbs
6 tablespoons (3 fl oz/90 ml) toasted
   walnut oil
2 tablespoons olive oil
3–4 tablespoons balsamic vinegar
salt and freshly ground pepper to taste
1 cup (4 oz/125 g) toasted walnuts
   (see glossary)

Trim the ends from the radicchio and
separate the leaves. Wash well if sandy
and dry well. Remove the tubular
stems from the fennel and cut the bulbs
into quarters; remove the hard center
cores and any discolored outer portions. Slice thin.
↋ In a bowl, combine the walnut
oil, olive oil and vinegar to taste with
a whisk. Season to taste with salt and
pepper. Marinate the walnuts in ¼ cup
(2 fl oz/60 ml) of the vinaigrette for
15 minutes. Toss the radicchio, fennel
and walnuts in the remaining vinaigrette.
Divide among 6 salad plates.

The facets of a cut-glass decanter highlight the deep color and clarity of fine red wine poured to accompany the Christmas dinner.

Onion Tart; Radicchio, Fennel & Walnut Salad

RIB-EYE ROAST WITH MUSTARD & BLACK PEPPER

SERVES 6

To ensure perfectly cooked beef, use an instant-read meat thermometer. You should have plenty left over for sandwiches.

FOR THE ROAST:
4–5 lb (2–2.5 kg) rib-eye roast
4 cloves garlic, cut into slivers
1 cup (8 oz/250 g) Dijon mustard
¼ cup (2 fl oz/60 ml) soy sauce
4 tablespoons (2 oz/60 g) coarsely
   ground or cracked pepper

FOR THE SAUCE:
¼ cup (2 oz/60 g) Dijon mustard
1 tablespoon soy sauce
1 cup (8 fl oz/250 ml) beef stock (see
   page 294)
1 tablespoon cracked pepper

To prepare the roast, cut incisions at even intervals in the surface of the meat and insert slivers of garlic. Place the meat in a roasting pan. Combine the mustard and soy sauce and spread the mixture over the roast. Top with the pepper. Let the roast sit at room temperature for up to 3 hours.

❧ Preheat an oven to 350°F (180°C). Roast the meat until a meat thermometer inserted in the center of the roast reads 120°F (50°C) for rare, about 1½ hours. Remove from the oven and let rest on a carving board, covered with aluminum foil, for 15 minutes.

❧ To make the sauce, in a small pan combine the mustard, soy sauce, beef stock and pepper with a whisk and heat through. Or, pour the stock into the degreased drippings in the roasting pan and stir to free any browned bits. Whisk in the mustard, soy sauce and pepper.

Rib-Eye Roast with Mustard & Black Pepper;
Potato & Sage Gratin; Winter Greens with Pancetta & Mint

WINTER GREENS WITH PANCETTA & MINT

SERVES 6

Mint and pancetta perfectly offset the mild bitterness of the greens. Make this at the absolute last moment for the freshest color and taste.

¼ cup (2 fl oz/60 ml) olive oil
8 slices bacon or pancetta (see glossary),
   about ¼ inch (6 mm) thick,
   cut into dice or small strips
1 large onion, chopped, about 2 cups
   (8 oz/250 g)
3 cloves garlic, minced
¼ cup (2 fl oz/60 ml) red wine
   vinegar
1½ lb (750 g) well-washed greens
   (dandelion, kale, chard, mustard
   greens or a combination), stemmed
   and cut into thin strips
salt and freshly ground pepper to taste
6 tablespoons chopped fresh mint

Heat the olive oil in a large sauté pan with high sides. Add the diced bacon or pancetta and cook until translucent but not browned, about 3 minutes. Add the onion and cook until soft, about 8 minutes. Add the garlic and cook for 1–2 minutes. Add the vinegar and greens and cover the pan. Cook the greens until wilted, stirring occasionally, about 5 minutes. Season with salt and pepper and stir in the fresh mint just before serving.

POTATO & SAGE GRATIN

SERVES 6

Fresh sage leaves and a hint of nutmeg perfume this classic dish of sliced and baked potatoes.

3 cups (24 fl oz/750 ml) heavy
   (double) cream
4 cloves garlic, sliced
8–10 fresh sage leaves, chopped, plus
   whole sage leaves for garnish
1½ teaspoons salt
1 teaspoon freshly ground pepper
¼ teaspoon ground nutmeg
6 large white boiling potatoes

Preheat an oven to 375°F (190°C). Butter a 12-cup (3-qt/3-l) baking dish. In a saucepan, bring the cream to a boil with the garlic and sage. Lower the heat and simmer for 15 minutes. Season with salt, pepper and nutmeg.

❧ Peel and slice the potatoes ¼ inch (6 mm) thick. Layer the potatoes in overlapping rows in the baking dish and pour the cream with sage and garlic over them. The cream should just cover the potatoes; if not, add a bit more. Cover with aluminum foil and set aside for up to 2 hours. Bake for 30 minutes, then remove the foil and continue to bake until potatoes are tender but still hold their shape, about 20 minutes longer. Garnish with a few whole sage leaves to serve.

Gold tones set the theme for a beguiling display of presents. Yet these elegant touches need not be costly. Use widely available Christmas ribbon, beads and ornaments in amber hues. To make pine cones gleam like treasures, spray them lightly with gold paint. Tuck a favorite card in a gilded mirror or picture frame.

APPLE CHARLOTTE WITH BRANDIED WHIPPED CREAM & APRICOT SAUCE

SERVES 6

For the most festive presentation, prepare the charlotte in a large mold. The apple purée must be very thick to support the bread casing, so cook it until you get the right consistency.

FOR THE CHARLOTTE:

12 McIntosh, Empire or Rome Beauty apples, peeled, cored and cubed
12 tablespoons (6 oz/180 g) unsalted butter, melted
¾ cup (6 oz/185 g) granulated sugar
½ teaspoon ground cinnamon
1 tablespoon grated lemon zest
1 teaspoon vanilla extract (essence)
12–15 slices white bread, about ¼ inch (6 mm) thick, crusts removed

FOR THE BRANDIED WHIPPED CREAM:

1 cup (8 fl oz/250 ml) heavy (double) cream
¼ cup (1½ oz/45 g) sifted confectioners' (icing) sugar
3 tablespoons brandy, optional

FOR THE APRICOT SAUCE:

1 cup (8 oz/250 g) apricot jam
¼ cup (2 fl oz/60 ml) water
¼ cup (2 fl oz/60 ml) brandy, optional

FOR THE GARNISH:

apricot halves, optional
orange peel, optional

Preheat an oven to 425°F (220°C). In a large, heavy sauté pan over moderate heat, cook the apples with 2 tablespoons of the butter for about 5 minutes. Add the sugar, cinnamon and lemon zest and combine well. Cook until the apples break down into a very thick purée, about 15 minutes. Stir in the vanilla. If the apples are very tart, add a bit more sugar. You should have about 5–6 cups (40–48 fl oz/1.2–1.5 l) apple purée.

❧ Cut the bread into pieces to fit the bottom and sides of a 6-cup (48-fl oz/1.5-l) round charlotte mold or soufflé dish. Dip the bread in the remaining melted butter and place, without overlapping, on the bottom and sides of the mold or dish. Spoon in the apple mixture and top with the remaining bread.

❧ Bake on the lower rack of the oven for 10 minutes, then reduce the oven temperature to 350°F (180°C) and bake until the bread is golden, about 30 minutes longer. Let the charlotte sit for 30 minutes before unmolding. (Or let sit for several hours, then rewarm in a low oven, then unmold.)

❧ To make the brandied whipped cream, in a bowl beat the cream and sugar until it forms soft peaks. Fold in the brandy, if desired. To make the apricot sauce, stir together the jam and water in a small saucepan and warm over low heat. Stir in the brandy if desired. Top the charlotte with some of the whipped cream and serve with the remaining whipped cream and the apricot sauce. Garnish with the apricot halves and orange peel, if desired.

Apple Charlotte with Brandied Whipped Cream & Apricot Sauce

NEW YEAR'S EVE FOR SIX

WITH THE NEW YEAR COMES A SPIRIT of optimism and an eager anticipation of new achievements, of resolutions soon to be fulfilled. As a result, New Year's Eve celebrations can be the most sparkling events of the year. This is a good time to invite your closest friends for a celebratory evening that doesn't end until well after midnight.

To observe New Year's Eve in style, we planned a sit-down dinner for six, to be served late in the evening. We selected elegant floral arrangements, including white tulips, roses, narcissus and orchids with green hydrangeas and bay laurel, but you can use any kind of blossoms, greens, or potted plants to make the setting as informal or formal as you wish. A party favor, wrapped in silver foil and streamers, adds intrigue to each place setting.

TO HIGHLIGHT THE once-a-year mood of New Year's, we chose to splurge with a menu featuring duck livers, lobster, shrimp, scallops and crème brulée, the richest of custards. The star of the meal is a hands-on bouillabaisse, the classic Provençal fish soup. For this course, you might want to provide your guests with over-sized bib napkins to use.

To help you put together this special meal, consult the preparation list at right and the tips given with each recipe. The soup can be pre-pared in steps so that the last-minute cooking is minimal. You could also serve fewer dishes or incorporate recipes from other menus in this book, if you like. The most important thing is to plan the evening so that you can enjoy the revelries as much as your guests.

Menu

A richly polished dining table reflects the elegance of fine silver, china, crystal and white floral arrangements.

WINE RECOMMENDATIONS

Start with a non-vintage brut Champagne, or a sparkling wine from California or Spain. Then move on to either a Chardonnay-based cuvée Champagne, or, if you want a still wine, a bracing white such as French Muscadet or Chablis. With dessert and midnight toasting, pour an extra-dry or demi-sec sparkling wine or Champagne.

*Duck Livers
with Apple-Ginger Butter*

Rice Croquettes

❧

Winter Bouillabaisse

Green Salad

❧

Blood Orange Crème Brulée

Ginger Florentines

*A side table holds a silver coffee service. Beside it,
leather-bound books form a casually elegant backdrop.*

PREPARATION LIST

◆ The day before, prepare the apple-ginger butter; assemble the croquettes; make the florentines and store them in an airtight container.

◆ The morning of the party, make the soup base, prepare and refrigerate the aïoli and the rouille and clean the seafood for the bouillabaisse. Make the crème brulée custard.

◆ One hour before, prepare the potatoes, fennel and bread for the soup.

◆ Fifteen minutes before guests arrive, cook the livers and croquettes. Bring the soup base to a simmer. Just before serving, finish the soup and the crème brulée.

EACH RECIPE YIELDS 6 SERVINGS.

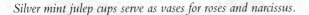

Silver mint julep cups serve as vases for roses and narcissus.

DUCK LIVERS WITH APPLE-GINGER BUTTER

SERVES 6

Perfumed by the apples and ginger, the duck livers make an unforgettable hors d'oeuvre for a special occasion.

about 6 tablespoons (3 oz/90 g) unsalted butter
1 small apple, peeled, cored and finely chopped
one 2-inch (5-cm) piece fresh ginger, peeled and grated
2 tablespoons Calvados (see glossary)
salt and freshly ground pepper to taste
12 large duck or chicken livers

In a small sauté pan, melt 2 tablespoons of the butter. Add the apple and ginger and cook until the apple is very soft, about 10–15 minutes. Add the Calvados and cook 1–2 minutes longer. Transfer the mixture to a blender or food processor and purée. Add about 4 tablespoons (2 oz/60 g) of the remaining butter or enough to make a thick, creamy compound. Season with salt and pepper. This butter may be made up to 1 day ahead of time, covered and refrigerated, then softened at room temperature before serving.

≈ Trim the livers carefully of fat and sinew; thread on skewers and sprinkle with salt and pepper. Preheat a broiler (griller). Broil the livers, turning once, until browned on the outside and medium rare in the center, about 2 minutes on each side. Remove the livers from the skewers, place 2 on each plate and top equally with the apple-ginger butter.

RICE CROQUETTES

MAKES 12–16 CROQUETTES

In Italy, these croquettes are known as suppli al telefono, or "telephone wires," which aptly describes the strings formed by biting into their cheese filling.

2 cups (16 fl oz/500 ml) lightly salted water
1 cup (7 oz/220 g) Arborio rice
2 eggs, beaten
5 tablespoons (1¼ oz/35 g) freshly grated Parmesan cheese
salt, freshly ground pepper and ground nutmeg to taste
8 ounces (250 g) fresh mozzarella cheese, cut into 12–16 small cubes
1 tablespoon chopped fresh marjoram or sage
¾ cup (3 oz/90 g) dried bread crumbs
peanut oil for deep-frying

In a saucepan, bring the water to a boil and stir in the rice; reduce heat and simmer, covered, until it has absorbed all the water and is cooked through but still sticky, about 20 minutes. Stir in the eggs and Parmesan and season with salt, pepper and nutmeg. Spread out evenly in an oiled baking sheet with sides and cool in the refrigerator.

≈ Line a baking sheet with baking parchment and set aside. Roll the cheese cubes in the chopped herb. Scoop up a heaping tablespoonful of the rice, make a well in it and tuck a piece of mozzarella in the center. Push the rice over the cheese and form it into a ball about 1½ inches (4 cm) in diameter. Repeat until all the rice is used. Dip the croquettes in the bread crumbs, place on the lined baking sheet and refrigerate until just before serving (up to 1 day).

≈ To serve, heat about 3 inches (7.5 cm) of peanut oil in a deep-fat fryer or wok to 350°F (180°C). Drop in a few croquettes at a time and fry until golden brown, lifting them in and out of the oil a few times with a slotted spoon so that the cheese will have time to melt in the center before the croquettes get too brown. Drain on paper towels and keep warm in a low oven for no more than 10 minutes before serving. Repeat until all the croquettes are cooked; serve at once.

New Year's Eve is synonymous with effervescence, so position iced champagne and several crystal flutes near the entryway, then pour a welcoming glassful for each guest as he or she arrives.

Rice Croquettes; Duck Livers with Apple-Ginger Butter

WINTER BOUILLABAISSE

SERVES 6

While shellfish are not traditionally used in bouillabaisse, for New Year's Eve they make it seem especially festive. Use as much as you can afford. If you don't eat shellfish, leave it out and increase the fish to 3 pounds (1.5 kg) total.

The key to success with this dish is organization. Make the soup base, rouille and aïoli the morning of the party and boil the lobster and crab (or purchase already cooked ones from your fishmonger), then prepare all the fish and shellfish and chill it (debeard mussels just before cooking). The ingredients for the accompaniments can be cooked up to an hour before eating. At the last minute, reheat the soup base and add the seafood.

FOR THE SOUP BASE:

¼ cup (2 fl oz/60 ml) olive oil

2 leeks, cut in half lengthwise and rinsed well, thinly sliced

2 large onions, diced, about 2 cups (8 oz/250 g)

2–3 ribs celery, diced

6 cloves garlic, minced

3–4 strips orange zest, ½ inch (12 mm) wide and 3 inches (7.5 cm) long (see glossary)

¼ teaspoon saffron threads, steeped in ¼ cup (2 fl oz/60 ml) white wine

12 fresh thyme sprigs

2 bay leaves

1 tablespoon ground fennel seed

½–1 teaspoon red pepper flakes

3 cups (1⅛ lb/560 g) drained and diced canned plum tomatoes

12 cups (3 qt/3 l) fish stock (see recipe on page 294) or 6 cups (48 fl oz/1.5 l) *each* chicken stock (see page 295) and bottled clam juice

salt and freshly ground pepper to taste

FOR THE ROUILLE:

3 slices bread, crusts removed, torn up

4 cloves garlic, minced very fine

1 teaspoon cayenne pepper

2 tablespoons tomato paste

6 tablespoons (3 fl oz/90 ml) olive oil

fish stock or bottled clam juice as needed

FOR THE BOUILLABAISSE:

2 lb (1 kg) boneless, skinless angler, flounder, bass or snapper cut into 3- by 2-inch (7.5- by 5-cm) chunks

1 live Atlantic (Maine) lobster, 1½ lb (750 g), boiled for 10 minutes, cleaned, cracked and cut into chunks (see glossary)

1 large crab, boiled for 10 minutes, cleaned, cracked and cut into chunks

18 large shrimp, shelled and deveined

18 sea scallops

about 1 cup dry white wine

2 lb (1 kg) mussels, scrubbed well and debearded (see glossary)

½ cup (¾ oz/20 g) chopped fresh parsley

¼ cup (⅜ oz/10 g) chopped fennel fronds

FOR THE ACCOMPANIMENTS:

3 fennel bulbs, quartered, cored and blanched until tender

18 very small potatoes, boiled

12 slices toasted French bread, rubbed with garlic

1 cup (8 oz/250 g) aïoli (recipe on page 295), optional

To make the soup base, heat the olive oil in a large, heavy pot. Add the leeks, onions and celery and cook until tender, about 10–15 minutes. Add the garlic, orange zest, saffron and wine, thyme, bay leaves, fennel seed, red pepper flakes, tomatoes and stock and bring to a boil. Reduce the heat; simmer until flavors are melded, about 15 minutes. Season with salt and pepper. Refrigerate, uncovered, until serving time.

❧ To make the rouille, combine the bread, garlic, cayenne and tomato paste in a blender or food processor. With the motor running, gradually pour in the oil. Transfer to a bowl and stir in enough fish stock or clam juice to make a spoonable sauce. Cover and refrigerate until serving time.

❧ To make the bouillabaisse, bring the soup base to a simmer. Add the fish and cook about 2 minutes; add the lobster, crab and shrimp and cook 2 minutes longer, then add the scallops and cook until all the seafood is firm, about 2 minutes longer. Meanwhile, in a large sauté pan, bring the wine to a boil. Add the mussels, reduce the heat, cover and steam until the mussels open, about 6–8 minutes; discard any unopened mussels. Add the mussels and their cooking liquid to the bouillabaisse. Ladle into soup bowls and top with chopped parsley and fennel fronds. Serve the rouille, fennel, potatoes, French bread and, if using, aïoli, in bowls alongside to add as desired.

After the soup, you could offer a fresh salad of mixed winter greens including crisp lettuces, frisée and radicchio.

Winter Bouillabaisse

Blood Orange Crème Brulée; Ginger Florentines

BLOOD ORANGE CRÈME BRULÉE

SERVES 6

Use regular oranges if you can't find blood oranges for this extra-rich custard.

1 cup (8 fl oz/250 ml) fresh-squeezed
    blood orange or regular orange juice
½ cup (4 fl oz/125 ml) Grand Marnier
    or other orange-flavored liqueur
2 cups (16 fl oz/500 ml) heavy
    (double) cream
grated zest of 2 blood oranges or
    regular oranges (see glossary)
¾ cup (6 oz/185 g) plus 2 table-
    spoons sugar
6 egg yolks, beaten

In a small saucepan, combine the orange juice and liqueur and cook over high heat to reduce to ½ cup (4 fl oz/125 ml). Set aside. In another small saucepan, combine the cream, orange zest and 6 tablespoons of the sugar. Bring to a simmer, stirring, over moderate heat. Remove from heat and cover. Let steep for 30 minutes.

❧ Preheat an oven to 300°F (150°C). Place the egg yolks in a bowl and stir in the cream mixture. Add the juice and liqueur. Pour the mixture into one 5-cup (40–fl oz/1.2-l) shallow baking dish or six small (6–fl oz/180 ml) rame-kins. Place in a baking pan and add hot water to come halfway up the sides of the custard container(s). Bake until just set, 45–60 minutes. Remove from the baking pan and place in the refrigerator. When cold, cover and chill thoroughly.

❧ To serve, preheat a broiler (griller). Sprinkle the remaining sugar over the custard(s). Place under a very hot broiler until the sugar has caramelized, about 3–4 minutes. Let sit until the melted sugar has hardened, then serve.

GINGER FLORENTINES

MAKES 12 DOUBLE COOKIES

Candied ginger adds an exotic flair to these crisp-textured, lacy cookies.

4 tablespoons (2 oz/60 g) unsalted butter
1½ cups (6 oz/185 g) sliced almonds
½ cup (4 oz/125 g) sugar
⅓ cup (3 fl oz/90 ml) heavy (double) cream
¼ cup (3 oz/90 g) honey
¼ cup (1 oz/30 g) chopped candied
    orange peel
¼ cup (1½ oz/45 g) candied ginger
½ teaspoon vanilla extract (essence)
¼ teaspoon ground cinnamon
¼ cup (1½ oz/45 g) all-purpose
    (plain) flour
4 oz (125 g) bittersweet chocolate

Preheat an oven to 325°F (170°C). In a small saucepan, melt 2 tablespoons of the butter. Line 2 baking sheets with baking parchment and brush the paper with the melted butter. Chop 1 cup (4 oz/125 g) of the almonds. Finely chop the remaining almonds in a food proces-sor or blender; do not let it turn to paste.

❧ In a small, deep saucepan, place the sugar, cream, honey and remaining 2 tablespoons butter. Bring to a boil, stir-ring once or twice, and cook until a candy thermometer reads 238°F (114°C). Stir in the candied orange peel, candied ginger, vanilla, cinnamon, flour and almonds. Let cool; then drop by the teaspoonful onto the baking sheets, leaving 3 inches (7.5 cm) between each cookie. Flatten with a fork or spread out with a spoon.

❧ Bake until golden brown, about 12 minutes. Let cool on the pans for several minutes, then transfer to racks. Mean-while, melt the chocolate in the top of a double boiler over simmering water. Coat one side of each cookie with chocolate and top with a second cookie.

NEW YEAR'S BUFFET

THE FIRST DAY OF THE NEW YEAR calls for entertaining of the most relaxed kind. With that in mind, we planned a late-lunch party of familiar, easy-to-eat foods that could be enjoyed while watching televised parades or sports. Whether you gather midday or in early evening, it's easiest to set the dishes on a coffee table near the fire or the television and let guests serve themselves. To promote a cozier feeling, we pulled in sofas and chairs from around the room.

In keeping with the casual feel of this menu, everyday dishware, cutlery and napkins are the best choice; stack them close by the food. There's no need to fuss over decorations, either. We used a few palm fronds and banana leaves to bring a touch of tropical warmth to the room and incorporated them into the personal items already on display.

A serene study in Asian artifacts is an oasis of calm.

Menu

THE FOLLOWING BUFFET MENU is particularly appealing for holiday entertaining because most of it can be made ahead of time and finished just before the guests arrive. These dishes are so versatile, you also could serve them for a New Year's Eve party, an après-ski gathering or a Sunday supper. In fact, any chilly day of the year would be appropriate for this medley of soup, salad and sandwiches.

You could begin the meal with bowls of black bean soup set atop dinner plates; place the quesadillas alongside. These plates can then be used for the sandwiches, potatoes and salad, while dessert can be eaten out of hand. The plan for this party is to make life easy for both the guests and the host, a great way to start the year.

A wooden planter, left on the deck or moved inside,
becomes an ice chest for beer and mineral water.

Quesadillas

*Black Bean Soup
with Dark Rum & Orange Zest*

❧

Barbecued Chicken Sandwiches

Sweet & White Potato Gratin

*Spinach Salad with Pecans
& Balsamic Vinaigrette*

❧

Chocolate Pound Cake

PREPARATION LIST

◆ Up to 1 month ahead, make and refrigerate the barbecue sauce.

◆ The day before, make the soup and bake the pound cake.

◆ The morning of the party, wash and stem the spinach and prepare the dressing; assemble the quesadillas, to be fried before serving.

◆ Up to several hours before, assemble and bake the potato gratin, to be rewarmed before serving.

EACH RECIPE YIELDS 12 SERVINGS.

WINE RECOMMENDATIONS

To complement the somewhat spicy food, select a slightly smoky red wine loaded with ripe fruit, such as Zinfandel or Burgundy. If you wish to continue toasting the new year, pour a rose Champagne or sparkling wine. Beer could also be enjoyed throughout the meal; choose a medium-bodied amber ale or lager. For dessert, add a dash of Kahlúa to the coffee.

*Set out some classic games, along with mugs of coffee,
to amuse guests all afternoon long.*

285

Quesadillas

SERVES 12

One of the great snacks of Mexico, these filled tortillas are the Latin American equivalent of the grilled cheese sandwich.

6 large fresh poblano chili peppers
6 ripe avocados
6 cups (1½ lb/750 g) grated Monterey jack cheese
24 flour tortillas
2 cups (6 oz/185 g) finely chopped green (spring) onions
½ cup (¾ oz/20 g) finely chopped cilantro (fresh coriander)
salt and freshly ground pepper to taste
salsa, optional

Roast, peel and derib the peppers as directed in the glossary. Cut the flesh into ¼-inch (6-mm) dice.

☙ Cut the avocados in half, remove the pit, scoop from the shell with a large spoon and cut into thin slices.

☙ Spread about ¼ cup (1 oz/30 g) grated cheese over half of each tortilla. Top equally with some diced peppers, a few slices of avocado, the minced green onions and cilantro; sprinkle with salt and pepper. Fold each tortilla gently in half without pressing down on it or it will crack. Repeat until all the ingredients are used. Cover and refrigerate until ready to cook (up to several hours).

☙ Place a griddle or large frying pan over medium-high heat and lightly oil it. Place as many filled tortillas as can fit on the griddle or in the pan, weight slightly with a pan lid and cook until golden brown on each side, turning once. Repeat until all the quesadillas are cooked. If desired, cut each quesadilla in half and serve with salsa.

Black Bean Soup with Dark Rum & Orange Zest

SERVES 12

Robust and warming, this Caribbean-style soup gains an unusual twist from rum and citrus.

6 cups (2½ lb/1.25 kg) dried black beans
12 cups (3 qt/3 l) cold water
1 ham bone or hock or prosciutto bone
3 tablespoons olive oil
3 large onions, diced, about 6 cups (1½ lb/750 g)
8 cloves garlic, minced
1½ teaspoons ground cinnamon
½ teaspoon ground cloves
1 teaspoon ground cumin
2 teaspoons dry mustard dissolved in 1 tablespoon sherry vinegar
2 tablespoons grated orange zest (see glossary)
½ cup (4 fl oz/125 ml) dark rum
1 cup (8 fl oz/250 ml) fresh orange juice
salt and freshly ground pepper to taste
sour cream, optional
thin slices of orange, optional

Pick over the beans to remove any debris. Soak the beans overnight in water to cover amply. Drain. Place the beans in a large pot, add the cold water and the hock or bone and bring to a boil. Reduce the heat to a simmer.

☙ In a large sauté pan, heat the olive oil. Add the onions and cook until tender, about 10 minutes. Add the garlic, cinnamon, cloves, cumin, mustard mixed with vinegar, and orange zest and cook 2 more minutes. Add this mixture to the beans. Cook, partially covered, until the beans are very ten-

der, about 60 minutes. Remove the bone or ham hock and discard. Purée the soup in batches in a blender or a food processor. If desired, cool, cover and refrigerate for up to 1 day.

☙ Return the soup to the heat and bring to a boil. Stir in the rum and orange juice. Season well with salt and pepper. Ladle into bowls and garnish each serving with sour cream and a thin slice of orange, if desired.

Plan on potting flowering bulbs in a large urn or stoneware vase early in the season so they'll be in full bloom on New Year's Day.

Quesadillas; Black Bean Soup with Dark Rum & Orange Zest

BARBECUED CHICKEN SANDWICHES

MAKES 12 SANDWICHES

Serve the sandwiches either open-faced or closed, slathered with as much barbecue sauce as you like. If made without the optional orange or lemon juice, this sauce will keep for several months under refrigeration.

FOR THE BARBECUE SAUCE:

2 tablespoons dry mustard
3 tablespoons chili powder
1 teaspoon ground ginger
½ cup (4 fl oz/125 ml) cider vinegar
1½ cups (12 fl oz/375 ml) tomato
  purée (see glossary)
2 tablespoons Worcestershire sauce
½ cup (3½ oz/105 g) light brown
  sugar, packed
½ cup (4 fl oz/125 ml) fresh orange
  juice or ¼ cup (2 fl oz/60 ml) fresh
  lemon juice, optional
1 tablespoon freshly ground pepper
cayenne pepper and salt to taste

FOR THE SANDWICHES:

12 boneless, skinless chicken breast
  halves
12 sandwich rolls, such as Kaiser rolls
  or poppy-seed rolls

To make the barbecue sauce, in a small bowl combine the mustard, chili powder and ginger and moisten with some of the vinegar. When smooth and dissolved, add the remaining vinegar. In a medium saucepan, stir together the tomato purée, Worcestershire sauce, brown sugar and, if desired, orange or lemon juice. Whisk in the vinegar mixture. Bring to a boil, reduce heat and simmer for 5 minutes. If the sauce seems too thick, thin it with a little water. Season with the ground pepper, cayenne and salt to taste. Cover and refrigerate until ready to serve.

❧ To make the sandwiches, preheat a broiler (griller) and broil the chicken breasts, brushing occasionally with the barbecue sauce, until cooked through, about 3 minutes on each side. Reheat the barbecue sauce in a small saucepan. Cut the chicken into ¼-inch (6-mm) slices. Dip in the sauce and place on the rolls. Or, serve the sauce alongside.

SWEET & WHITE POTATO GRATIN

SERVES 12

Its slight edge of sweetness makes this side dish of sliced and baked potatoes a nice complement to the barbecue sandwiches.

6 cups (48 fl oz/1.5 l) heavy
  (double) cream
6 cloves garlic, smashed with the flat
  of a knife
salt, freshly ground pepper and ground
  nutmeg to taste
6 large russet potatoes
6 large yams

Preheat an oven to 375°F (190°C). In a saucepan, bring the cream to a boil with the garlic, lower the heat and simmer for 10 minutes. Remove the garlic and season the cream with salt, pepper and nutmeg to taste. The mixture should be a little salty, as the potatoes are very bland and will absorb the cream and salt.

❧ While the cream is simmering, peel and slice the potatoes and yams ¼ inch (6 mm) thick. Layer the potatoes and yams in overlapping rows in a deep baking dish or lasagne pan. Pour the warm cream over the potatoes and yams. The cream should just cover the potatoes; if not, add a bit more. Bake until the potatoes and yams are tender, about 45 minutes.

SPINACH SALAD WITH PECANS & BALSAMIC VINAIGRETTE

SERVES 12

By mixing two types of olive oil for the dressing, you get a more balanced flavor for this light spinach salad.

6–8 bunches small-leafed spinach
1 bunch green (spring) onions,
  sliced thin
½ cup (4 fl oz/125 ml) olive oil
¼ cup (2 fl oz/60 ml) extra-virgin
  olive oil
⅓ cup (3 fl oz/90 ml) balsamic vinegar
salt and freshly ground pepper to taste
2 cups (8 oz/250 g) toasted pecans
  (see glossary)
3 ripe pears, cored and sliced, optional
  (peels may be left on)

Remove the stems from the spinach, rinse the leaves well and pat dry. You should have about 18 cups loosely packed leaves (about 12 oz/375 g). If desired, refrigerate the spinach in a plastic bag for several hours.

❧ To serve, combine the spinach and green onions in a large salad bowl. In another bowl, whisk together the olive oils and vinegar and season with salt and pepper. Toss the pecans in ½ cup (4 fl oz/125 ml) of the vinaigrette. Add the pecans and the optional pears to the spinach. Dress the salad with the remaining vinaigrette, toss well and serve at once.

Barbecued Chicken Sandwiches; Sweet & White Potato Gratin;
Spinach Salad with Pecans & Balsamic Vinaigrette

Arrange personal collectibles with tropical or regular greenery on a side table for an eye-catching decoration.

CHOCOLATE POUND CAKE

MAKES ONE 9- BY 5- BY 3-INCH
(23- BY 13- BY 7.5-CM) CAKE

Dust the pound cake with powdered sugar if you wish. To serve, slice it to be eaten by hand, or serve on plates topped with whipped cream or ice cream.

1½ cups (6 oz/185 g) sifted all-purpose
  (plain) flour
½ cup (2 oz/60 g) sifted unsweetened
  Dutch-process cocoa
¼ teaspoon salt
2 oz (60 g) bittersweet chocolate
1 cup (8 oz/250 g) unsalted butter at
  room temperature
2 cups (14 oz/440g) light brown
  sugar, packed
3 eggs
1 teaspoon vanilla extract (essence)
1 cup (8 oz/250 g) sour cream

Preheat an oven to 350°F (180°C).
Butter a 9- by 5- by 3-inch (23- by
13- by 7.5-cm) loaf pan. Sift the flour,
cocoa and salt together. Set aside. Place
the chocolate in the top of a double
boiler and melt over simmering water.
☙ In a large bowl, beat the butter and
brown sugar together until fluffy. Beat
in the eggs, one at a time. Add the
vanilla and the melted chocolate and
mix well. Fold a third of the dry ingredients, then half the sour cream into the
chocolate mixture; repeat, ending with
the dry ingredients. Pour the batter into
the prepared loaf pan.
☙ Bake until a toothpick inserted in
the center of the cake comes out clean,
about 1 hour. If the cake is browning
too quickly, cover it loosely with
aluminum foil. Let the cake cool in the
pan on a rack for 10 minutes, then turn
out onto the rack to cool completely.
Slice and serve.

Chocolate Pound Cake

Elements of Entertaining

❧

At its simplest, entertaining involves presenting guests with appetizing food in a welcoming setting. Most likely, there will be times when your schedule allows you to do nothing more than that. But many hosts like to endow even a casual event with qualities that set it apart from the everyday. And gala occasions such as big parties and holiday meals seem to call for more elaboration.

To add distinction to your menus, you may want to make basics such as stocks, breads and pie pastry from scratch. Your entertaining can also be personalized with homemade pasta, salsa, pesto and other menu elements. On pages 294–300, you'll find recipes for such staples and special touches. If your schedule is tight, however, do not hesitate to substitute a good-quality store-bought item.

To create a suitable setting, choose cutlery, dishes and glasses to complement one another, the mood of the occasion, and the food (see pages 308–9). Select table coverings and napkins with the same criteria in mind, and consider one of the napkin-folding techniques illustrated on pages 310–1. Flowers and other decorative arrangements (pages 312–4) will help set the mood for a festive event that is truly memorable.

FISH STOCK

MAKES ABOUT 2½ QT (2.5 L)

Delicate and quick-cooking, fish stock, or fumet, is the basis for successful fish soups and stews. Ask your fishmonger for fish frames, or buy a whole fish and have the fillets removed to be used in another recipe.

6–8 lb (3–4 kg) fish frames (bones) with heads and tails (gills removed) from mild-flavored fish such as snapper, rockfish or halibut
2 tablespoons olive oil
8 cups (64 fl oz/2 l) water or to cover
3 cups (24 fl oz/750 ml) dry white wine
3 onions, chopped
4 celery stalks, chopped
3 strips lemon zest (see glossary)
5 fresh parsley sprigs
2 fresh thyme sprigs
10 peppercorns
4 coriander seeds
3 allspice berries
1 bay leaf

Rinse the fish frames well. Heat the olive oil in a large, heavy pot over moderate heat and cook the fish frames, stirring often, until they give off some liquid, about 10 minutes.

❧ Add the water, wine, onions and celery. Place the lemon zest, parsley sprigs, thyme sprigs, peppercorns, coriander seeds, allspice and bay leaf on a square of cheesecloth (muslin) and tie up with cotton string. Add to the stockpot and bring to a boil. Reduce heat and simmer, uncovered, for 30 minutes, skimming the scum from the surface occasionally. Strain into a bowl through a strainer lined with cheesecloth (muslin). Discard the solids. Let the stock cool to room temperature, then cover and refrigerate until cold. Use within 1 or 2 days, or transfer to one or more tightly covered containers and store in the freezer for up to 6 months.

BEEF STOCK

MAKES ABOUT 2½ QT (2.5 L)

Incomparably rich and deep in color, this stock will add an intense depth of flavor to soups, stews and sauces. It takes all day to simmer, but you don't have to hover over the stove while it's cooking.

6 lb (3 kg) meaty beef shanks (shins)
10 cups (2½ qt/2.5 l) cold water
beef scraps or other trimmings, optional
2 onions, coarsely chopped
1 leek, trimmed, carefully washed and coarsely chopped
2 carrots, peeled and coarsely chopped
1 celery stalk, coarsely chopped
about 1 cup (8 fl oz/250 ml) hot water
mushroom stems, optional
6 cloves garlic
4 fresh parsley sprigs
10 whole peppercorns
3 fresh thyme sprigs
2 small bay leaves

Preheat an oven to 450°F (230°C). Place the beef shanks in a large metal roasting pan and roast, turning occasionally, until browned, about 1½ hours. Transfer the shanks with tongs to a large stockpot and add the cold water.

Add beef scraps, if using. Bring to a boil and skim off any scum on the surface. Reduce the heat to a simmer and cook, uncovered, adding water as needed to keep the bones submerged. Skim the surface occasionally.

❧ Meanwhile, place the roasting pan on the stovetop. Add the onions, leek, carrots and celery to the juices in the pan. Cook over high heat, stirring often, until the vegetables are browned, about 20 minutes. Add the vegetables to the stockpot. Pour the hot water into the roasting pan, bring to a simmer and stir to dislodge any browned bits. Add to the stockpot.

❧ Place the optional mushroom stems and the garlic, parsley sprigs, peppercorns, thyme sprigs and bay leaves on a square of cheesecloth (muslin) and tie up with cotton string. Add to the stockpot. Simmer the stock, uncovered, over low heat, at least 6–8 hours, or preferably all day.

❧ Remove the stockpot from the heat and lift out the solids with a slotted spoon. Strain the liquid into a bowl through a strainer lined with cheesecloth (muslin). Discard the solids. Let the stock cool to room temperature, then cover and refrigerate until cold. Lift or spoon off the solidified fat on top and discard. Store the stock in one or more tightly covered containers in the refrigerator for up to several days or in the freezer for up to 6 months.

Turkey or Chicken Stock

MAKES 2–2½ QT (2–2.5 L)

The turkey stock is made from the carcass of the holiday bird and can be used in soups, sauces and rice dishes. Chicken stock, a kitchen standby, has dozens of uses.

1 turkey carcass, broken up, or
 2 pounds (1 kg) chicken parts
water, as needed
3 fresh flat-leaf (Italian) parsley sprigs
2 fresh thyme sprigs
1 bay leaf
1 large yellow onion, coarsely chopped
1 or 2 carrots, peeled and chopped
1 celery stalk, chopped

To make the stock, in a large stockpot, combine the turkey carcass or chicken parts and water as needed to cover the poultry fully. Bring to a boil, regularly skimming off any foam and scum that forms on the surface. Cover, reduce the heat to medium-low and simmer for about 1 hour.

❧ Make a bouquet garni by combining the parsley and thyme sprigs and bay leaf on a small piece of cheesecloth (muslin) and then bringing the corners together and tying securely with kitchen string to form a small bag. After 1 hour of simmering, add the bouquet garni, onion, carrots and celery, cover partially and continue to simmer for 1½ hours longer.

❧ Strain the stock through a fine-mesh sieve into a jar or other container and place, uncovered, in the refrigerator. When cooled completely, skim off all the fat that has solidified on top. You should have 2–2½ qt (2–2.5 l) stock. At this point the stock can be covered and refrigerated for up to 2 days.

Aïoli

MAKES ABOUT 2½ CUPS (20 FL OZ/625 ML)

This garlic-laced mayonnaise is served as a traditional dip in France.

1 tablespoon finely chopped garlic
½ teaspoon salt
2 large egg yolks
3–4 tablespoons fresh lemon juice
2 cups (16 fl oz/500 ml) olive oil

In a mortar, grind the garlic and the salt into a paste. In a blender or food processor, blend the egg yolks with 3 tablespoons of the lemon juice. With the machine running, gradually add olive oil a few drops at a time until sauce emulsifies; slowly add remaining oil. Add the garlic paste. Add more lemon juice and salt if desired. Put in a bowl, cover and refrigerate up to 8 hours.

Fruit Salsa

MAKES ABOUT 1 CUP (8 FL OZ/250 ML)

This sauce can replace the mustard with the pork tenderloin (recipe on page 56). It can be made 4–6 hours ahead.

1 cup (6 oz/185 g) diced mango,
 papaya or pineapple
1 or 2 small fresh chili peppers, seeded,
 if desired, and minced
1 clove garlic, minced
2 tablespoons sugar
¼ cup (2 fl oz/60 ml) fresh lemon or
 lime juice
1 tablespoon Thai fish sauce (*nam pla*)
 or 1 teaspoon anchovy paste, optional

In a bowl, mix well the mango, papaya or pineapple, chilies, garlic, sugar, lemon or lime juice and the fish sauce or anchovy paste, if using. Cover and refrigerate until serving.

TOMATO PURÉE

MAKES ABOUT 6 CUPS (48 FL OZ/1.5 L)

This easy-to-make purée is a good base for pizza toppings or can be used almost any time a simple tomato sauce is needed. If flavorful fresh plum (Roma) tomatoes are in the market, they can be used in place of the canned: Peel and seed 2½ pounds (1.25 kg) fresh tomatoes, coarsely chop them and then simmer until soft. Proceed with the recipe as directed.

1 can (2½ lb/1.25 kg) plum (Roma)
   tomatoes, seeded and diced
2 tablespoons olive oil
3 tablespoons minced garlic
2 tablespoons dried oregano
salt and freshly ground pepper

In a food processor fitted with the metal blade or in a blender, place the tomatoes and pulse until puréed. Transfer to an enamel or stainless steel saucepan and place over medium heat. Bring to a simmer, then reduce the heat to low and simmer very gently, uncovered, until thick, about 20 minutes.

❧ Stir in the olive oil, garlic and oregano. Season to taste with salt and pepper and additional garlic and oregano, if desired.

SUN-DRIED TOMATO SPREAD

MAKES ABOUT 1½ CUPS (12 FL OZ/375 ML)

Serve with cooked vegetables, pasta or grilled fish, or spread on pizza or bread. This purée can be made ahead and stored in a covered container in the refrigerator for up to 1 week.

1 cup (8 oz/250 g) chopped, drained
   oil-packed sun-dried tomatoes
   (oil reserved)
1 tablespoon minced garlic
4 tablespoons fresh basil leaves, optional
4–6 tablespoons coarsely chopped
   roasted red bell pepper (capsicum),
   about 1 medium pepper (see glossary),
   or 1 medium roasted pepper
   from a jar, rinsed, drained and
   coarsely chopped
pinch of cayenne pepper, optional
extra-virgin olive oil

In a food processor fitted with the metal blade or in a blender, combine the tomatoes, garlic, basil, if using, roasted red bell pepper and cayenne pepper, if using. Measure the reserved oil from the tomatoes. Add enough extra-virgin olive oil to measure ¼ cup (2 fl oz/60 ml). Add to the food processor or blender and purée until smooth. Transfer to a covered container and store in the refrigerator.

TAPENADE

MAKES ABOUT 1½ CUPS (12 FL OZ/375 ML)

This Provençal olive purée is great on pizza or grilled bread or mashed with hard-cooked eggs for a spread. It is also delicious stuffed under the skin of a roasting chicken, or slathered on grilled fish or tossed with steaming hot pasta. Niçoise olives are small, black, brine-cured olives packed in olive oil. They are available in well-stocked markets and specialty-food stores. Tapenade will keep in the refrigerator for up to 2 weeks.

1 cup (5 oz/155 g) pitted niçoise olives
2 tablespoons capers, rinsed and drained
1 tablespoon minced garlic
2 teaspoons chopped, drained
   anchovy fillet
½ teaspoon freshly ground pepper
6 tablespoons (3 fl oz/90 ml)
   extra-virgin olive oil
finely grated zest of 1 lemon or orange,
   optional (see glossary)
2 tablespoons Cognac, optional

In a food processor fitted with the metal blade or in a blender, combine the olives, capers, garlic, anchovy, pepper, olive oil and the lemon or orange zest and Cognac, if using. Purée until smooth. Transfer to a covered container and store in the refrigerator.

PESTO

MAKES ABOUT 3 CUPS (24 FL OZ/750 ML)

Pesto keeps well in the refrigerator for up to 1 week. Be sure to pour a thin layer of olive oil on top; this keeps it from discoloring. It can also be frozen for up to 6 months, but do not add the cheese until after it is defrosted. Use pesto on pasta, pizza, crostini and grilled vegetables. It can also be thinned with olive oil or vinegar for a tasty salad dressing or sauce for grilled fish.

2 cups (2 oz/60 g) firmly packed fresh basil leaves
2 teaspoons minced garlic
2–3 tablespoons pine nuts or walnuts
½–1 teaspoon salt, or to taste
½ teaspoon freshly ground pepper
1 cup (8 fl oz/250 ml) mild olive oil
½ cup (2 oz/60 ml) freshly grated Parmesan cheese

In a food processor fitted with the metal blade or in a blender, combine the basil, garlic, nuts, salt and pepper. (Be cautious when adding the salt, as the cheese that is added later can be quite salty.) Process until well combined. Add ½ cup (4 fl oz/125 ml) of the olive oil and purée using short off-on pulses. Stir between the pulses to blend well. Add the remaining ½ cup (4 fl oz/125 ml) oil and the cheese and process to form a thick purée. Do not overprocess; the mixture should have a little texture.
☙ Taste and adjust the salt and pepper. Transfer to a covered container and store in the refrigerator.

MANGO CHUTNEY

MAKES ABOUT 4 PINTS (64 FL OZ/2 L)

This chutney can be made 6 months in advance and processed as described in the glossary. Or it can be made 2–3 weeks ahead and refrigerated. It must stand for at least 1 week to mellow.

1 large yellow onion, diced
2 cloves garlic
2 limes, cut into small pieces
¼ lb (125 g) fresh ginger, peeled and thinly sliced across the grain
2 cups (16 fl oz/500 ml) cider vinegar
3–4 lb (1.5–2 kg) medium-ripe mangoes, peeled, pitted and cut into large dice
2 cups (14 oz/440 g) firmly packed brown sugar
1 teaspoon salt
1½ teaspoons ground cinnamon
½ teaspoon ground allspice
½ teaspoon ground cloves
¼ teaspoon cayenne pepper, or to taste
1 cup (6 oz/185 g) raisins

In a food processor fitted with the metal blade or in a blender, combine the onion, garlic, limes and ginger and process until finely chopped. Add 1 cup (8 fl oz/250 ml) of the vinegar and purée until smooth.
☙ Place the mangoes in a large, heavy enameled or stainless-steel pan. Stir in the onion mixture, brown sugar, salt, cinnamon, allspice, cloves, cayenne and the remaining 1 cup (8 fl oz/250 ml) vinegar. Bring to a boil. Reduce the heat to medium and simmer uncovered, stirring from time to time, until thick, from 45 minutes to 1½ hours (depending on the thickness and size of the pan). Add the raisins during the last 15 minutes. Stir often now to prevent scorching. Chutney is ready when a

teaspoonful sets up within 2 minutes of being dropped into a frozen saucer or when a candy thermometer registers 215°F (102°C) (see glossary).
☙ Ladle the hot chutney into 4 hot, sterilized pint (16-fl oz/500-ml) canning jars, leaving about ½ inch (12 mm) head space. Top with lids and metal bands. Process in a hot-water bath for 10 minutes. Check for a good seal, then store for up to 6 months; refrigerate once opened. Alternatively, pack into covered containers and store in the refrigerator for up to 3 weeks.

HOT FUDGE SAUCE

MAKES ABOUT 1½ CUPS (12 FL OZ/375 ML)

The fudge sauce can be made up to 2 weeks in advance and stored in the refrigerator.

3 oz (90 g) unsweetened chocolate
1 cup (8 fl oz/250 ml) heavy (double) cream
1 tablespoon corn syrup
1 cup (8 oz/250 g) sugar
2 teaspoons vanilla extract (essence)
pinch of salt

In a heavy-bottomed saucepan over medium heat, combine the chocolate, cream, corn syrup and sugar. Cook, whisking often, until the sauce registers 234°–240°F (112°–116°C) on a candy thermometer, the soft-ball stage. To test, scoop a little on a wooden spoon, dip the spoon into ice water and gather the chocolate mixture in your fingertips; it should feel soft and pliable.
☙ Remove from the heat and stir in the vanilla and salt. Serve immediately or let cool, cover and refrigerate. Reheat in the top pan of a double boiler over simmering water or in a small saucepan over low heat. Stir until hot.

BAGUETTES

MAKES THREE 1-LB (500-G) LOAVES

Slender batons of homemade bread are the quintessential accompaniment to many European meals. This is one of the easiest breads to make. Spraying with water during the first 10 minutes of baking ensures a crisp crust.

1 tablespoon active dry yeast
2½ cups (20 fl oz/625 ml) warm
  (110°F/43°C) water
6 cups (30 oz/940 g) unbleached
  all-purpose (plain) flour
1 tablespoon salt

Dissolve the yeast in the warm water in the bowl of an electric mixer (or a large bowl). Gradually add the flour and salt and mix with the paddle attachment to combine (or beat with a wooden spoon). Change to the dough hook and knead on moderate speed (or knead by hand on a lightly floured board) until the dough is smooth and elastic, 5–10 minutes, adding more flour as necessary to prevent sticking. Transfer to an oiled bowl or container, cover with a towel and let rise in a warm place until doubled, about 1 hour. Punch down, cover and refrigerate overnight.

❧ The next day, remove the dough from the refrigerator and allow it to rest for 1 hour. Shape into 3 baguettes; put on baking sheets. Cover with kitchen towels and let rise in a warm place until doubled in size, about 1 hour.

❧ Preheat an oven to 425°F (220°C). With a sharp knife or razor blade, cut diagonal slashes in the top of each baguette. Bake until golden brown, about 20 minutes, spraying the bread with a water mister 3 or 4 times during the first 10 minutes of baking. Remove from the oven and let cool on racks.

COUNTRY BREAD

MAKES TWO 1¾-LB (875-G) LOAVES

Known as pane integrale *in Italian, this bread gets a distinctive tang from a sour-dough-like starter. You can double the starter.*

FOR THE STARTER:
1 cup (8 fl oz/250 ml) warm
  (110°F/43°C) water
⅛ teaspoon active dry yeast
2 cups (10 oz/315 g) unbleached
  all-purpose (plain) flour

FOR THE BREAD:
1 tablespoon active dry yeast
2¼ cups (18 fl oz/560 ml) warm
  (110°F/43°C) water
2 tablespoons olive oil
¾ cup (3 oz/90 g) pumpernickel rye
  meal or dark rye flour
¾ cup (4 oz/125 g) coarse whole-
  wheat flour
4¾ cups (1½ lb/750 g) unbleached
  all-purpose (plain) flour
1 tablespoon salt

To make the starter, place the water, yeast and flour in the bowl of an electric mixer (or a large bowl) and beat with the paddle attachment at medium speed for 3 minutes or until the starter pulls away from sides of the bowl (or beat with a wooden spoon). Place the starter in a container large enough to allow it to triple in size. Cover and let sit at room temperature overnight. Use the next day or, preferably, refrigerate for 1–2 days longer to develop the flavor.

❧ To make the bread, place the yeast and the starter with the warm water in the bowl of an electric mixer (or in a large bowl). With the paddle attachment (or a wooden spoon), mix until it is dissolved, about 5 minutes. The water will be chalky white and foamy.

❧ Change to the dough hook and add (or stir in) the olive oil, the rye meal, the whole-wheat flour, the all-purpose flour and the salt. Knead on moderate speed until a stiff, firm dough pulls completely away from the side of the bowl; continue kneading for 5 minutes (or knead by hand on a lightly floured board) until smooth and elastic, adding more all-purpose flour as necessary to prevent sticking. Transfer to an oiled bowl, cover and refrigerate overnight.

❧ The next day, shape the dough into 2 loaves and place on greased baking sheets, or place in greased loaf pans. Cover with kitchen towels and let rise in a warm place until doubled in size, about 1½–2 hours.

❧ Preheat an oven to 450°F (230°C). With a sharp knife or razor blade, cut 3 diagonal slashes in the top of each loaf. Place in the oven, reduce the heat to 400°F (200°C) and bake until golden brown, 45–60 minutes, spraying the bread with a water mister about 4 times during the first 20 minutes. Remove from the oven and let cool on racks.

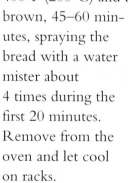

BASIC PIE PASTRY

Use this recipe for a failsafe crust for the pies throughout this book. If you want a sweet crust, add the sugar; for savory pies, leave it out. To achieve a flaky texture, make it with butter; for tender crusts, use the vegetable shortening, or use half of each. After rolling out the dough and placing it in the pan, put it in the freezer to rest for at least 30 minutes so that it will shrink less in baking.

FOR A SINGLE-CRUST PIE SHELL:

½ cup (4 oz/125 g) chilled unsalted
   butter or vegetable shortening
   (vegetable lard), or half of each
1½ cups (7½ oz/235 g) all-purpose
   (plain) flour
½ teaspoon salt
1 tablespoon sugar, optional
about 3–4 tablespoons cold water

FOR A DOUBLE-CRUST PIE SHELL OR 2 PIE CRUSTS:

¾ cup (6 oz/180 g) chilled unsalted
   butter or vegetable shortening
   (vegetable lard), or half of each
2¼ cups (11½ oz/360 g) all-purpose
   (plain) flour
¾ teaspoon salt
2 tablespoons sugar, optional
about 6–7 tablespoons (3–3½ fl oz/
   90–95 ml) cold water

Hand Method:

Cut the butter or shortening into small bits. Combine the flour, salt and sugar, if using, in a medium bowl. Add the butter or shortening. With your fingertips, 2 knives or a pastry blender, quickly blend the ingredients together until the mixture resembles coarse crumbs. Sprinkle on the water 1 tablespoon at a time, stirring with a fork after each addition. Add just enough water for the dough to mass together. Turn out onto a lightly floured board and, with floured hands, pat the dough into 1 or 2 smooth cakes, one just slightly larger than the other if you are making a double-crust pie. Roll out the dough and place it in the pan as directed in the recipe. Put the pie shell in the freezer and let it rest for at least 30 minutes before baking.

Food Processor Method:

Cut the butter or shortening into large pieces. With the steel blade attached, place the flour, salt, sugar (if using) and butter or shortening in the work bowl. Process with rapid off-on pulses until the mixture resembles cornmeal; do not overprocess or the pastry will be tough. Add the water, a little at a time, and process until blended; do not let the mixture form a ball. Stop and feel the dough (taking care not to touch the blade); it should be just damp enough to mass together. If necessary, add more water by teaspoonfuls, processing for just an instant after each addition. Turn out onto a lightly floured board and, with floured hands, pat the dough into 1 or 2 smooth cakes, one just slightly larger than the other if you are making a double-crust pie. Roll out the dough and place it in the pan as directed in the recipe. Put the pie shell in the freezer and let it rest for at least 30 minutes before baking.

To Fully Bake a Pie Shell:

Preheat an oven to 400°F (200°C). Line the pie shell with aluminum foil and fill with dried beans or pie weights. Bake for 10 minutes, then lower the heat to 350°F (180°C) and continue baking until the shell is golden brown, about 15–20 minutes longer. Remove the weights and aluminum foil during the last 5 minutes of baking. Let cool completely on a rack.

Baguette; Country Bread; Basic Pie Pastry

HOMEMADE PASTA

MAKES ABOUT 1½ LB (750 G); SERVES 6

Making pasta at home is easy if you have a food processor for mixing the dough and a small hand-cranked pasta machine for rolling it out into thin sheets. The pasta machine can also be used for cutting the dough sheets into a variety of noodles, from narrow taglierini to fettuccine or tagliatelle. Wider noodles, such as pappardelle, are easily cut with a pastry wheel. For those who lack a food processor and/or pasta machine, directions for making pasta by hand follow. The pasta dough can be made and the noodles cut up to 8 hours in advance of cooking.

3 cups (15 oz/470 g) all-purpose
   (plain) flour
1 teaspoon salt
4 eggs
about ½ cup (2½ oz/75 g) cornmeal

In the bowl of a food processor fitted with the metal blade, combine the flour and salt. Break the eggs into a small bowl and whisk together lightly. With the processor motor running, drizzle in the eggs. The ingredients will gather together into a rough mass that will look like cornmeal. Turn off the processor and squeeze a handful of the mixture; it should hold together. Transfer the dough from the processor to a work surface. If the dough is crumbly, add a few drops of water. Now, knead the dough with the palm and heel of your hand, repeatedly pushing it against the surface and turning it, until it is smooth and elastic but not too soft, about 5 minutes.

❧ Flatten the dough into a disk and place in a plastic bag. Let rest at room temperature for 30–60 minutes.

❧ Divide the dough into 6 equal portions. Lightly dust 1 portion with flour; keep the remaining portions covered. Set the rollers of a hand-cranked pasta machine at the widest opening. Flatten the portion slightly and crank it through the rollers. Reset the rollers one notch narrower. Lightly dust the dough with flour again, fold it into thirds and pass it through the rollers. Repeat this process, being sure to fold the dough each time and dust it with only enough flour to prevent the dough from sticking. Reduce gradually the width of the rollers, until the dough sheet reaches the desired thinness. When it is very thin, lightly sprinkle a kitchen towel with some of the cornmeal and transfer the pasta to it.

Let the pasta dry for about 10 minutes—or less if the air is very dry. It should be neither sticky nor too dry. Repeat with the remaining 5 portions.

❧ To cut the noodles, using the pasta machine, secure the desired cutting attachment to the machine. Cut the dough sheets into easily manageable lengths and crank each length through the cutter to make pasta strands about ⅜ inch (1 cm) wide for fettuccine or tagliatelle and a scant ⅛ inch (3 mm) wide for taglierini. For pappardelle, lay the dough sheet on a floured work surface and, using a pastry wheel, cut into long ribbons about 1 inch (2.5 cm) wide. Transfer the pasta to a large tray and toss with some of the cornmeal to prevent the strands from sticking together. Repeat with the remaining dough sheets, then cover the tray with plastic wrap and refrigerate for up to 8 hours. Remove the noodles from the refrigerator just before cooking.

Hand Method:

To make the pasta by hand, mix together the flour and salt on a work surface and shape into a mound. Make a well in the center and add the eggs to it. Using a fork, lightly beat the eggs, and then gradually combine the flour and the eggs. Knead the dough until smooth and elastic but not too soft, about 5 minutes. Let rest as directed, then divide in half and roll out each half on a lightly floured surface as thinly as possible. Let the pasta dry for about 10 minutes, less if the air is very dry. Using a pastry wheel, cut into long strips of desired width.

ROASTING & CARVING

Golden brown on the outside, moist and tender within, whole roast poultry, prime rib of beef, or leg of lamb makes a magnificent main course for any dinner party. The guidelines here will help you achieve the best results whenever you prepare one of these roasts.

❧ Cooking times will vary with the size of the roast and, for red meats, the degree of doneness you desire. Bear in mind, too, that roasts put into the oven straight from the refrigerator will take longer to cook, so it's best to let the meat stand at room temperature for about 1 hour before roasting. Be sure you allow enough time to cook the roast and let it stand before carving so that dinner is not delayed.

❧ To check the roast for doneness, use a meat thermometer; the instant-read kind is accurate and easy to use. After cooking, let roasts rest at room temperature, loosely covered with aluminum foil, for about 15 minutes before carving. This lets the meat reabsorb its juices and makes it moist and tender. The meat also continues to cook, adding 5°–7°F (2°–3°C) to the final temperature.

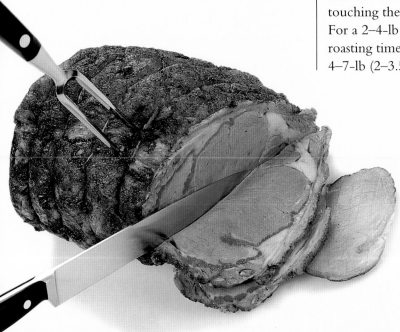

Roasting Turkey

❧ Preheat an oven to 350°F (180°C). Place the turkey breast-side down on a rack in a roasting pan and tent it loosely with aluminum foil.

❧ Place the turkey in the oven and roast, turning it breast-side up for the last 45 minutes of cooking, until it is golden brown all over and an instant-read thermometer inserted into the thickest part of the thigh, not touching the bone, registers 180°F (82°C). For an 8–12-lb (4–6-kg) turkey, total roasting time will be 2–3¼ hours. For a 12–16-lb (6–8-kg) turkey, 3¼–4¼ hours. For a 16–20-lb (8–10-kg) turkey, 4¼–5 hours.

❧ For a stuffed turkey, add 30–45 minutes to the total roasting time.

Roasting Chicken

❧ Preheat an oven to 325°F (165°C). Place the chicken on its side on a rack in a roasting pan.

❧ Roast the chicken until it is golden brown, turning it on the other side, and then finishing it breast-side up, at even intervals during cooking.

❧ Remove the chicken from the oven when an instant-read thermometer inserted into the thickest part of the thigh, not touching the bone, registers 180°F (82°C). For a 2–4-lb (1–2-kg) chicken, total roasting time will be 1–1½ hours. For a 4–7-lb (2–3.5-kg) chicken, 1½–2 hours.

Roasting Prime Rib of Beef

❧ Preheat an oven to 500°F (260°C). Place the prime rib roast rib-side down in a roasting pan and roast it for 15 minutes.

❧ Reduce the heat to 325°F (165°C) and continue roasting until the meat is browned and reaches the desired degree of doneness.

❧ For rare beef, remove the roast when an instant-read thermometer inserted into the center of the meat, not touching the bone, registers 120°F (50°C), about 15 minutes per pound (500 g). For medium beef, remove when an instant-read thermometer registers 135°F (57°C), about 20 minutes per pound (500 g).

Roasting Leg of Lamb

❧ Preheat an oven to 350°F (180°C). Place the lamb on a rack in a roasting pan and roast in the oven until it is browned and cooked to the desired doneness.

❧ For rare to medium-rare lamb, remove when an instant-read thermometer inserted into the thickest part, not touching the bone, registers 135°–140°F (57°–60°C) about 1½ hours for a 6–7-lb (3–3.5-kg) leg.

❧ For medium lamb, remove when an instant-read thermometer inserted into the thickest part, not touching the bone, registers 150°F (65°C), about 2 hours.

CARVING TURKEY

Carve only as much dark leg meat and white breast meat as you need to serve at one time, completing one side of the turkey before starting the next. Use a slicing knife with a long, flexible, but sturdy blade.

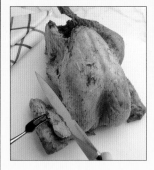

1. Remove the leg and the wing.
Cut through the skin between the leg and breast to locate the thigh joint; cut through the joint to sever the leg. To remove the wing (shown at left), cut through the shoulder joint where it meets the breast.

2. Slice the drum-stick and thigh.
Cut through the joint to separate the drumstick and thigh. Serve them whole or carve them, cutting the meat into thin slices parallel to the bone.

3. Carve the breast.
Just above the thigh and shoulder joints, carve a deep horizontal cut toward the bone to create a base cut. Starting near the breastbone, carve thin slices vertically, cutting parallel to the rib cage and ending at the base cut.

CARVING CHICKEN

Carving a chicken is similar to carving a turkey. But because the bird is smaller, you may use a smaller knife, which is easier to handle. The breast can be removed in several slices, as for turkey, or in one piece.

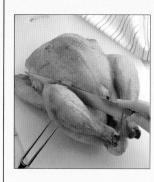

1. Remove the leg and the wing.
Cut through the skin between the leg and breast to locate the thigh joint; cut through the joint to sever the leg (shown at left). Cut through the shoulder joint where it meets the breast to remove the wing.

2. Separate the drumstick and thigh.
If the chicken is small, serve the whole leg as one portion. If it is large, cut through the joint to separate the drumstick and thigh into two pieces.

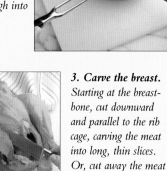

3. Carve the breast.
Starting at the breastbone, cut downward and parallel to the rib cage, carving the meat into long, thin slices. Or, cut away the meat from the breastbone in one piece.

CARVING PRIME RIB OF BEEF

A prime rib is fairly simple to carve, provided you have a large, sharp knife for slicing and a sturdy fork to steady the roast. Serve some slices still attached to the ribs for guests who like the bones.

1. Cut the first slice.
Place the roast, ribs down, on a carving surface and steady it by inserting a carving fork into the top. Cut a vertical slice against the grain down to the rib bone; cut along the bone to free the slice.

2. Continue carving.
Cutting parallel to the first slice, continue to carve slices of the desired thickness. As individual bones are exposed, cut between them to remove them; or leave them attached to a slice for guests who request them.

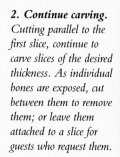

CARVING LEG OF LAMB

Shaped like an irregular, elongated pear, a leg of lamb presents something of a challenge to the carver. The keys to successfully carving the leg lie in cutting parallel to the bone and providing guests with slices from both sides of the leg.

1. Slice the rounded side of the leg.
Grasp the end of the shank bone with a kitchen towel and tilt it slightly upward. Carve a slice from the rounded outer side of the leg at its widest point, cutting away from you and parallel to the bone.

2. Cut parallel slices.
Cutting parallel to the first slice, continue carving the meat in thin slices until you have cut enough to serve each guest a slice.

3. Carve the inner side of the leg.
Rotate the leg of lamb to expose its other, flatter side—the inner side of the leg, which is slightly more tender. Still cutting parallel to the bone, carve one slice of meat for each guest.

GLOSSARY

The following list describes special ingredients and techniques used throughout the recipes in this book.

AL DENTE
An Italian term, literally "to the tooth," used to describe the ideal degree of doneness for cooked pasta or vegetables—tender, but still firm to the bite.

ALMONDS
See *nuts*.

AQUAVIT
A clear, dry Scandinavian spirit distilled either from potatoes or grains and usually flavored with caraway, or sometimes with citrus and spices.

ARMAGNAC
A dry brandy, similar to Cognac, distilled in the Armagnac region of southwestern France from wine produced there. Other good-quality dry wine–based brandies may be substituted.

ARUGULA
A green leaf vegetable with slender, multiple-lobed leaves that have a peppery flavor. Often used raw in salads; also known as rocket.

BELGIAN ENDIVE
A leaf vegetable with refreshing, slightly bitter spear-shaped leaves, white to pale yellow-green—or sometimes red—tightly packed in cylindrical heads 4–6 inches (10–15 cm) long. Also known as chicory or witloof.

BELL PEPPERS
See *peppers*.

BREAD CRUMBS
To make fresh bread crumbs, choose a good-quality, country-style loaf made of unbleached wheat flour, with a firm, coarse crumb. Cut away the crusts and crumble the bread to the desired consistency by hand or in a blender or a food processor fitted with the metal blade.

BRUSSELS SPROUTS
Small, spherical green vegetables, usually 1–2 inches (2.5–5 cm) in diameter, resembling tiny cabbages, to which they are related.

BUTTER, CLARIFIED
Butter is often clarified—that is, its milk solids are removed—when it is to be used for cooking at higher temperatures or as a sauce. To clarify butter, melt it in a small, heavy saucepan over very low heat; watch carefully to avoid burning. Remove from the heat and let sit briefly. Then, using a spoon, skim off and discard the foam from the surface. Finally, carefully pour off the clear yellow butter, leaving the milky solids behind in the pan.

CACHACA
A smooth, colorless Brazilian rum with a strength and dryness reminiscent of brandy.

CALVADOS
A dry French brandy distilled from apples and bearing the fruit's distinctive aroma and taste. Dry applejack may be substituted.

CANDY THERMOMETER
A thermometer specially designed to register temperatures in the 230°–350°F (110°–177°C) range to which sugar syrup–based mixtures are heated in dessert and candy making.

CANNING
Many of the preserves recipes in this book can be stored for long periods if they are packed into hot sterilized jars and then hot-water processed to prevent spoilage. While books on preserving will offer charts with specific times and procedures necessary to preserve different kinds of ingredients, the basic steps are as follows:

1. Thoroughly wash all jars, lids and screw bands. Place them in a large pan, add hot water to cover and bring to a full boil. Boil 10 minutes, then remove from the heat and let the jars stand in the water.
2. Using tongs, drain the jars and, while they are still hot, fill them with the preserves, leaving about ½ inch (12 mm) of head space. Gently tap and shake the jars to force out any air bubbles. Using a dampened cloth, wipe any spillage from the jar mouths, then seal the jars with the lids.
3. Meanwhile, fill a large pot with water, insert a jar rack or place a folded cloth on the bottom and bring the water to a bare simmer; bring a separate pot of water to a boil. Put the filled jars in the rack or on the cloth and add enough boiling water to cover them by at least 1 inch (2.5 cm). Bring the water to a full boil, cover and begin counting processing time: 10 minutes for chutneys, jams, marmalades and conserves; 25–30 minutes for whole or halved peaches, plums and apricots.
4. Turn off the heat and remove the jars with canning tongs to a flat surface. After several hours, all of the jars should be sealed. Check the lids by touching them to see if they are concave, indicating a secure seal. If a lid is not concave, refrigerate the preserves and eat within a few weeks.

CARAWAY SEEDS
See *seeds*.

CARDAMOM
See *seeds*.

CAYENNE PEPPER
A very hot spice derived from ground dried cayenne chili peppers.

CELERIAC
Also known as celery root. The large, knobby root of a species of celery plant, with a crisp texture and flavor closely resembling the familiar stalks. Choose smaller, younger roots, to be peeled and eaten raw or cooked.

CHANTERELLES
See *mushrooms*.

CHESTNUTS
Raw chestnuts have glossy brown shells and a dark fuzzy membrane beneath the shells. Both the shells and the membrane must be removed before use. Shelled whole chestnuts or chestnut pieces, dry-packed, candied or packed in water or syrup, as well as sweetened and unsweetened chestnut purées, are available in some specialty-food shops.

CHILI PEPPERS
See *peppers*.

CIPOLLINE
Cipolline are small, flat, brown-skinned onions, prized in Italy for their sweetness; available in some vegetable markets, they may be replaced with pearl onions.

CITRUS FRUITS
A wide variety of citrus fruits enliven festive meals. Two in particular are well worth seeking out at good-quality greengrocers or well-stocked food markets:
Blood Oranges are a variety of the fruit with red pulp and orange skins tinged with red. Their flavor is more pronounced than that of regular oranges, which may be substituted for blood oranges.
Meyer Lemons are slightly larger and have thinner skins than common lemons, and they have a more pronounced, slightly sweeter aroma and taste. A mixture of 2 parts fresh lemon juice to 1 part fresh orange juice may be substituted for Meyer lemon juice in some recipes.

SECTIONING CITRUS FRUIT

Some recipes call for segments, or sections, of citrus fruit, free of pith and membranes.

❶ To section a citrus fruit, first use a small, sharp knife to cut a thick slice off its bottom and top, exposing the fruit beneath the peel. Then, steadying the fruit on a work surface, thickly slice off the peel in strips, cutting off the white pith with it.

❷ Hold the peeled fruit in one hand over a bowl to catch the juices. Using the same knife, carefully cut on each side of the membrane to free each section, letting the sections drop into the bowl as they are cut.

❶ *Use a small, sharp knife to cut off the citrus peel and white pith.*

❷ *Cut the sections free, letting them drop into a bowl below.*

CLAMS

Bivalve mollusks prized for their sweet, tender flesh. Sold live in their shells, or sometimes already shucked, in fish markets or good-quality food markets with seafood departments. Check all the clams and discard any whose shells do not close tightly to the touch.

COCONUT

To toast flaked coconut, spread it evenly on a baking sheet and bake in a 350°F (180°C) oven, stirring once or twice, until pale gold, 10–20 minutes.

COGNAC

A dry spirit distilled from wine and, strictly speaking, produced in the Cognac region of France. Other good-quality dry wine–based brandies may be substituted.

CORIANDER

See *seeds*.

CORN, SWEET

Before use, fresh sweet corn must be stripped of its green outer husks and the fine inner silky threads must be removed. If a recipe calls for removing the raw kernels from an ear of corn, hold the ear by its stalk end, steadying its other end on a cutting board. With the ear at a 45-degree angle to the board, use a sharp, sturdy knife to cut down and away from you along the ear, stripping off the kernels from the cob. Continue, turning the ear with each cut.

CORNICHONS

French-style sour pickled cucumbers no more than 2 inches (5 cm) in length, available in specialty food stores.

CRAB

Already-cooked crab meat is widely available in fish markets or the seafood counters in most food markets. Most often, it has been frozen; for best flavor and texture, seek out fresh crab meat. When crab is in season, fish markets will often sell crabs boiled or steamed whole; ask for them to be cracked, so that you can open the shells by hand and remove the meat.

CUMIN

See *seeds*.

CURRANTS, DRIED

Produced from a variety of small grapes known as Zante, these dried fruits resemble tiny raisins but have a stronger, tarter flavor. Sold in the baking section of food markets. If they are unavailable, substitute raisins.

EMMENTHALER

A variety of Swiss cheese with a firm, smooth texture, large holes and a mellow, slightly sweet, nutty flavor.

FENNEL SEEDS

See *seeds*.

FETA

A white, salty, sharp-tasting cheese made from sheep or goat's milk and with a crumbly, creamy-to-dry consistency.

FIGS

Summer fruit characterized by their many tiny edible seeds, sweet, slightly astringent flavor and soft, succulent texture. It is best to buy fresh figs ripe and use them immediately.

FILO

Tissue-thin sheets of flour-and-water pastry. The name derives from the Greek word for *leaf*. Usually found in the freezer case of a food market, or purchased fresh in Greek and Middle Eastern delicatessens; defrost frozen filo in the refrigerator thoroughly before use. As you work with the filo, cover the unused sheets with a very lightly dampened towel to keep them from drying out.

GINGER

The rhizome of the tropical ginger plant, which yields a sweet, strong-flavored spice. Whole ginger may be purchased fresh in a well-stocked food shop or vegetable market. Ginger pieces are available crystallized or candied, or preserved in syrup. Ground dried ginger is easily found in the food market spice section.

GOAT CHEESE

Any of a number of cheeses made from goat's milk; also commonly known by the French word *chèvre*. Most goat cheeses are fresh and creamy, with a distinctively sharp tang; they usually are sold shaped into rounds or logs.

GRAPE LEAVES

In Greek and other Middle Eastern cuisines, grapevine leaves are commonly used as edible wrappers. If fresh leaves are available, wash them thoroughly before use. Bottled leaves, available in ethnic delicatessens and the specialty-food section of well-stocked food markets, should be gently rinsed of their brine.

GRUYÈRE

A variety of Swiss cheese with a firm, smooth texture, small holes and a strong, tangy flavor.

HAZELNUTS

See *nuts*.

HOT-WATER PROCESSING

See *canning*.

JALAPEÑO CHILIES

See *peppers*.

EGGS

Beaten eggs add richness, lightness and body to a wide variety of recipes. Eggs are often separated before beating.

WHISKING EGG WHITES

❶ Put the whites into a large bowl with a pinch of cream of tartar. With a wire balloon whisk, or an electric beater set on medium speed, beat the whites with broad, sweeping strokes to incorporate as much air as possible. As the whites begin to thicken and turn a glossy, snowy white, lift out the whisk or beater: If a soft peak forms, then droops back on itself, the whites have reached the "soft peak" stage.

❷ For the "stiff peak" stage, continue beating until the whites form stiff, unmoving moist peaks when the whisk or beaters are lifted straight out.

WHISKING EGG YOLKS WITH SUGAR

❸ Put the egg yolks and sugar into a large bowl, place the bowl in hot water and beat until warm to the touch. Remove from the hot water and, with a wire whisk or an electric beater set on high speed, beat until thick and pale, about 8 minutes. To test if beaten sufficiently, lift out the whisk or beater: The mixture should flow in a ribbon that takes about 3 seconds to fall back onto the surface and then slowly dissolve.

❶ *The whites have reached "soft peak" stage when the peak is soft and droops back on itself after the beater is lifted.*

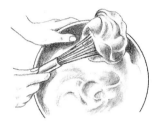

❷ *For the "stiff peak" stage, look for firm, unmoving peaks when the whisk or beaters are lifted out of the bowl.*

❸ *When egg yolks and sugar have been properly beaten, a ribbon of egg will take 3 seconds to fall back onto the surface when the whisk or beaters are lifted.*

JULIENNE

Refers both to cutting food into long, thin strips and to the strips themselves. To julienne vegetables, thinly slice lengthwise, then stack several slices and slice again into thin strips; alternatively, use a mandoline or the julienne-cutting disk of a food processor.

LEMONS, MEYER

See *citrus fruits*.

LEMON VERBENA

A strongly lemon-scented herb, native to South America. Available in some fruit and vegetable markets, or you can grow your own.

LOBSTER

Although many seafood stores and some food markets sell lobsters already cooked, cleaned and shelled, it is usually far more economical, and yields better results, to buy a live lobster and cook it yourself.

TO REMOVE LOBSTER MEAT

❶ After cooking a whole lobster as specified in the recipe, let it rest until cool enough to handle. Then, steadying the body with one hand, firmly grasp a claw where it joins the body; twist and pull to remove it. Repeat with the other claw.

❷ To enable the claw meat to be extracted, crack its shell with a lobster cracker or mallet. Peel away the shell and gently remove the meat, taking care to keep it in one piece if possible. Twist and pull off the four small legs arrayed along each side of the body.

❸ To split the lobster in half, turn it underside up on the work surface. Steadying it with one hand, use a large, sharp knife to cut through the soft shell from head to tail. Continue cutting through the head and tail sections and downward through the harder shell along the back. If a black vein is visible along the center of the tail meat, remove it with the knife tip and discard.

❹ Using a small, sharp-edged spoon, scoop out the stomach sac and other soft matter from the head portion of the shell halves. Using a fork, spear one end of the tail meat and gently pull it out of the shell. If the recipe requires the shell halves for presentation, clean and reserve them.

❶ *Firmly grasp each claw where it joins the body and twist it off.*

❷ *Crack the shell in several places to enable the claw meat to be extracted.*

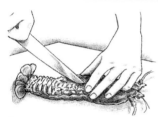

❸ *Turn the lobster over and cut it in half lengthwise with a sharp knife.*

❹ *Remove the tail meat with a fork.*

MADEIRA

A sweet, amber dessert wine originating on the Portuguese island of Madeira.

MARSALA

A dry or sweet amber Italian wine from the area of Marsala, in Sicily; widely used to flavor meats, poultry, vegetables and desserts.

MASCARPONE

A thick Italian cream cheese, usually sold in tubs and similar to French crème fraîche. Look for mascarpone in the cheese case of an Italian delicatessen or a specialty-food shop.

MOZZARELLA

A rindless white, mild-tasting Italian cheese. Look for fresh mozzarella sold immersed in water.

MUSHROOMS

Cultivated white and brown mushrooms are available in food markets and fruit and vegetable markets. Porcini, the widely used Italian term for *Boletus edulis,* are popular wild mushrooms with a rich, meaty flavor; also known by the French term *cèpe,* they are most commonly sold in dried form in Italian delicatessens and specialty-food shops, and are reconstituted in liquid to use.

Chanterelles (shown below), subtly flavored, pale yellow, trumpet-shaped wild mushrooms about 2–3 inches (5–7.5 cm) in length, are also cultivated commercially, and may be found in specialty-food markets and fruit and vegetable stores.

MUSSELS

Before cooking, these bluish black–shelled bivalves require special cleaning. Rinse the mussels thoroughly under cold running water. One at a time, hold them under the water and scrub with a firm-bristled brush to remove any stubborn dirt. Firmly grasp the fibrous beard attached to the side of each mussel and pull it off. Discard any mussels whose shells do not close tightly to the touch.

NUTS

To toast almonds, hazelnuts, pecans, pine nuts and walnuts, preheat an oven to 325°F (165°C). Spread the nuts in a single layer on a sided baking sheet and toast in the oven until they just begin to change color, 5–10 minutes. Remove from the oven and let cool to room temperature. Toasting also loosens the skins of hazelnuts and walnuts, which may be removed by wrapping the still-warm nuts in a cotton towel and rubbing against them with the palms of your hands.

To chop nuts, spread them in a single layer on a nonslip cutting surface. Using a chef's knife, carefully chop the nuts with a gentle rocking motion. Alternatively, put a handful or two of nuts in a food processor fitted with the metal blade and use a few rapid on-off pulses to chop the nuts to desired consistency; repeat with the remaining nuts in batches. Be careful not to process the nuts too long, or their oils will be released and the nuts will turn to a paste.

OILS

Extra-virgin olive oil, extracted from olives on the first pressing without use of heat or chemicals, is preferred for most recipes in this book. Many brands, varying in color and strength of flavor, are available; choose one that suits your taste. Pure olive oil, derived from the later pressings, has less of the fruit's distinctive flavor and may be used for sautéing and frying, or to mix with extra-virgin oil in salad dressings

for a milder flavor. Walnut oil has a rich, nutty taste prized in dressings; that made from toasted nuts has the deepest color and fullest flavor.

OLIVES

Ripe black olives are cured in combinations of salt, seasonings, brines, vinegars and oils to produce pungently flavored results. Good-quality cured olives, such as niçoise, Moroccan, or Kalamata varieties, are available in ethnic delicatessens, specialty-food shops and well-stocked food markets.

ORANGE FLOWER WATER

A sweet, aromatic essence distilled from the natural oils present in orange petals and used as a subtle flavoring in Middle Eastern and other cuisines.

ORANGES, BLOOD

See *citrus fruits.*

OYSTERS

Buy fresh oysters from a reputable fish market. They vary in size from area to area. They are available live in the shell as well as shucked and in their liquor.

PANCETTA

Italian-style unsmoked bacon cured with salt and pepper. Available in Italian markets and specialty-food stores.

PARMESAN CHEESE

A hard, thick-crusted Italian cow's milk cheese with a sharp, salty, full flavor. Buy in block form, to grate fresh.

PEARS

Several pear varieties are available seasonally in fruit and vegetable markets and food markets. Comice pears (below left) are large, with short necks and greenish skin highlighted with a red blush; they are excellent for eating and in desserts. Bartlett pears (below middle), also called Williams' pears, are fine-textured, juicy and mild; they are equally good for cooking or eating. Long, slender, tapered Bosc pears (below right), with their yellow and russet skins and slightly grainy, solid-textured flesh, are good for cooking.

PECANS

See *nuts.*

PEPPERS

Widely varied in shape, size and hue, and ranging in taste from mild and sweet to fiery hot, peppers are used to add flavor, color and texture to many savory recipes.

Bell Peppers, also known as capsicums, have a sweet, mild taste and a bell shape; they come in a range of colors and flavors.

Chili Peppers include a wide variety of peppers prized for the mild-to-hot spiciness they impart as a seasoning. Red ripe chilies are sold fresh and dried. Fresh green chilies include the mild-to-hot dark green poblano; the long, mild Anaheim, New Mexico or green chili; and small, fiery serranos and jalapeños. When handling most chili peppers, it is advisable to wear rubber gloves to prevent your skin from coming in contact with the pepper's volatile oils.

TO ROAST, PEEL AND DERIB PEPPERS

❶ When a recipe calls for roasted peppers, there are several ways to achieve this. One method (shown at right) is to spear each pepper individually on a long fork and hold it directly over an open flame, turning until the skin is evenly blackened. Alternatively, place the whole peppers on a baking sheet and roast in a 400°F (200°C) oven, or under a broiler (griller), turning occasionally with tongs, until the skins are evenly blackened.

❷ After roasting, place the peppers in a paper bag or plastic container and let them sit until cool enough to handle, about 10 minutes. When cool, use your fingers to peel off the charred skins. Cut the peppers in half and pull out and discard the stems, seeds and ribs. Then use the peppers as directed in the recipe.

❶ *To roast a pepper, rotate it directly over a gas flame until the skin is charred.*

❷ *After letting the pepper cool, pull off the skin with your fingers.*

PINE NUTS
See *nuts*.

POLENTA
Coarsely but evenly ground yellow cornmeal. Available in Italian grocers or some well-stocked food shops.

PORCINI
See *mushrooms*.

POUSSIN
A small, immature chicken, weighing no more than about 1 pound (500 g), prized for its tender, sweet flesh.

PROSCIUTTO
Italian raw ham, a specialty of Parma, cured by dry-salting, then air-drying for half a year or longer. Usually cut into tissue-thin slices to eat.

QUAIL
A small game bird, usually a single serving, with moist, tender, very flavorful dark meat.

SAFFRON
Saffron threads are the dried stigmas of a species of crocus. Saffron is used to perfume and color many classic Mediterranean and East Indian dishes and also is sold in powdered form. Look for products labeled *pure saffron*. Saffron threads have more flavor and should be crushed before use: First, put them in a metal kitchen spoon and hold the spoon over a hot burner

for a few seconds; then use the back of a teaspoon to crush the threads, or pulverize in a mortar with a pestle.

SCALLOPS
Bivalve mollusks that come in two common varieties: The round flesh of the sea scallop is usually 1½ inches (4 cm) in diameter, while the bay scallop is considerably smaller. Usually sold already shelled.

SEEDS
Toasting before use enriches and releases the flavor of spice seeds. To toast seeds, stir them in a small, dry heavy frying pan over moderate heat until you can smell their aroma, 1–2 minutes. If grinding is required, let them cool slightly, then place in an electric spice mill or a clean coffee grinder and pulverize, or crush them in a mortar with a pestle.

SHERRY
Fortified, cask-aged wine, ranging from dry to sweet, enjoyed as an aperitif and used as a flavoring in both savory and sweet recipes.

SHRIMP
Fresh, raw shrimp (prawns) are usually sold with the heads already removed but the shells intact. They may be peeled and their thin, veinlike intestinal tracts removed before cooking.

1. To peel, with your thumbs split open the shrimp's thin shell along the concave side, between its two rows of legs. Peel away the shell; leave the last segment with tail fin intact and attached to the meat, if desired.

2. With a small, sharp knife, carefully make a shallow slit along the peeled shrimp's back, just deep enough to expose the long, usually dark-colored, veinlike intestinal tract. With the tip of the knife or your fingers, lift up and pull out the vein, discarding it.

SQUAB
A delicate-flavored, tender pigeon raised specifically for the table. The single-serving birds, usually weighing about 1 pound (500 g), are available either fresh or frozen from good-quality butchers.

STAR ANISE
A small, hard, brown seedpod resembling an eight-pointed star, used whole or broken into individual points to lend its distinctive anise flavor to savory or sweet dishes.

TOMATOES
During summer, when tomatoes are in season, use the best sun-ripened tomatoes you can find. Large beefsteak tomatoes have a robust flavor and meaty texture to match their name. Bite-sized cherry tomatoes are prized for their sweet flavor and juiciness. Plum tomatoes, sometimes called Roma or egg tomatoes, are likely to have the best flavor and texture when other tomatoes are not at the peak of season. Whole, crushed or puréed plum tomatoes are also the best canned product, adding their rich flavor to sauces, braises and stews; look for good-quality imported Italian brands.

TOMATOES, SUN-DRIED
When dried in the sun, tomatoes develop an intense, sweet-tart flavor and a pleasantly chewy texture. Available either packed in oil or packaged dry in specialty-food shops and some food markets.

TOMATO PURÉE
Good-quality canned tomato purées are available in most food markets. To make your own tomato purée, peel and seed the tomatoes, then purée in a blender or a food processor.

WALNUT OIL
See *oils*.

WALNUTS
See *nuts*.

ZEST
The brightly colored, outermost layer of a citrus fruit's peel, the zest contains most of the fruit's flavorful oils, unlike the bitter white under layer, or pith. The zest can be removed with a simple tool known as a zester by drawing its sharp-edged holes across the fruit's skin to remove the zest in thin strips, or by using the fine holes on a hand-held grater. Alternatively, remove strips of zest with a vegetable peeler, taking care not to remove any white pith. Thinly slice the strips with a small, sharp knife.

SETTING A TABLE

As the photographs on these pages illustrate, a wide array of specialized items is available for setting the dining table. The actual tableware you select, however, will vary with the menu, style and level of formality you desire. An informal setting (below right) draws on all-purpose, everyday pieces. A formal setting (facing page) employs more varied and elegant tableware. ප Whatever kind of table you set, some basic rules govern its arrangement. Plates, glasses, knives, forks and spoons are all placed in their accustomed spots with efficiency in mind, each set in the most convenient spot for your guests to use as the meal progresses.

Specialized glassware, distinguished by its shape, includes from left to right: white wineglass; rounded glass for Burgundy or other red wines; oversized balloon glass for red or white wine or water; all-purpose wineglass; snifter for Cognac or brandy; Champagne flute; sherry or dessert wineglass.

Additional flatware, which could supplement the standard pieces used in the place settings on these pages, includes from left to right: luncheon fork; luncheon knife; fish fork; fish knife, which also may be used for butter service; round-bowl spoon for cream soups; oval-bowl spoon for other soups; serving fork; serving spoon; slicer/server for appetizers, main courses or desserts.

ප Logic lies behind the rules of serving and clearing at informal and formal tables alike. Food is always passed or served to each guest's left-hand side and cleared from the right. While the directions themselves are set in tradition, what matters most is the consistency that these rules bestow, literally keeping the meal's service flowing in a uniform direction.

INFORMAL SETTING

The setting shown below is informal in two basic ways. First, it uses everyday tableware—in this case, three pieces of stainless-steel flatware, a country-style pottery plate, a cotton napkin and an all-purpose glass.

ප More significantly, the setting reflects the simplicity of the meal to come. A small fork awaits a first-course salad, to be followed by a main course for which the larger fork and the knife will be used. The single all-purpose glass indicates that one kind of wine, or perhaps water or some other nonalcoholic beverage, will be poured.

ප Some general lessons for setting any informal table may be readily drawn from this basic arrangement. All implements are placed in the order in which they will be used. The napkin goes to the left of the plate and forks, its folded side facing the

plate, ready to be picked up by a corner, opened and placed in the lap when a guest sits down. Next comes the first-course fork, then the dinner fork, closest to the plate.

ප The dinner knife goes to the right of the plate, its blade facing inward, ready for the guest to pick it up for cutting. If soup were planned as a preliminary course, its spoon would be placed just to the right of the knife, since most people eat soup with their right hand. The glass is positioned above and just inside the knife, within easy reach but well clear of cutlery and plates.

ප Other implements are notable by their absence. For an informal meal, dessert forks or spoons arrive at the table with that course, placed on the side of each plate. Likewise, teaspoons are offered only when coffee is passed, placed on the side of each saucer, thus avoiding unnecessary table clutter earlier in the meal.

ප Whatever informal setting you arrange, you might also want to consider using place mats. They not only protect an attractive table, but also highlight each individual setting and add to the ambience with their color or pattern.

Napkin

Salad Fork

Dinner Fork

Dinner Plate

All-Purpose Glass

Dinner Knife

FORMAL SETTING

This setting reflects the more elegant style and the greater complexity of a formal meal. Fine china is complemented by silver flatware, an embroidered linen napkin and cut-crystal glasses with gold rims. As a backdrop for these fine accessories, a linen tablecloth could cover the table or, if the table's surface is beautiful in its own right, it could be left bare.

ɛ► Each item is carefully positioned in the order in which it will be used. The napkin, folded into a simple rectangle to highlight its monogram, is on the far left, ready to be unfolded and placed in the lap; a more elaborate fold such as one of those shown on pages 310–1 might be placed in the center of the dinner plate.

ɛ► To the right of the napkin go the forks, arranged left to right in their order of use. In most cases, the dinner fork is placed closest to the plate, although a salad fork might take that position if the menu calls for salad to be served after the main course, in the European fashion. Above the forks, a small plate awaits bread, with an individual butter knife laid across

the top rim with its handle pointing to the right, since most people will pick it up with their right hand.

ɛ► The dinner knife, as always, goes just to the right of the plate, its blade facing inward. A soup spoon to the right of the knife indicates that soup is part of the menu.

ɛ► Glassware should also be arranged in order of use. Traditionally, the glasses are placed in a linear fashion, but we've chosen a more contemporary arrangement that saves room on the table: Within closest reach of the right hand is a glass for the white wine that is usually poured with first courses. To its left, a larger glass awaits the red wine that would be poured next. Above both glasses goes an even larger goblet for guests who might request water.

ɛ► In a formal setting such as this, dessert utensils may be placed on the table before the meal, just above the dinner plate. Logic, again, determines their exact positioning: The dessert spoon's handle faces right, since most guests are likely to pick

it up with their right hand, and the fork's handle points to the left, to be picked up easily with the left hand. Alternatively, the utensils could be placed on the sides of the dessert plates when they are served.

ɛ► Depending on your own formal menu, you can further elaborate the setting. Many different shapes and sizes of glasses and more than two dozen kinds of table utensils have evolved over the centuries; some of the most common appear in the box on the opposite page. But while their combination of elegance and functionality is appealing, such specialized items are not absolutely essential to a formal menu. Any table set with simplicity, order and, above all, a regard for the convenience and comfort of your guests will be elegant.

Butter Knife

Water Goblet

Red Wineglass

Dessert Spoon

Bread Plate

Dessert Fork

White Wineglass

Dinner Fork

Dinner Knife

Salad Fork

Soup Spoon

Napkin

Dinner Plate

NAPKIN FOLDING

A napkin folded into one of the five simple, classic patterns shown here can add variety and style to any party table.

❧ We recommend using sturdy-weave cotton or linen, which is more absorbent and soil-resistant than synthetic or coated fabrics. For the crispest folds, iron the napkins first; you may also want to apply a light spray starch. A final decorative touch such as ribbon, twine, string or flowers adds extra charm.

❧ The illustrations here use 20-inch-square (50-cm) linen napkins. But feel free to choose any fabric, pattern and size that suit the setting and mood of your party.

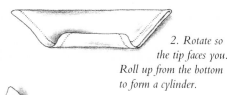

A simple linen napkin rolled and knotted to form a bow tie, then draped diagonally across a dinner plate, adds casual elegance to an everyday place setting. The fabric and placement may be varied.

BOW TIE

This easiest of folds has universal appeal. As effortless in effect as it is quickly achieved, the bow tie works well with napkins of any fabric or size. This fold is ideal with a casual setting or even on a semi-formal table.

❧ For a striking effect, use this fold for such unconventional napkins as Western-style bandanas or large swatches of Indian madras cotton. You may also want to tuck little gifts inside the knots to add an amusing touch that carries out the theme or ambience of your party.

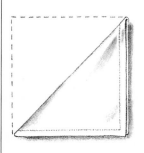

1. Fold the upper left corner of the napkin to the lower right corner, forming a triangle.

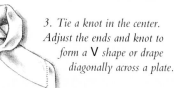

2. Rotate so the tip faces you. Roll up from the bottom to form a cylinder.

3. Tie a knot in the center. Adjust the ends and knot to form a V shape or drape diagonally across a plate.

BOUQUET

Two napkins of complementary or contrasting colors and patterns may be folded together to create a bouquetlike arrangement. Widely available wooden napkin rings neatly hold the bouquets, which are placed to the left of or on the dinner plate.

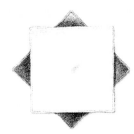

1. Open one napkin flat. Place the other napkin on top and rotate 45 degrees, forming an eight-pointed star.

2. Using your fingertips, grasp the centers of the two napkins together and pick them up.

3. Arrange the sides and points of the two napkins into neat overlapping folds. Insert the stem of the resulting bouquet into a napkin ring and pull halfway through. Rearrange the points to form a full, attractive bouquet.

BISHOP'S HAT

The bishop's hat has adorned fine tables for centuries and lends distinction to today's more formal occasions. You can present it either standing up or lying flat.

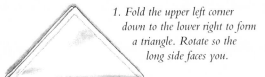

1. Fold the upper left corner down to the lower right to form a triangle. Rotate so the long side faces you.

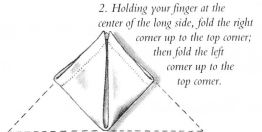

2. Holding your finger at the center of the long side, fold the right corner up to the top corner; then fold the left corner up to the top corner.

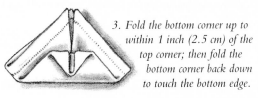

3. Fold the bottom corner up to within 1 inch (2.5 cm) of the top corner; then fold the bottom corner back down to touch the bottom edge.

4. Carefully turn the napkin over and fold the left side into the center.

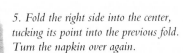

5. Fold the right side into the center, tucking its point into the previous fold. Turn the napkin over again.

POINTED POCKET

Folded into a tidy pocket, a napkin doubles as a creative holder for a set of flatware, an especially convenient bundle for guests to pick up at a buffet table.

1. Open the napkin flat. Fold it into quarters, rotating it so the open points are at the top.

2. Fold the point of the topmost layer downward until it almost—but not quite—touches the bottom corner.

3. Turn the napkin over. Fold the two side corners inward so they meet in the center.

4. Again, fold the sides inward so they meet in the center.

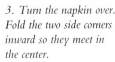

5. Carefully turn the napkin back over to reveal the pocket and tuck cutlery into it. If you like, lightly tie a piece of raffia or ribbon around the napkin just below the pocket.

THE FAN

One of the most spectacular of napkin folds, the fan really dresses up a festive table such as the one set for the Heritage Christmas menu (see page 263). To make the napkin stand up stiffly, iron the pleats.

1. Fold the napkin in half vertically to form a rectangle.

2. Starting at the bottom, fold back and forth into ½-inch (12-mm) accordion pleats, stopping when the unfolded portion is half as tall as it is wide.

3. Fold the napkin in half with the pleats on the outside.

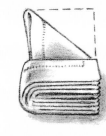

4. Fold all the layers of the top square in half diagonally, tucking the point under the pleats. Lift the napkin from the right side so it stands up and the pleats fan out.

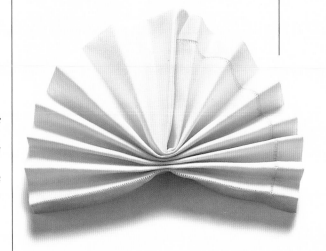

FLOWER ARRANGING

Examples of casual, easily achieved flower arrangements—such as the swagged flowerpot shown on this page—may be found throughout this book. For some festive occasions, you may want elaborate decorations of the kind you might order from a florist, but on the following pages we present four arrangements that can be done at home with lovely results. All that's required is a little time, imagination and patience, as well as simple tools and materials available at a florist's supplier or variety or hardware store.

Basic flower-arranging equipment (clockwise from top left): **1. florist's tape**, *for wrapping fragile stems, binding flowers together and strapping down florist's foam;* **2. florist's foam**, *or oasis, to be cut to fit into a bowl, soaked in water and used as a base into which flower stems are pushed;* **3. frogs**, *spiked metal disks into which stem or branch ends may be pushed to secure them;* **4. chicken wire**, *available in hardware stores, for use inside a bowl as a mesh to support branches and stems;* **5. clippers**, *to cut thicker stems or branches;* **6. shears**, *for cutting flower stems;* **7. gardening gloves**, *for handling thorny or prickly flowers;* **8. florist's wire**, *ranging from thin to thick gauges, for reinforcing stems or binding them together.*

SWAGGED FLOWERPOT

Small potted plants already growing in your home—or purchased from a local nursery or florist—easily become attractive living decorations. A view of their soil, however, can be unpleasant in close proximity to food, so it is best to conceal the base of the plant. Sphagnum moss, available where plants are sold, offers one attractive, natural solution. Or with some inexpensive fabric scraps, tape and florist's wire, you can fashion swags that transform each pot into a colorful, country-style decoration (see pages 82–3).

1. Cut fabric as long as twice the circumference of the pot's rim and 12 inches (30 cm) wide. Place wrong side up, fold both sides to the center and secure the seam with masking tape.

2. With a ruler and pencil, mark the tape in the middle and 2 inches (5 cm) from each end. Then mark the remaining length at regular intervals of 2–3 inches (5–7.5 cm).

3. For every mark on the tape, cut one 6-inch (15-cm) length of florist's wire.

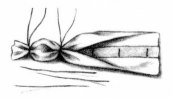

4. Starting at one end, gather the fabric together at each mark, concealing the tape inside. Lightly twist a piece of wire around each gather to secure it in place.

5. Starting at one end of the swag, secure the ends of a wire twist inside the pot's rim with masking tape. Continue tucking the swag around the pot and securing the wires inside. Place the plant inside the swagged pot.

VEGETABLE POTAGER

In spring or summer, fresh herbs and baby vegetables make visually appealing decorations—and serve as a healthy treat to be nibbled on by your guests. Any assortment of small containers in sizes and shapes that are easily grouped together can display them. Or, as shown here, create an attractive centerpiece using small terra-cotta pots stacked to construct a grouping that recalls, in miniature, the provender of a French country garden, or potager (see page 79).

1. Using glue, attach sheet moss or carpet moss to cover the top and edges of a circular piece of particle board or an upturned old circular tray.

2. Stack 2 good-sized terra-cotta pots and glue or place them securely in the center of the moss.

3. Arrange and secure smaller pots of varying sizes and heights around the center pots, to form a pleasing composition. Plant pots with fresh herb plants and baby vegetables.

FESTIVE ARRANGEMENT

Equally at home as a centerpiece or on a side table, this all-purpose arrangement may be created with a wide variety of flowers and greens. For the version shown here, we selected an array of white blossoms and delicate greenery: tulips, hyacinths, lilies of the valley, snowballs and ferns. You could

1. Secure the florist's foam in place in the container with strips of florist's tape.

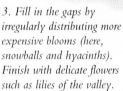

3. Fill in the gaps by irregularly distributing more expensive blooms (here, snowballs and hyacinths). Finish with delicate flowers such as lilies of the valley.

vary the elements with your own favorite flowers in any pleasing combination, defining the overall shape with sturdier and less expensive blossoms and filling in with more delicate or costly blooms.

❧ To prepare this arrangement, you will need a container with a wide mouth and low base; a chunk of florist's foam cut to fit the container; and florist's tape. At your flower shop, select eight to ten green fronds; about two dozen sturdy blossoms; and approximately a dozen each of two or more kinds of more delicate flowers. Use flower shears to cut all stems diagonally and put the flowers in warm water until ready to use; soak the foam in warm water for 30 minutes.

2. Create a fringe of ferns, inserting the stems around the base of the foam. Evenly insert less expensive, sturdy-stemmed flowers (we used tulips).

ROSE BRAID

A special occasion becomes even more memorable when decorated with roses. To give additional elegance to a rose bouquet, you could add a braid that cascades down the side of the vase.

⤷ You'll need about four dozen roses in all. Depending on the style of your party, choose either a mix of colors or blossoms of a single hue. The loose, open petals of garden roses gives a more luxuriant look to the bouquet and braid; if you plan to use hot-house roses, buy them two days ahead of time so they can unfurl a bit. An urn-shaped vase will complement the elegance of the bouquet and provide height to lift the braid. Cut a piece of florist's foam to fit the container and presoak it in warm water for 30 minutes; place it inside the vase and add water. Arrange about three dozen of the roses, ends trimmed, in a bouquet shape and fill in any gaps with small roses or tight buds.

⤷ To prepare the braid, select about 15 roses, in an even range of blossom sizes from small to large. Trim all their stems to a uniform 6-inch (15-cm) length. Place the roses in warm water until ready to use. As a base for the braid, use two 18-inch-long (45-cm) strips of variegated ivy, which has

small, delicate leaves that contrast nicely with roses. If you like, you could make the braid longer, buying about a dozen more roses for each additional foot in length. Have on hand both florist's tape and thin florist's wire to secure the arrangement.

1. Hold the two 18-inch-long (45-cm) strands of ivy parallel to one another. At one end, attach three small partially opened roses with 6-inch (15-cm) stems, wrapping florist's wire around the stems and ivy.
Trim the rose stems to 1 inch (2.5 cm) past the wire.

2. Continue attaching bunches of three roses, using the blossoms to conceal the wire of the previous bunch. Use fuller roses as you progress from beginning to end. Leave 5 inches (12.5 cm) of ivy bare at the end.

3. Tuck the ends of the bare ivy into the vase, sticking it into the florist's foam, and secure the braid inside and along the rim with florist's tape.

HOLIDAY TREE

Other attractive objects besides flowers make excellent candidates for festive arrangements. This centerpiece presents a tree-shaped composition of vegetables and fruits—an arrangement similar to the fruit tree in the Christmas dinner (see page 265). You can give your imagination free rein when planning a holiday tree's elements, selecting from a wide range of foods and other materials and opting for either a monochromatic or a varied color scheme.

⤷ A 12-inch (30-cm) Styrofoam cone serves as the base for the tree, with wooden toothpicks used as fasteners. Because foods arranged in this way will not keep long, assemble the tree the day of the party.

1. Insert wooden toothpicks into the largest items (here, limes, Brussels sprouts and baby artichokes) and attach them to the base of the cone in several layers.

2. Fill the gaps with smaller items, such as broccoli, skewering them on toothpicks or, in the case of string beans, inserting them directly into the foam.

3. Top the tree with an attractive object (here, a small artichoke). Add final decorations (here, whole jalapeño chilies) by skewering them onto toothpicks so that they rest atop the other items.

INDEX

CREDITS

Unless otherwise noted, all items pictured are from private collections.

INTRODUCTION
Pages 10–1: Crystal vase — Pottery Barn. Pewter vase and damask napkins — Sue Fisher King Company. Notebook, place cards — Oggetti. Place card holders — Dandelion. Square vase with marbles, silver note paper holder, pen, napkin rings and candlesticks — Fillamento.

WELCOME HOME DINNER
Pages 14–5: Candles — Pottery Barn. **Pages 16–7:** Flowers — Silver Terrace Nurseries. Green charger — Sue Fisher King. Grape leaf napkin — Fillamento. **Pages 22–3:** Serving spoon — Sue Fisher King.

DATE DINNER FOR TWO
Pages 26–7: Tin vase — Fioridella. Dot glass, linen napkins — Fillamento. Gold-edged tumblers, napkin rings — The Gardener. Dinner plates, votives — Sue Fisher King. **Pages 28–9:** Pewter vase — Sue Fisher King. Tin vase — Fillamento. **Page 29:** Amber glass plate — The Gardener. Flatware — Pottery Barn. **Page 35:** Napkin, square bowl — Fillamento. Oval glass dish — The Gardener. **Page 36:** Cream demitasse cups, mother-of-pearl–handled spoons — Sue Fisher King. **Pages 36–7:** Wood chargers, black-edged plates, napkins — Fillamento.

FAMILY BIRTHDAY PARTY
Pages 38–9: Napkins, glasses — R.H. Glazed vases, footed compotes — Fillamento. Multi-colored plates — Sue Fisher King. Woven napkin rings, "Montana" flatware — Pottery Barn. Flowers — Silver Terrace Nurseries. **Page 39 (inset):** Blue frosted vase — Pottery Barn. **Pages 40–1:** Basket — Forrest Jones. Gift cards, plate — Sue Fisher King. **Page 42 (inset):** Glass decanters — Fioridella. **Pages 42–3:** Glass bowls, wire tray — R.H. **Pages 44–5:** Platter — Virginia Brier. Souffle dish in basket — Forrest Jones. Checked bowl — Tancredi & Morgan. **Page 47:** Aqua bowl—Fillamento. Yellow plates — R.H. **Pages 48–9:** Striped plate, tablecloth — Sue Fisher King. Green bowl — Pottery Barn. Blue napkins — R.H.

BACKYARD BARBECUE
Pages 50–1: Chairs, table, straw hats, candleholders — Gardeners Eden. Yellow bowl — Sue Fisher King. Baskets — Chambers/Gardeners Eden. Tumblers, wicker carafes — Pottery Barn. Dish towels and potholder —

Williams-Sonoma. **Page 51:** Chair — Pottery Barn. Green pot — Gardeners Eden. **Page 53:** Metal container — Gordon Bennett. Concrete urns — Gardeners Eden and American Ornament. Antique crock — J. Goldsmith Antiques. **Pages 54–5:** Yellow tray — Pottery Barn. **Page 57:** Red straw hat — Forrest Jones. **Page 58:** Red flatware — J. Goldsmith Antiques. **Page 59:** Serving spoons — Forrest Jones. **Pages 60–1:** Glass oval baker — Forrest Jones.

ENGAGEMENT PARTY
Pages 62–3: Sangría glasses — Williams-Sonoma. **Page 64:** Ribbon — Paulette Knight. Gift cards — Brown Bag. Glass pitcher — Antique Dept., Williams-Sonoma Post Street. **Pages 68–9:** Terra-cotta dish — Forrest Jones. "Casbah" serving pieces — Pottery Barn. Mortar and pestle — Biordi Imports. **Page 71:** Cherry pitter — Williams-Sonoma.

CASUAL PIZZA PARTY
Pages 72–3: Place mats, napkins — Candelier. Flatware — Williams-Sonoma. Glasses — Pottery Barn. **Page 74:** Basket and aprons — Forrest Jones. **Page 75:** Stemmed glasses, terra-cotta pot — Pottery Barn. **Page 77:** Checked dish towel — Williams-Sonoma. Cordovan bowls — R.H. **Page 79:** Antique orchid pots — Gordon Bennett. **Page 80:** Glass-footed bowl — Antique Dept., Williams-Sonoma Post Street. **Page 81:** Large footed bowl — Gordon Bennett. Ceramic bowls — Williams-Sonoma.

KITCHEN BREAKFAST
Pages 82–3: Potted flowers — Silver Terrace Nurseries. Embroidered napkin, shell-patterned flatware — Williams-Sonoma. Luneville pottery — Forrest Jones. Red place mats — Fillamento. Stools — Pottery Barn. Fabric on flowerpots — Pierre Deux. **Page 83 (inset):** Tea strainer, teapot, trivet, striped cup and saucers, teapot infuser — Williams-Sonoma. **Pages 84–5:** Tumblers, goblets, glass pitcher — Williams-Sonoma. **Page 90:** French-press coffee pot — Forrest Jones. Coffee grinder and canister — Williams-Sonoma.

AUTUMN SUNDAY SUPPER
Pages 92–3: Basket — Rod McLellen Company. Iron candleholder — Pottery Barn. **Page 94:** Teapot, clay teacups — Fillamento. **Pages 94–5:** Napkin ring, black stoneware plate, glasses — Fillamento. Bamboo-handled flatware — Sue Fisher King. **Page 97:** Orchids — Rod McLellan Company. Red lacquer chair — T. Keller Donovan. **Page 100:** Dot soup bowl — Fillamento.

AFTER-WORK SUPPER
Pages 102–3: Wine glasses — Fillamento. **Page 104:** Martini glass, square silver bowl — Sue Fisher King. **Page 105:** Napkin, Bridgewater salad plate — Candelier. Maryse boxer bowl — Fillamento. Place mat — Forrest Jones. **Page 108:** Napkin — Sue Fisher King. **Page 109:** Lemon reamer — Williams-Sonoma. **Pages 112–3:** Glass bowl, compotes — Fillamento. Napkin — Williams-Sonoma. Metal "Bongo" vase — Pottery Barn.

SOUP SUPPER BY THE FIRE
Pages 114–5: Coconut boxes, ebony flatware — Sue Fisher King. Metal urns and fruit candelabra — Brambles. Napkins — R.H. **Page 115 (inset):** Leaf votive holder — Brambles. Beeswax candle — Pottery Barn. **Page 116:** Glazed pots — Sue Fisher King. Wine glasses — Fillamento. **Page 117:** Striped plate — Fillamento. Napkin — R.H. **Pages 118–9:** Soup tureen with lid — R.H. Dishware, salt and pepper grinders — Fillamento. **Pages 120–1:** Striped salad bowl, black salad plates — Fillamento. **Page 121:** "Leaf" plate — R.H.

DINNER WITH DEAR FRIENDS
Pages 126–7: Raffia table runner — Bell'occhio. Plants — Silver Terrace Nurseries. Chairs — Pottery Barn. Flatware, celadon plates, green pot — Forrest Jones. Trunks, sailboat, glove, binoculars — Beaver Bros. Antiques. Palm tree print — Candelier. **Page 128:** Green batik napkin — Sue Fisher King. Woven place mat, glasses — Forrest Jones. Tray, glass decanter, ice bucket, corkscrew, glass pitcher — Beaver Bros. Antiques. **Page 129:** Iron lantern — Candelier. **Page 134:** Palm tree plates — Sue Fisher King. Wooden salad bowl and servers — Forrest Jones.

TREE-TRIMMING SUPPER
Pages 136–7: Cashmere throw, suede pillows, taffeta sachets — Sue Fisher King. Fireplace garland — Laura Lorenz. Douglas Fir tree — Marnie Donaldson. Ribbon — Paulette Knight. **Page 138:** Toile cachepots — Sue Fisher King. Topiaries, greens, wreath — Laura Lorenz. **Page 139:** Flatware — Sue Fisher King. Utensil caddy — Pottery Barn. Goblets and plates — R.H. Cream plates — Candelier. **Page 140 (inset):** Twig tray — R.H. Patterned bowl — Sue Fisher King. **Page 141:** Yellow quilted tablecloth, green "woven" bowl — Sue Fisher King. Cheese grater — Forrest Jones. **Page 143:** Pedestal salad bowl, silver-handled salad servers — Fillamento. Green glass plates — R.H. Yellow print napkin —Vanderbilt & Company. **Page 144:** Lavender bushels — Pottery Barn. **Page 145:** Glass ramekins — Forrest Jones. Cordial

glasses — Fillamento. Wood-handled teaspoons — Sue Fisher King. Candles — Pottery Barn.

ROMANTIC DINNER FOR TWO
Pages 148–9: Fringed Marseilles table cover, Venetian velvet throw — Sue Fisher King Company. Gold-rimmed oval glass platter — Fillamento. Arm chair — Mike Furniture. **Page 149 (inset):** Gold-rimmed glass bowl — Fillamento. **Pages 150, 153, 155:** Napkins, flatware, "Gaudron" salad plates, "Gio Ponti" dinner plates, heart bud vase, gold-rimmed wine glasses — Fillamento. Gold basket salt cellar and spoon — Sue Fisher King Company. **Page 152:** "Camelot" serving plate, votive holder, gold-rimmed champagne glasses — Fillamento. **Page 157:** Brandy snifters — Williams-Sonoma.

RITE-OF-SPRING BRUNCH
Pages 158–9: "Paris" wicker dining chairs, table — Pottery Barn. **Page 159 (inset), page 161:** Juice glasses — Crate & Barrel. Glass bud vases — Bloomers. **Pages 160, 163:** "Flip Flop" dinner plate, star napkin ring, "Double Helix" flatware, salt and pepper shakers — Fillamento. **Page 161:** Pen — Fillamento. **Page 162:** Ash occasional table, "Volumetric" charger plate — Fillamento. **Page 165:** Tea kettle, coffee pot, "Flip Flop" cups, saucers, and dessert plates, glass vases — Fillamento.

MEDITERRANEAN EASTER
Pages 166–7: Herb topiaries — R.H. **Page 171:** Ochre dinner plate and green salad plate — Vanderbilt & Company. Plaid placemats and napkins, flatware — Pottery Barn. "Giotto" wine glasses — Sue Fisher King Company. **Page 172:** Venetian velvet table cover, carving set — Sue Fisher King Company. Octagonal serving dish — Biordi Art Imports. **Page 174:** Napkin, serving spoon and leaf spheres — Sue Fisher King Company. **Page 175:** Aperitif glasses — Pottery Barn. "Bistro" cake server — Sue Fisher King Company.

TEATIME FÊTE
Pages 176–7: Floral throw pillows — Shabby Chic. Garden roses — Green Valley Growers. Antique tablecloth, damask napkins — Antique Dept., Williams-Sonoma Post Street. Colored cups and saucers — Ralph Lauren china for Waterford Wedgwood. Pressed glass pitcher and glasses — Pottery Barn. Three-tiered caddy — Sue Fisher King Company. **Page 180:** Miniature tea set, tea strainer — Fillamento. **Page 181:** Antique ivory-handled bread knife — Sue Fisher King Company. **Page 182:** Vintage oval silver tray, linen luncheon napkins — Sue Fisher King Company.

AL FRESCO LUNCH

Pages 188–9: Awning stripe linen tablecloth — Sue Fisher King Company. Directors chairs — Pier 1 Imports. Seashells — Seascape. **Page 189 (inset):** "Almost Round" dinner plates, glass beaded-edge salad plates, wine glasses, "Bullet" salt and pepper shakers — Fillamento. White linen hemstitched napkins — Sue Fisher King Company. **Page 190:** Mosaic shell and tile urn — Sue Fisher King Company. Seagrass occasional table — Pottery Barn. **Page 193:** "Column" salt and pepper shakers — Vero. **Page 197:** Square dessert plates — Fillamento.

GALA BUFFET

Page 200: Cream dinner plates — Williams-Sonoma. Wine and water goblets — Pottery Barn. Blue and white Chinese porcelain cachepots — Forrest Jones. Blue cricket stripe napkin — Williams-Sonoma. Antique blue and white salad plates — Antique Dept., Williams-Sonoma Post Street. **Page 201:** Double old-fashioned glasses — Pottery Barn. Vintage pressed-glass pitchers — Antique Dept., Williams-Sonoma Post Street. **Page 203:** Antique blue and white platters and dinner plates — Antique Dept., Williams-Sonoma Post Street. **Page 206:** "Optic" champagne glasses — Williams-Sonoma.

HARVEST LUNCH

Pages 208–9, 210, 217: Ceramic plates, cups and jug — Villa Italiana (Australia). **Page 212:** Wooden lug — Appley Hoare Antiques (Australia). **Page 214:** Cutlery and large platter — Accoutrement (Australia).

PRE-THEATER COCKTAILS

Page 220: Embroidered cotton cocktail napkins — Antique Dept., Williams-Sonoma Post Street. **Page 221:** Martini glasses — Sue Fisher King Company. Monogrammed double-old fashioned glasses — Williams-Sonoma. **Page 223:** Hemstitched linen cocktail napkins — Sue Fisher King Company. **Page 224:** Scalloped-edge linen cocktail napkins — Sue Fisher King Company.

TRADITIONAL THANKSGIVING

Pages 228–9, 234: Pheasant feathers — Coast Wholesale. **Page 230:** Linen damask napkins — Sue Fisher King Company. **Pages 232–3:** Wheat wreath — Sue Fisher King Company.

CASUAL HANUKKAH BUFFET

Page 242: Wire menorah — Fillamento. **Page 244:** Dinnerware, placemats — Pottery Barn. **Page 245:** Rectangular serving tray, twisted iron candlesticks — Pottery Barn. **Page 246:** Basket, wreath — Pottery Barn. **Page 248:** Fruit labels — Smith & Hawken. **Page 249:** Sherry glasses — Fillamento. Napkin — Pottery Barn.

CHRISTMAS SEASON OPEN HOUSE

Page 251 (inset): Vintage pressed-glass cake stand — Antique Dept., Williams-Sonoma Post Street. **Page 253 (top):** Birdhouse — Sue Fisher King Company. Bird's nest and finch eggs — Bell'occhio. **Page 253 (bottom):** Plaid cotton napkins — Polo-Ralph Lauren Shop. **Page 255:** Antique metal reindeer — J. Goldsmith Antiques. **Page 256:** Gold-leafed starburst — Sue Fisher King Company. **Page 257:** Antique wooden bowl — J. Goldsmith Antiques. **Page 261:** Cross-stitch sampler — J. Goldsmith Antiques. Wooden bear candlestick — Candelier.

HERITAGE CHRISTMAS DINNER

Page 263: Wreath — Green Valley Growers. **Page 266:** Decanter and wine glasses — Waterford Wedgwood. **Page 270:** Pleated gold sachet, gold cachepot — Sue Fisher King Company. Script wrapping paper — Oggetti. Gold wrapping paper — Bell'occhio. Leaf ornament — Dandelion. Acorn ornament — Pottery Barn.

NEW YEAR'S EVE FOR SIX

Page 274: Candlesticks, candle shades and antique silver compote (for flowers) — Sue Fisher King Company. **Page 275 (top):** Demitasse cups and saucers — Fillamento. **Page 276:** Crystal vase — Fillamento. **Page 277:** Hors d'oeuvres plate — Fillamento. **Page 278:** Silver mint julep cups — Sue Fisher King Company. "Earthscape," "Starstruck" and "Moonscape" dinnerware, "Meier" silver bowl — Fillamento.

NEW YEAR'S BUFFET

Page 284: Pint glasses — Crate & Barrel. **Page 286:** Greek Key patterned linen napkins, "Thames" flatware, rectangular platter, bowls and plates, salt and pepper shakers — Fillamento. **Page 289:** Dinner plates — Fillamento. **Page 290–1:** Wire urn — Fillamento. Cake server — Pottery Barn. Coffee pot — Fillamento. Plaid cotton napkins — Crate & Barrel.

SETTING A TABLE

Stemware (page 308): Williams-Sonoma. **Flatware (page 308):** Pavillon Christofle. **Informal Setting (page 308):** Plate — Waterford Wedgwood. Flatware — Pavillon Christofle. Napkin — Candelier. **Formal Setting (page 309):** Plate — Waterford Wedgwood. Crystal — Paul Bauer Inc. Flatware — Pavillon Christofle.

FLOWER ARRANGING

Festive Arrangement (page 313): Footed compote — Waterford Wedgwood. **Rose Braid (page 314):** White ceramic urn — Candelier.

SOURCES (USA):

American Ornament, (415) 543-1363
Beaver Bros. Antiques, (415) 863-4344
Bell'occhio, (415) 864-4048
Biordi Art Imports, (415) 392-8096
Bloomers, (415) 563-3266
Brambles, (707) 433-1094
The Brown Bag, (415) 922-0390
Candelier, (415) 989-8600
Chambers, (800) 334-9790
Coast Wholesale Dried Flowers & Baskets, (415) 781-3034
Crate & Barrel, (415) 986-4000
Dandelion, (415) 563-3100
Fillamento, (415) 931-2224
Fioridella, (415) 775-4065
Forrest Jones, (415) 567-2483
Galisteo, (415) 861-5900
The Gardener, (510) 548-4545
Gardener's Eden, (800) 822-9600
J. Goldsmith Antiques, (415) 771-4055
Gordon Bennett, (415) 929-1172
Great American Collective, (415) 922-2660
Green Valley Growers, (707) 823-5583
Laura Lorenz Floral Styling and Events, (510) 652-1746
Mike Furniture, (415) 567-2700
Oggetti, (415) 346-0631
Paul Bauer Inc., (415) 421-6862
Paulette Knight, (415) 626-6184
Pavillon Christofle, (415) 399-1931
Pier 1 Imports, (415) 387-6642
Pierre Deux, (415) 296-9940
Polo-Ralph Lauren Shop, (415) 567-7656
Pottery Barn, (800) 922-5507
RH, (415) 346-1460
Rod McLellan Co., (415) 362-1520
Seascape, (415) 681-2666
Shabby Chic, (415) 771-3881
Silver Terrace, (415) 543-4443
Smith & Hawken, (415) 381-1800
Stroud's Linen Warehouse, (415) 979-0460
Sue Fisher King Company, (415) 922-7276
Susan Eslick Custom Ceramics, (415) 255-2234
T. Keller Donovan, (212) 759-4450
Tancredi & Morgan, (408) 625-4477
Vanderbilt & Company, (707) 963-1010
Vero, (415) 255-0707
Vignette, (415) 567-0174
Virginia Brier, (415) 929-7173
Waterford Wedgwood, (415) 391-5610
Williams-Sonoma, (800) 541-2233
Williams-Sonoma Post Street store, (415) 362-6904

(SYDNEY, AUSTRALIA):

Accoutrement, (02) 969-1031
Appley Hoare Antiques, (02) 362-3045
Villa Italiana, (02) 960-1788

ACKNOWLEDGMENTS

The publishers would like to thank the following people and organizations for their assistance and support in producing this book. For lending, giving or making props: Chuck Williams; Alexandre Saporetti; Kevin Littlefield of Pierre Deux; Marnie Donaldson; Iris Fuller and her group at Fillamento; Sue Fisher King and her team; Rick Herbert and Chris Moss of RH; Marty, Phillipe and Forrest of Forrest Jones; everyone at Green Valley Growers; Alta Tingle at The Gardener; Beaver Bros. Antiques; Michelle Carrara; Stephen Griswold; Dennis Leggett; Janice Nicks Fisher; D.D. Stoner; and Connie, Travis and Mr. and Mrs. Robert Ruggeri of Silver Terrace Nurseries.

Special thanks to Bob Long and Pat Perini of Long Vineyards; the Niebaum-Coppola Estate; Jane and John Weil; D. Scott Ruegg; Mr. and Mrs. Ruegg; Carol Davis; Mr. and Mrs. J. Van Lott; Mr. and Mrs. John B. Ritchie; Jennifer Millar; Dan Glazier; Stephen W. Griswold; and the entire staff at Square One Restaurant. For additional food styling: Janice Baker. For food prep assistance: Daniel Becker and Nette Scott. For photography assistance: Brian Mahany, Mark Eakle, Sharon C. Lott and Susanna Allen. For styling assistance: Tessa Barroll; Danielle D. DiSalvo and Elizabeth Ruegg. For their editorial and design help: Steven Wooster, Maria Cianci, Ken DellaPenta, Jonathan Schwartz, Lynn Meinhardt, Sharon Silva, Yolande Bull, Mick Bagnato, Tarji Mickelson, Jim Obata, Janique Poncelet and Claire Sanchez. For their general advice and location information: Stephanie Le Gras of 20 Ross Commons, Jim Caldwell, Phoebe Ellsworth, Sara Bennett, Sally Tantau of Tantau Designs, Margo Tantau Kearney, Keven Clancy, Sharon Lott, Wade Bentson and Al Karstensen.

The following people kindly provided the use of their homes and properties as settings for the menus in this book: Barbara, Spencer and Lindsay Hoopes; Stephen Shubel; Ivy Rosequist; Beth and John Allen; Kaye and Eric Herbranson; Tom Dunker and Barbara Brooks; William and Kathleen Collins of Collins Vineyards; Richard Crisman and Jeff Brock; John and Kittina Powers; Mr. and Mrs. Stephen W. Griswold; Mary and Howard Lester; Wendely Harvey; John and Dawn Owen; Chuck Williams; Joyce Goldstein; Edward and Cynthia Mackay; Paul Vincent Wiseman; Ken Monnens; Sue Fisher King; Robert Cave-Rogers; and Richard and Ann Grace of Grace Family Vineyards.